Babies: the Mumsnet Guide

mumsnet.com

Babies: the Mumsnet Guide

by Natasha Joffe and the Mumsnet Mums

Edited by Justine Roberts and Carrie Longton

Illustrated by Mia Nilsson

BLOOMSBURY

LONDON · BERLIN · NEW YORK · SYDNEY

First published in Great Britain 2010

Copyright © 2010 by Mumsnet Limited

Illustrations © Mia Nilsson

The moral right of the authors has been asserted

Bloomsbury Publishing, London, Berlin and New York

36 Soho Square, London W1D 3QY

A CIP catalogue record for this book is available
from the British Library

ISBN 978 1 4088 0148 2
10 9 8 7 6 5 4 3 2

Typeset by RefineCatch Ltd, Bungay, Suffolk
Printed in Great Britain by Clays Ltd, St Ives plc

FSC
Mixed Sources
Product group from well-managed
forests and other controlled sources
Cert no. SGS-COC-2061
www.fsc.org
© 1996 Forest Stewardship Council

www.bloomsbury.com/mumsnet

For Mumsnetters whose countless everyday acts of kindness and support make the gargantuan task of baby rearing just a little easier.

Foreword

So you've done it – you've given birth. The end of a gruelling nine-month journey, culminating with an exhausting, elating and quite possibly traumatising finale. But there's not a moment to rest on your tender behind because now is, of course, only the beginning: with no instruction manual included, you suddenly have in your possession possibly the most complicated thing ever invented.

In the old days your mum might have moved in, offering an alternative to chilly figures like the psychologist John B. Watson who admonished parents to 'never hug or kiss your children, never let them sit in your lap' and to 'shake hands in the morning'.

What we now know, and probably didn't need Professor Erich Seifritz, of Basel University's Department of Psychiatry, to tell us (though thanks anyway Erich) is that the brains of parents, mothers especially, are hard-wired to respond to the cries of babies. So the bad news is that it will be a good few weeks, possibly months, before you manage to sleep through even the slightest nocturnal whimper from the direction of the Moses basket. And even if your newborn does miraculously sleep like a baby, chances are you won't: more than one Mumsnetter recalls prodding her baby out of his slumber, so convinced was she that the newborn had stopped breathing altogether, each time he drifted off.

If this is your first baby you are almost guaranteed, it seems, to develop Precious Firstborn Syndrome: a well-documented phenomenon on the Mumsnet Talkboards involving strangely obsessive parental behaviours like rubbing shampoo into one's own eyes to test it doesn't sting, pulling prams backwards for miles to avoid direct sunlight and even sterilising the steriliser.

So while most of your memories of the actual birth will soon be selectively erased (how else would so many choose to reproduce a second and third time?), you're destined to look back on this first year with a rueful 'if only I'd known then what I know now' shake of the head.

If only, for instance, I'd known that breasts really do only produce minute amounts of yellowy colostrum for the first few days but that that really is enough for a baby; or that a damp cotton-wool ball is no match for those first bitumen-like poos; or indeed that I really didn't need half of the £4,000 worth of kit the average expectant mother spends on her babe... I could have saved myself an awful lot of bother.

In the days before Mumsnet, mothers like me had to make do with the mildly terrifying admonitions of 'experts' like Gina Ford (you may have heard of her), but how much better to have access to vast archive of expertise – collected the hard way – by thousands of real parents? Whatever the parenting poser you are facing, chances are a Mumsnetter will have faced it already. And their advice is offered in a rather different tone of voice to the tablets of stone delivered by the parenting gurus: not so much 'do this because it's the right way' as 'this worked for me, maybe it could work for you'.

No single piece of advice should be read as 'a Mumsnet way of doing things'. One of the first things we learned from Mumsnetters is that different folk really do take different strokes. The aim of this book is simply to provide you with a bank of solutions many thousands of mums have found to the countless thorny dilemmas, problems and panics every parent faces in the first year of their child's life. And to have a bit of a giggle along the way.

We're confident that, whatever the subject, you'll find some advice that works for you. And if you can't, or if you'd like to share your own ingenious cure for colic, boast about your previously untested levels of endurance or just chew the fat about the extraordinary soft milkiness of your newborn's head, we're just a click away at www.mumsnet.com.

Justine Roberts (Co-founder, Mumsnet.com)

P.S. A long time ago, a friend called up to pick my brains about her pregnancy palpitations. Somewhat ruthlessly I replied that I'd only answer her question if she posted it on the talkboard of the website I'd started a few months earlier. But by the time I hurriedly and rather guiltily logged on, someone else had got there first. It was at that moment that I knew Mumsnet was coming to life. That friend never left Mumsnet, and even better, though it took about ten years, she eventually agreed to write this book. Sometimes even the longest gestations are worth the wait.

P.P.S. Mumsnetters go by a variety of weird and wonderful pseudonyms. Please do not be put off however – just because someone's goes by the moniker of IAteRosemaryConleyFor Breakfast it doesn't mean she did (far too many high-GI calories).

Contents

Chapter Three: You, Yourself and You

Chapter Four: The Sleep of the Damned

Chapter Five: Food, Glorious Food

Chapter Six: Baby's Health

Chapter Seven: Parenting – Or What to Do With Babies All Day

Chapter Eight: Relationships

Chapter Nine: Childcare and Going Back to Work

Chapter Minus One

The Readiness Is All

In this chapter …

'If it be now, 'tis not to come; if it be not to come, it will be now; if it be not now, yet it will come – the readiness is all.' William Shakespeare, *Hamlet*

The End of the Beginning

By the end of pregnancy, many of you, frankly, will just be looking forward to sleeping on your stomachs again. Or sleeping at all (which – it has to be said – is a somewhat far-fetched expectation). And eating soft cheese. And being able to see your pubic hair. Somewhere along the way (maybe during those last few months when your feet swelled up like unpricked sausages and stopped fitting in real-person shoes?), you may – understandably – have lost sight of where it's all heading. And the transition from lumbering baby-on-the-inside person to strangely lightened baby-on-the-outside person can seem more improbable the closer it gets, as you start to feel like you always have been and will be heavily pregnant.

But any day now, there really will be a new, small person in your home and there are some things you can do to prepare for landing.

Some women are struck in very late pregnancy by a kind of deranged nesting instinct. They rise from their chaise longues, brush aside the chocolate wrappers, turn off Jeremy Kyle and start filling dressers with muslins and stencilling murals of fluffy bunnies on changing tables. If this is you, just be careful. You wouldn't be the first woman to put her back out in late pregnancy trying to paint the nursery ceiling ...

You could use some of that energy to batch cook and freeze meals for the early weeks. Or just do an internet shop for lots of nourishing snacks which can be eaten one-handed while feeding a baby.

'If you don't have a dishwasher, get paper plates.' Marina

Many mothers think this is the time to look after yourself:

'Book some beauty treatments and pamper yourself. It will be your last chance for some time. The same goes for a haircut. I went to the cinema on my own during my maternity leave. The daytime screenings were cheaper and I got a chance to watch loads of chick flicks that I couldn't drag my hubby along to. The vast consumption of sweets, ice cream and popcorn were a bonus too.

Go swimming. The feeling of weightlessness is second to none when you've been feeling like a heifer for months. Even if you only do a few laps, you'll feel the Mars bar from the vending machine in the reception is more than justified.

Antenatal yoga is a great way of stretching out those aches and pains. It can be a bit tricky to get into some of the poses in the final weeks, but it's quite an accomplishment when you do.

And, if you can be arsed, give the house a deep clean. It won't get done again for a long time. Lie in and nap during the day. Why not? If you are going to be a first-time mum, you probably won't have this opportunity again.'
ILikeToQuickStepItTangoIt

Give some thought to how you are going to keep your mind busy when your body is mostly devoted to servicing your new baby. Lay in some books or magazines.

'Sky Plus all your favourite shows and stock up on DVD box sets – because chances are that for the first few weeks you will spend an inordinate amount of time sitting on the sofa nursing a never-full newborn. Likewise, make sure you have your laptop charged and within reach, so you can call upon Mumsnet when you need to (and you will need to!).

If you have the energy you could also build a small rocket on which to blast your maternity clothes into space, as you will be THAT fed up of them by the time the baby arrives.' AvonBarksdale

Washing all the baby clothes and linen is a useful, soothing, sometimes tear-inducing activity for the late weeks of pregnancy.

'But don't wash all newborn clothes. I unpacked and washed all of mine, and my daughter was a big baby and went straight into 0–3-month clothes and the newborn ones couldn't go back.'
Tillyscoutsmum

'Buy a nice notebook which will start off being a list of feed times/sides, but will morph into being a lovely diary of baby's first year.'
AnybodyHomeMcFly

'Be prepared for terminal boredom and crying fits after you've done all of the above and there's still no sign of the baby.' LionStartBigpants

And then, of course, there is the shopping ...

Stuff (and Nonsense): What to Buy and What Not To

In the world of baby kit, one mum's meat is another mum's trans-fat-laced sausage roll. And while some of us approach the prenatal shopping excursion with a greedy glint in our eyes – oh, brave new world of consumer indulgence that has the John Lewis baby department in it! – others will be flummoxed by the array of infant technology and wonder which items their baby really requires. Do always bear in mind that just because something exists, it doesn't mean that anyone actually *needs* it. The world is chock-full of multinationals and mumtrepreneurs finding new 'gaps' in the baby goods market and articles in women's magazines encouraging you to buy flim-flammery. And they are all well aware that you are awash with hormones and ready to buy anything that is covered in bunnies or adorably tiny.

The bare essentials: you don't actually need all that cr*p

As one seasoned veteran says: 'Don't buy much in advance; get the absolute minimum and wait to see what you need. And then borrow it all!' 'Only buy essentials; all the cutesy stuff will be given as gifts anyway,' says another thrifty pragmatist. If you do find yourself postnatally inundated with tiny sleepsuits, consider trading a proportion in for larger sizes; otherwise, your hefty three-month-old may find himself with nothing to wear.

'My top tip would be to take a (recent) mother with you when you go baby-stuff shopping and, if possible, take a child with you when pram shopping. Get the shop assistants to demonstrate everything, and experiment to see what's right for you.' aligard

If, like most of us, you are watching what you spend, think about what you can borrow or get second-hand on eBay, Mumsnet's For Sale boards, through Freecycle or at NCT nearly-new sales. And, of course, you can also dispose of the odd rash purchase or unwanted gift item through the same channels.

Essentially, you'll need to feed your baby, keep her warm, dispose of her waste products, transport her in some fashion, wash her, provide her with somewhere to sleep and supply her with some very modest entertainment. You *actually* need:

- An age-appropriate car seat. There are some car seats that slot in like carrycots, but in general, newborn car seats will be rear-facing and should be fitted in the rear seat of the car. Your baby won't graduate to a forward-facing seat until he is at least a year old and 9kg (20lb) in weight.

  'Don't forget to try the car seat before you need it. We couldn't manage to get the seat belt round it first time we tried and had to ask a friend to show us how it went in. Very glad we didn't try for the first time coming home from hospital.' *tb*

  And don't be tempted to buy a second-hand car seat – it may be an older model which does not comply with current government safety standards; it could even have been in an accident.

- Nappies – you have a choice of disposable or reusable, and although newborn-size nappies look like they'd be too small for a doll, they still often swamp brand-new bottoms!
- Cotton wool or baby wipes – most parents, particularly of precious firstborns, kick off with cotton wool and water, graduating to wipes once they start heading out to places without ready access to water, but basically, it's up to you.
- Sleepsuits and vests (and perhaps some cardies, if it is winter – those acrylic ones made by grannies and sold in some charity shops are cheap and wash and wear well; or, if you've managed to track down wealthy godparents, you could always go the cashmere route).
- Some cellular blankets – great for swaddling newborns and stopping them waking themselves up by hitting themselves in the eye with flailing arms.
- Your breasts (preferably housed in a well-fitted maternity bra) and/or some bottles and formula. Bottles are a bit of a

trial-and-error thing in that no bottle seems to suit all babies. And some babies suit no bottles:

'I must have spent £100 buying up every bottle on the market – but my daughter never took expressed breast milk, despite me pumping out litres of the stuff for months on end.' *morningpaper*

'We love the Haberman Feeder which was recommended by a friend who is a midwife. Quite expensive, but well worth it for us, as my son will not take any other teat! Little monkey! The feeder has a valve system which means the milk will only come out when they are sucking – it doesn't shoot down their throats as soon as you turn up the bottle, which our baby hates!' *kiwikid*

- Cot/cot bed. Many Mumsnetters agree that decisions about pricey sleep equipment may be better left until after the birth, when you think about co-sleeping versus your baby's own cot (or when the baby makes them for you). If you are going to buy early, there is much to be said for a cot bed (i.e. a cot which converts to a toddler-sized bed) because of the longevity factor. A drop-side feature in a cot is also generally highly rated. If you go for a second-hand cot, remember to buy a new mattress which is firm and well-fitting, to help reduce the risk of sudden infant death syndrome (SIDS).
- A sling of some sort – for when you have accepted that you will never walk alone for more than, say, five minutes. These are indispensable for dancing colicky babies about to Classic FM, can be very useful indeed on public transport and are reckoned by some to provide mums with a respectable upper-body workout. Slings come in many varieties. (If you are very nimble-fingered you can even fashion your own wrap sling out of a long piece of fabric. Apparently.) You will need to work out which type is least likely to knacker your back and works with your personal body shape and breast layout. Try some on, test them out and remember that what works for you now may change as your baby gets bigger. Some can fit on front or back, allow multiple carrying positions, and some allow breastfeeding in situ. For the large of bosom, the kind that drapes the baby across your body can be most comfortable, while others will feel more secure with a more structured harness-style arrangement which dangles the baby vertically. Oh, and unless they are hopelessly unattractive, dads generally look hot wearing a baby in a sling (although possibly not to their actual partners).

The dissenters: some negative thoughts about slings

- The body-shape objection: 'Big knockers and slings don't go.' *cod*
- The aesthetic objection: 'I don't like to see new babies hanging in front of their parents like a big old handbag.' *JoolsToo*
- The aesthetic objection (for men): 'The Baby Bjorn is fine, but it does look a bit ridiculous on larger men – the scale is all wrong for them. Sort of like a hairy-arsed trucker carrying a Fendi "baguette" bag.' *Issymum*
- The health and shopping objection: 'It's like doing origami with an octopus; and it does your back in. Hooray for the pram! Also, if you use a sling instead, you don't have anywhere to put your shopping!' *aloha*

- A pram of some sort. At the light-industrial end of the market, you may find yourself attracted to a 'travel system'. These are lie-down prams which convert into pushchairs for larger babies and toddlers and also have a car seat attachment. They tend to be heavy, and you need to make sure the model you fancy fits into the boot of your car, or you won't be doing much travelling (legions of Mumsnetters have made this very mistake). They are valued by those who want to move a sleeping baby seamlessly from pram to car, but that's not much use if you then have to abandon the base by the roadside. Most Mumsnetters agree that by the time the baby is big enough for a stroller, what you'll want is one of those lightweight foldable ones (indispensable for anyone trying to get on a bus which already has two prams in the wheelchair space), so the travel system may be a short-lived piece of kit, though many these days are very stylish.

  What you need in the pram department is really very much dependant on your lifestyle. Some relatively light, foldable pushchairs are suitable from birth; if you use public transport a lot, this is likely to be the pushchair for you. But be aware that they are unlikely to be suitable for a young baby to sleep in for long periods. Fancier (and heavier and pricier) contraptions often have other advantages – some are much more manoeuvrable, ergonomically designed to be easier to push and more comfortable for you and baby if you walk long distances. The very old-fashioned lie-down Mary Poppins-style baby carriage has a very limited lifespan, and many are impossibly cumbersome for public transport. Do also consider how important shopping is to you – some buggies have good shopping bags or baskets or at least good handles for hanging bags on; others are pants. Read your Mumsnet reviews and test drive a selection before you buy (even if you then hurry home from the shop to order on the internet).

- Nursing bras. Don't buy more than one of these now though and do allow room for growth; your breasts may well change size radically after the birth. And you also need to get properly fitted. A bra which is too tight can lead to discomfort and blocked ducts. The good news for the particularly well endowed or floppy, is that there are now some good underwired varieties to rival what one mother feelingly called 'the monoboob-sausage look', but it is particularly important that these are fitted, so that the underwire lies correctly.

And that's probably about all you really *need*. Realistically, however, you are probably not going to stop there. So here are ...

... a few of our favourite things

If we're getting all fancy, consider these:

- Muslin squares – phenomenal multitaskers for 'mopping up, protecting, using as a tiny towel, covering the changing mat' – or even as comforters. 'When I first heard about muslins I thought, "What are they for?" Then I had a baby and knew. Never sit down to feed without muslins or kitchen roll,' says one convert. Most mums find them invaluable with sicky babies, but there are always exceptions:

'Neither of my sons would ever be sick on a specific piece of cloth; they always tended to go for maximum impact.' *Demented*

- Breast pads – to stop your cups running over. These can be disposable or reusable, but whichever you choose, make sure they are soft and absorbent – don't skimp and get rougher ones, at least not at the start, when your norks are at their most sensitive.
- A changing mat – or preferably two, including a folding travel one, so you've always got one to hand. You could use towels, but

you'd be doing an awful lot of laundry. 'Don't bother with fabric covers on the changing mat – they'll poo on them every time. We used two separate bits of kitchen roll – one for under head and shoulders, the other for under bum. If you leave them joined, the inevitable runny yellow poo spreads up the kitchen paper to the head, but a break in the paper keeps it under control.' *monkey*

- A baby gym, nest or mat – so that you *can* put that baby down, even if only for a few minutes. You may never walk (or shower, or wee) alone without one, otherwise.
- Bouncy chairs – go basic with these; it's not the buck, it's the bounce. Do not be blinded by bells, whistles and vibrating systems.

'Get the really cheap sort with a bendy wire frame that bounces when the baby moves. The more expensive ones don't. And the babies often ignore the toy bars and all the fancy extras, anyway. It's nice to have lots of different places to "put" the baby cos they get bored after ten minutes. And they like to be in the same room as you, although with your first baby you can just lay them on the floor, as you won't have a toddler stomping around.' *fruitful*

- A breast pump – but you may well want to see how things go on the breastfeeding front before making an expensive investment. Some mums profess themselves happy with a good manual pump, but many recommend buying or renting an electric one. As one thrifty Mumsnetter points out, 'eBay has loads of nearly-new ones'. (See Chapter Two for more detailed information on the relative merits of the different types of pump.)
- Baby sleeping bags with shoulder straps (which eliminate the need for blankets) – loved by many mums, hated by a minority of babies: 'Borrow one first, if you can, before shelling out.' You must buy an age- and weather-appropriate sleeping bag, and be aware that they are not suitable for the very early weeks when the bag can end up over your baby's mouth. You will find that reputable manufacturers specify a recommended minimum weight for the smallest size of sleeping bag. Otherwise, old-fashioned cellular blankets are good for layering, swaddling and temperature control.
- Lansinoh or Purelan – pure lanolin cream for sore nipples:

'It's a lovely, gentle moist wound cream, and you don't need to wash it off before feeds.' *spidermama*

- Soothing music – CDs aimed at babies, a nice cot mobile with a soothing tune, Classic FM; whatever works for you both.

But don't bother with

- Changing tables – they have a few fans and may be useful if you have back issues, but most Mumsnetters recommend the top of an ordinary chest of drawers or the floor (the sofa, the back shelf of the car, the kitchen table …)
- Bottle warmers are 'a totally useless waste of plastic and electricity' in one user's view.

'By the time the bottle heats up, the whole neighbourhood is awake from the screaming baby.' *sansouci*

- Cot bumpers – 'pointless tat' that you gussy up a cot with; not recommended for infants who can sit up and use them to climb out of the cot.
- Nappy wrapper bins – where do we start? 'Nauseatingly "sweet-scented" deodorant does not hide the stench'; 'Didn't work properly and my husband got drenched in week-old pee'; 'Now an expensive adornment to my garage'; 'Baby faeces and urine mixed with some unbearable deodorant stuff. Arghhh! I'll remember that stink until I'm 90'; 'Useless, smelly, broken'. (But then aren't we all?)
- Most baby toiletries:

'You don't need baby soap, shampoo, talc, baby oil or any of the other million things Johnson's try to sell you. You're not supposed to use anything but water to wash them with for the first couple of months, anyway … Later on, you only need the "top-to-toe" wash stuff and a big tub of aqueous cream (moisturiser – behind the counter at the chemist). I've not had a baby that needed a hairbrush. And cotton buds? Baby powder? Baby oil? What are they for?' *fruitful*

- Top and tail bowl – you know, for washing tops and tails. Well, anyway…
- Scratch mitts – judging by Mumsnetters' experiences, almost no baby requires or will wear these but, again, there are always babies determined to go their own way:

'My daughter needed these so much – after about two minutes her face would be all marked – but none fitted her tiny little arms; so I bought those hair bobble things (the soft ones) and kept the mitts on with them.' *sweetkitty*

- Baby-wipe warmers – 'Who needs a baby-wipe warmer when you can just leave the packet on top of the radiator? They do clean poo off better when they are warm, honest!' reckons one scientifically minded mum. But once again, there is always that voice crying in the wilderness:

'Have to say, we do use the wipe warmer. Since my son can't talk yet, I have no idea if he really notices the difference or not though!' *Woodstock*

À chacun son goût ...

... because babies have individual tastes too.

- Moses baskets – these will seem adorably picturesque in those sentimental latter weeks of pregnancy, but just bizarre once you contemplate putting an actual baby down among all the frothy broderie anglaise frills; particularly if you have a Giant Haystacks-style infant who already fills the basket at birth. Some babies, however, do seem to enjoy them, possibly because they are a bit womblike and enclosing, and babies who are very small indeed may sleep in them until six months plus. And there are some parents who seem to like lugging baby from room to room in a Moses basket. One piece of equipment to borrow or inherit, if possible; and certainly a conversation piece if you actually name your baby Moses.
- Swinging cradle – as per Moses baskets, above; though we doubt many will be naming their baby Swinging, but who knows?
- Nappy-changing bags. Some more parsimonious Mumsnetters will tell you that you are just as well off with a cheap rucksack or a very large handbag and a foldable changing mat. But for the handbag aficionados among us, there is something hopelessly alluring about a modern-style changing bag with special compartments for bottles, wipes, a travel changing mat and lots of doohickies. Watch out for strap arrangements which interfere with your newly outsize breasts, though. Some bags fit well over pram handles (and some pram systems have their own changing bags as optional accessories), while others may be backpack style.

- Baby walkers (essentially a small table on wheels with a seat hanging from a hole in the middle, with or without built-in plastic entertainment) – a controversial item thought to be too dangerous by some Mumsnetters because of the potential for babies to drive them recklessly down flights of stairs. According to another (possibly bungalow-dwelling) mum though, they are 'only as dangerous as you let them be' and some babies are mad for them. The ones with no wheels and toys all over the tray are obviously completely safe and another useful place to keep a bigger baby entertained, while you enjoy a wee/glass of wine. But do bear in mind that these are not insignificant items budget-wise, and they don't have more than a few months' shelf life.
- Baby baths – these seem to be popular mostly with parents who have either back or C-section issues, because they allow you to bathe baby at waist height (although you won't want to be *carrying* a full baby bath post C-section). Some think 'a sink works perfectly and is the right height for your back', but this will depend on how capacious your sinks are. For bathing in the tub, there is a wide variety of bath seats or frames available for very small babies which are widely liked by Mumsnetters, or you could just hop in the bath with her (NB – it's worth having another adult standing by if you do, or you may never be able to get out of the bath).
- Door bouncers (small bungee arrangements which attach to door frames, for infants of at least three months, who can hold their heads up properly). It is strangely hilarious to see one's bemused darling dangling off the ground in one of these, and some parents find them a useful part of their putting-baby-down-for–five-minutes arsenal. However, a reasonable proportion of babies are unsurprisingly utterly freaked out by them. Borrow one if possible.
- Bumbos – seats for an older baby which look a bit like a squishy potty. They work particularly well for babies with, er, 'chunky' thighs, and allow your child to sit up from about three months, so they can sit and watch you tidying up after them. Don't leave a baby unsupervised in a bumbo though; nothing in nature moves faster than a baby experimentally bouncing itself out of a squishy rubber chair.
- Baby monitors – consider the size of your house and the acuity of your hearing (and whether you are going to be putting baby in a room by himself at any stage).

'For me, the baby monitor was a waste of money because we have a small house and could always hear them if they cried.' *blueteddy*

Incidentally, they are, of course, great for eavesdropping and indispensible in any self-respecting soap storyline.

- Fancy clothes, tiny hats and shoes – anything which looks like grown-up clothes: these are 'always covered in sick or a huge bib'. Even if your main motivation for reproducing was to produce a dressable mini-me, remember that newborns are essentially invertebrate and don't make good clotheshorses. So step away from that teensy, weensy biker jacket. Rest assured that there is a window of opportunity between about nine months and two years (when they often start to get their own ideas) when you are likely to be able to have your sartorial way with them.

- Snowsuits – 'The really big, puffy all-in-one things that engulf babies and are impossible to get on, and then, when you do, you can't then stuff the baby into the car seat or pram', as described by one frustrated mum. These are probably going to be too hot if your baby is in a pushchair with a cositoes (a kind of padded bag with zips and poppers which fits on to a pushchair to keep an infant cosy) or a pram with blankets, but can be useful for babies dangling in slings, or if you go for a stroller with no cositoes.

- Sterilisers – some say stoutly that a 'pan on the hob does the job', but others rate a microwave steriliser (a kind of plastic container into which some water and the items needing to be sterilised go before a sojourn in the microwave) for ease and speed. The plug-in steam variety also has fans for safety and certainty, but is a bulky piece of kit if space is an issue. Check out Chapter Two for some bottle-sterilising guidelines.

- Travel cots – foldable cots which double as playpens or containment devices. Love 'em, hate 'em – another Marmite-category item for babies. Not much point for co-sleepers. (See Chapter Four for some guidelines on safe use of travel cots.)

Finally, don't stress too much about the inevitable odd bum purchase. You're not alone.

'I don't reckon you can stop someone buying the whole of Mothercare with a first baby! But hey!' wickedwaterwitch

But if you *are* buying all of Mothercare, do think a little bit about space. Nothing will bring on a bad bout of postnatal tristesse faster than being unable to find the TV remote under a heap of baby-related appliances.

Baby Names

Once your house is impassable with baby gear and/or you are too large and tired to shop, you may want to devote some of your sofa time to the question of what to call your baby. Some folks want to wait and have a look at the little creature before they start pondering the name issue. Others find it is a useful distraction from Thinking about the Birth ...

There is an argument for not discussing your name choices with anyone. Someone somewhere has a horrible aunt or a scrofulous dog with the name you fancy ... or thinks it sounds like a venereal disease ... or once lived in a country where it was the name for a venereal disease.

There is also an argument for donning a hard hat and posting the name you are considering on an internet chat board, especially if it is one you made up yourself by combining the names of your two all-time favourite pets:

'The thing is, if you post a name suggestion on here and 99 per cent of people think it's bonkers and you'd have to be as mad as a box of frogs to use it, you are within your rights (of course) to use it, but you know in advance how 99 per cent of the population is going to react. Which is useful, I think.' seeker

There are essentially two polarised schools of thought on unusual names (and some wiffly-wafflers in between who prefer to decide the issue on a name-by-name basis). Some people feel that the child with a very unusual name will spend his life repeating it, spelling it and fending off teasing (GAYlord, GAYlord, hahaha).

Others feel that actually kids need to be taught to get used to all sorts of names, that an unusual name can be a source of pride and pleasure to its bearer, that any name can be an excuse for teasing (PEEter, PEEter, hahaha) and that life would be unbearably dull if we were all called Mark or Susan (although it seems no one under 20 is these days, so these names are quite possibly due for a revival ...).

Mumsnetiquette of naming: some rules for you to ignore

- Think about your context, if you are concerned about your child having a burdensomely unusual name; you may find every child at the local Montessori nursery is called Bear or Star anyway.
- If you don't want your child to be one of 14 Ellas in her class, have a look at the national statistics for the past few years. You could also try to get to know your local demographic – by lurking in playgrounds, for example. If all the mummies are shrieking, 'Come here, Eurydice', you may want to strike that one off your shortlist.
- You can get a feel for trends by looking at the endless – and sometimes acrimonious – waffle on parenting chatboards. Some recent trends include Victorian maids' names (Lily, Evie, Mabel, Ruby) and old men's names (Archie, Arthur, Herb, Fred).
- While conducting your research, delicately consult your own feelings on the question of class associations: you may be anxious either overtly or secretly to avoid names which might be considered either 'poncey' or 'chavvy'; you may firmly reject the notion of chaviness or ponciness (and consider the first word in particular to be offensive); or you may happily embrace your own inner (or outer) ponce or chav.
- 'Every baby goes out into the world with a secret name he or she would have been given had its mummy's pregnancy hormones prevailed.' *ninedragons*
  This is worth remembering when you are fighting with your partner about the merits of 'Shark' (what a great name, sigh).
- Think about the meaning of a name and its associations. Again, the internet is useful here. Beelzebub has manifest drawbacks,

(continued)

but who knew Kennedy meant 'ugly head'? Then again if no one knows, you may not care either – at least until young Kennedy Googles it, that is.

- Test the name in question out with the accompanying surname, in terms of both meaning and initials (you know, 'Ima Hogg', 'Percy Octavius Organ' – that kind of thing), but also consider issues of rhythm, rhyme and alliteration. You may like Willy Wonka or you may feel like a fool for calling your child Kris Kristofferson.

Much debate rages on the question of giving the child a shortened version of a traditional name, i.e. a nickname. Will she feel silly as Dottie when she's running the Large Hadron Collider, for example? Conversely, can you bear the name Archibald?

'My daughter has a long name for High Days and Holidays and for when I tell her off. She likes her short name, but has the option of reverting to her long name when she gets her PhD and becomes a respectable lady.' Gingerbear

'I have a longish name and was always, always known by a shorter nickname as a child, but gradually, I started using the longer formal name – especially for CVs, job interviews, etc. I am extremely glad that I have the long name as a fallback for more 'formal' occasions, although I always think of myself by the short name. So for that reason I am firmly in the "put the long name on the birth certificate" camp.' LuLuBai

'They're called what you want them to be called – we preferred the shortened versions, end of. The only problem is when you need a longer name for when they're in trouble – I have solved this by extending their names in an Italian style for these occasions, a bit like: Cod – Codarina. I have an extremely short name (three letters, not shortened from anything) and my own mother used to call me "InTheseShoes Elizabeth" when I was in trouble.' InTheseShoes

What's in a name?

The 'bring-back-real-names' camp
'Hannah and Sophie are real names and Hannahs and Sophies won't spend their whole lives: a) spelling out their name; b) repeating their name; c) explaining why they are called that; d) wanting to *punch* their stupid parents for lumbering them with a bizarre jumble of letters instead of a name.' MaloryDon'tDiveIt'sShallow

The, ermm, 'nominative-determinism' camp
'Can I just put in a word about nominative determinism and Murphy's Law?

If you name your baby after the Sleeping Beauty, you are tempting fate. You could end up with a child who sleeps no more than ten minutes for its entire first year. Disclaimer: call your child what you like, everyone else can bugger off. PS: Then again, DO NOT let her take up embroidery, sewing or stitchery of any kind. You never know.' FabioCatello

The 'Eddie-Stobart-method' camp
'I have struck upon a rich seam indeed. Struggling to find the perfect name for your daughter? Torn between traditional or unusual? Tearing your hair out on the baby name talkboard?

(continued)

Use the Eddie Stobart Method (for the uninitiated, Eddie Stobart is a haulage company whose lorries are individually named):

Get in car. Drive on motorway. Come alongside Eddie Stobart lorry. Read name of lorry on front right-hand corner. There you go. You cannot back out once you have seen your name. The method is all about chance and living on the edge.' *Slubberdegullion*

The 'sausage-variety-method-for-boys' camp

'I met someone recently who came up with a novel way of choosing a name for a boy. She and her husband got a selection of sausages and named their son after the one they liked most.' *LuLuBai*

The 'ceased-caring' camp

'I used to love this topic. It was my ultimate relaxation. Now I think I have overdosed. I no longer CARE what other mums call their infants. I don't MIND whether people call them Snarglegarglemeepersneep, or Zg, Fruition-Bumholey, FB for short. I have no view. Names don't matter overly, whatever anyone says. It's all fine. They're all fine, and it doesn't matter if your cat was called it, or a serial killer, or it's chavvy or poncey or reminds someone of a disease. IT'S ALL FINE! <goes off gnashing teeth, whimpering, as head falls off and then the wires explode KER-BAM!>' *LadyThompson*

If you've now done all the shopping, the batch cooking, the pedicures and daytime cinema trips, this is a good time to do a bit of advance reading. Have a look at Chapter Two to begin educating yourself about breastfeeding and bottle-feeding, check out the section on visitor management in Chapter One and maybe just peek at Chapter Three, so as to get an idea about what you might expect your body to be doing and feeling like once a baby has emerged from it.

Chapter One

Starting Out

In this chapter ...

After nine months on the runaway train of pregnancy, you may be mildly startled to find yourself sitting at home with an actual infant. But here you are, none the less, and the first few weeks with a new baby can all be a bit like a one-sided love affair in which ecstatic moments alternate with profound angst.

The ecstasy to angst ratios vary enormously from person to person, as do the degrees of exhaustion, boredom and bafflement that almost all mothers seem to feel in some measure. Not only do you have an entirely new and utterly dependent person to look after, you have a rather battered and ragged self with which to do the job. And all the while you're trying not to offend your mother-in-law (or at least not irretrievably), while wondering whether it's OK to have passed a blood clot the size of a full-grown hamster.

This chapter is designed to help you find your way through these early days, sometimes referred to as the 'babymoon', but dubbed by one Mumsnetter as 'a grey blur of horror'. (Or, failing that, to make you grimace wryly, as you sob into a maternity pad. For detailed thoughts on feeding, sleeping and health, turn to subsequent chapters.) It's about surviving the initial cataclysmic changes to your life, *feelings*, coping with visitors and getting to know your baby.

The shock of the newborn

Nothing can really prepare you for the profound surprisingness of having your own baby. And for the baffling fact that they just send you home from hospital without actually ascertaining that you have any idea at all about what you are supposed to do with it. The Cats Protection League are fussier about letting you adopt an old moggy...

'It's such a shock to go from being pregnant to being plunged into a world where 24/7 is devoted to the newborn ... feeding it, worrying about it, changing it, cleaning the stump, bathing the baby without it slipping out of your arms, trying to interpret the crying/screaming, coping with well-meant but confusing advice, being totally hormonal.' *sansouci*

(continued)

The First Night

Some women find they have the best sleep of their lives in hospital after they have had their babies. Especially if they are floating on a wave of postnatal euphoria and their babies are sleeping off the birth blissfully in their little plastic bassinets. However, this idyll can be shattered by any of the following: an assortment of other new babies and mothers arriving on the ward, being awoken to hysterical screaming, finding a substance much like tar in the baby's nappy.

The scary 'first night' is likely to be the one after you first get your baby home, and there is no one there to supervise the pair of you.

'Think of your baby as a human being only smaller. There is no one-size-fits-all-approach in my opinion. Anybody telling you what to do 'exactly' is likely to make you feel as if you are going wrong if your baby behaves differently. Babies haven't read manuals. If you feel up to it, go out, or stay in, if you prefer. Have visitors, if you like them; keep them away, if not. Keep your house the temperature you like it, unless you are freaks who like freezing houses. Put a cardigan on the baby, if it seems cold (their hands and feet are always chilly, so go by tummy or neck, but don't stress; they just need one more layer than you do, as a rule). At night you might want to give the baby a bath (plain water only is all you need) and change its clothes, etc. The baby won't know day from night, but you might like the ritual. Feed when the baby seems hungry. Expect the unexpected.' aloha

'Don't expect to get any sleep the first night or two; even if the baby sleeps you'll be checking that it's still breathing every five minutes. (So sleep during the day when you can!) Be proud of yourself if you get dressed at all the first few days.' janh

'Put everything you'll need to change your baby's nappy in a box or on the changing table. We had bits and pieces for a change all over the house and it took about 15 minutes with a screaming baby to find everything after an explosive poo. Try not to come home from the hospital too late to do everything before bedtime (although this may not be possible). Make the baby's bed and then put a pile of cloth nappies or soft cloths/sheets, one on top of the other. Then you are peeling off layers to get to a clean one, rather than changing a whole cot. Have a low-wattage lamp to turn on in the middle of the night and tons of water (for yourself) wherever you are feeding.' bobthebaby

Home Again, Home Again, Jiggety-jig

In some cultures, you would be lying around in a tent for forty days and having fragrant spices rubbed into your belly by female members of your family (an experience possibly not to everyone's taste). In our culture, however, you may not be long out of hospital before you are making cups of tea for your father-in-law, while trying to ensure that mad Auntie Irene doesn't feed your new baby chocolate fingers.

You may find yourself wishing you were back in your filthy sheets on the maternity ward, where at least someone else was making you tea and toast.

'In a lot of cultures, it is the norm for a new mum to move back to her mother's house for a month, where she does *nothing* except feed the baby. This is a really, really, really, really, really, really, really, really good idea.' acnebride

(Depending on your mother, of course.)

If money is not too tight, you might consider hiring a postnatal doula or maternity nurse to help you through the early weeks.

'A postnatal doula will cook, iron, take care of older children, take care of the new baby/ies (bath, walk, etc.). Whatever the new mum will find useful. She doesn't stay the night and is probably cheaper than a maternity nurse. Maternity nurses are baby-centred, while doulas are mother- and family-centred. A maternity nurse will give you 24-hour care for six days a week and will get up at night with the baby and set a routine for him or her. A doula will help the mother to do the mothering: she will give advice and help with breastfeeding, help calm her fears, help with housework, and encourage the mother to care of herself as well as the baby.' pupuce

> The best way to recruit is through a personal recommendation; otherwise there are professional websites you can try, see Resources, p. 434. Make sure you choose someone you genuinely like in interview, who has excellent references and (if she is a maternity nurse) has appropriate training and qualifications. Do also think about how you will feel about having someone else in the house all the time:

'I had a maternity nurse for four weeks after my son was born and have mixed feelings about them. It is *very* hard having someone living with you at such an amazing time of your life, when you just want to be "your own new family unit", and it didn't help that I didn't get on with mine at all. She picked at a lot of things I did and gave my son formula when I wanted to breastfeed only. In the end, my husband spoke to her about anything I couldn't face bringing up (I was very emotional). But, but, BUT – I managed to sleep a lot when she was here, which was great for getting over a C-section, and by the time she left my son knew the difference between night and day. So, I would have another maternity nurse next time (clearly not the same one), but would be much firmer about what I wanted at the interview stage, and if she didn't like it, find someone else.' Tinkerbell

It's Your Baby, You Can Cry If You Want to: the Baby Blues

The baby blues tend to occur any time in the first week after birth, and can last for several days or as little as half an hour (but they can be later or longer-lasting; don't fret too much if you feel moody/bloody miserable in a way you weren't expecting). They are generally ascribed to a combination of exhaustion, massive hormonal changes and the 'lifestyle' changes (hollow laughter) a new baby brings.

You may find yourself possessed by what you subsequently recognise to be strange thoughts and anxieties, such as: 'My baby is bald – he may never grow any hair, boo hoo hoo'; 'This bread is the wrong size for my toaster, boo hoo hoo'; 'I am afraid I'm going to trip and send my baby flying twenty feet across the room and out of that window, boo hoo hoo'. It takes everyone a bit differently and affects some women not at all, or perhaps not with every pregnancy. You may find yourself doing a lot of weeping, like one particularly lachrymose Mumsnetter: 'About twenty-four hours after giving birth, I just sobbed for hours. I have never sobbed like it; I couldn't breathe. And I had nothing to cry about either.'

But it can all have a paradoxical quality:

'On day three I cried at the World Cup match (England weren't even playing). And then cried because I was finding breastfeeding really difficult. And then cried because my baby boy was so beautiful that I couldn't believe he was mine. But looking back, it was one of the happiest days of my life.' thebecster

Or you may feel really, really grim. And the baby blues can be a particularly alarming prospect if you have suffered in the past from depression or panic attacks. Remind yourself that feeling a bit weepy/moody/panicky is normal and will pass. Feed yourself properly. Have a walk and get some fresh air, if you can. Follow any advice you find particularly helpful and *look after yourself*.

Baby blues which persist beyond a few weeks may be postnatal depression (PND) and you should consider seeking medical advice (see p. 146).

Beware of In-laws Bearing Gifts: the Art of Visitor Regulation

It can seem mightily unjust. You are beyond tired. Your breasts have started to leak and/or turned into boulders. You may still look pregnant. You may even be wearing incontinence pants (as recommended by some Mumsnetters for Caesarean wounds). You are trying to bond with your new infant. And suddenly you are thrust into the ferocious world of grandparent diplomacy.

Your family and other animals

'I enjoyed having some visitors, but my dad drove me crazy. He started camcording the minute he saw my son and myself (five hours post C-section, still bloated with drugs). They came again on the third day with my aunt. My son was just learning to latch on and again, out came the camcorder, at which point I did put my foot down. Then they wouldn't flipping leave for about two hours. It was like some Alan Bennett play: three oldies yapping on about how loud the music was in Tesco these days, and me wondering

(continued)

if the baby would ever let go of my boob and if breastfeeding was meant to hurt so much.' *rookiemum*

'My mother-in-law was waiting behind the door of the delivery suite and came in about fifteen minutes after the baby had been born – I had a second-degree tear and they wanted to stitch me up; my husband had to almost throw her out after that first cuddle! At the time, I wanted just my husband and me, but my mother-in-law is by herself now and my husband is her pride and joy; she was desperate to see the baby, so I just couldn't deny her the experience. My mum always used to say "offer it up to the Holy Souls"; I believe the modern idiom is "suck it up" – not quite as poetic, but you get my drift.' *quarkee*

'You never know how you will feel. When my son was born, I had a bad time, and was rather pleased to still be here to *see* my visitors! I was filled with love for all my family and friends and loved having the security of having them around.' *HonoriaGlossop*

'I had a home birth and the house was invaded for six hours straight for the next two days. We were not given a choice in the matter; no one cared that we hadn't eaten or slept, and we were too dazed to deal with it. It affected both of us deeply, to the point that it almost tipped me into PND. No way is that happening next time. I'm staying in bed for a week. People can come for 20 minutes and then bugger off, unless they're planning to cook or mop the floor for us. Some people know how to act around new parents, others don't. Those that don't need to be told. It's a learning curve: last time was hideous; this time will be different.' *bohemianbint*

Obviously everyone's family, friends and in-laws are different, but the one piece of advice that emerges from all the horror stories is to give some thought to the situation before your baby is born, if possible. Consider initially asking for no visitors at the hospital, or only those you feel very comfortable with, whether that be your own mother or sister, a close female friend or whoever. Then see how you feel before deciding what you want by way of visitors.

You may be physically a mess, or you may be euphoric and high on adrenaline. Or both.

It's also an idea to let visiting friends know if you'd rather receive a lasagne than some pink carnations in a ceramic stork.

'Tell people to bring a pressie for you, not the kid – a voucher for a facial is much more welcome in my house than another pink babygro.' lilymum

Think about how you are likely to feel about breastfeeding in front of particular audiences. Someone who will merrily breastfeed on the bus may feel uncomfortable doing so in front of her father-in-law. If you do feel awkward, you will want to keep visits pretty short while you are establishing breastfeeding.

'I personally found it very embarrassing to breastfeed in front of relatives. It was hard enough getting the baby's position right, without having to keep my boobs hidden from all and sundry. In the end, I shut myself in our bedroom to breastfeed – I felt a bit like a prisoner in my own home.' BigBadMouse

Don't end up doing all of the crowd control yourself:

'"Gatekeeping" is a very good job to give to your partner. I can't imagine anybody minding if they're told at the outset, "She's really tired – can we keep it to five minutes?" People usually like to feel they're doing their bit to take care of you by keeping it brief, I think.' HonoriaGlossop

Some veterans advocate a 'no-visitors-without-an-appointment' policy, or a 20-minute warning rule. Your heart may sink at the thought of the response of your nearest and dearest to such a rule, so just work with what you've got; there's no point stressing yourself out by trying to completely re-engineer your family. Even if you don't have any breastfeeding issues though, do still think about time-limiting visits – you are going to be tired.

If you are finding it all too much:

'Say something sooner rather than later. A quiet, "I need to find my own way with him," as my mother-in-law raced across the room when he squeaked, soon got the message across! And perhaps say something like, "It's been lovely seeing everyone, and it is so nice that everyone is so pleased about baby's arrival, but we'll have a few days on our own now, to settle down to being a family." Any response along the lines of, "We're family too/we only want to help/we're excited" can be rebuffed with the finding-our-own-way line. Much, much better to do it now than let it run and then become a source of long-term resentment. Not good for anyone.' mrschop

It's delicate ground, but for many Mumsnetters there are rational distinctions to be drawn between mothers and mothers-in-law (or simply between helpful and supportive relatives and those who are not):

'I want my in-laws to have close and loving relationships with my baby. But I also know that I am at risk of PND, and after the birth my mum is coming to stay to offer support. My mother-in-law (who my husband finds infuriating, never mind me) will be welcome to visit as often as she likes – but after a week, so I can recover from birth and becoming a mum.' Qally

Mumsnetiquette: Crowd control the Mumsnet way

'Consider staying in your PJs all day, for at least the first ten days. That way, visitors treat you more as an invalid.' *whatdayisit*

'If your parents or in-laws want to come and stay, suggest a B&B.' *LaTrucha*

'The best thing I did with baby no. 3 was to put a photo of the baby on a poster on the front door, saying: "Mum and I are fast asleep – please can you call back another time when we will be awake and pleased to see you!"' *lianey1802*

Above all, do what you feel is best for you, your partner and your baby. It's not really a time to be evaluating and considering everybody else's needs. If you need some time just to be together as you, baby and partner, you are well within your rights to ask for it (or get your partner to do so). But if all else fails:

'Just tell them all to bugger off and leave you alone. Then when you're ready for babysitters, apologise and blame it on the hormones.' *platesmasher*

I Will Survive (or Actually, I Might Not): the First Few Weeks

The visitors dry up, your partner goes back to work and you and your baby are alone together. All day. Every day. Breathe deeply into a brown paper bag.

'I remember that in the early days, when my husband left the house, I had an incredible urge to open the door and run down the street screaming, "Please don't leave me with the baby!"' bademployeur

The horror! The horror! – mixed feelings

'It is quite a shock becoming a parent and suddenly being totally responsible for a new human being on a permanent basis. It's something I don't think anyone is really prepared for, no matter how wanted their children are. The loss of self and the absolute necessity to put someone else before yourself is certainly something I struggled with when my son was born.' *Pheebe*

'Yes, you did do the right thing having a baby, you just don't realise it yet.' *Melrose*

'Undoubtedly, it is hard; there will be miserable times, but there are some absolutely brilliant ones too. It doesn't have to be a battle. I expected it to be and remember thinking I must have missed something when my husband and I sat having dinner while watching film the whole way through, with our week-old son happily washed, fed and sleeping next to us.' *stripeybumpsmum*

'Enjoy every minute because it goes by very, very fast.' *hollyboo*

'The first year is a nightmare. You'll want to divorce your husband about once a month – it's a normal part of parenting. All that bollocks about "enjoying" your screaming baby, "he'll grow up so fast". Shite. Every hour felt like a lifetime in that first year.' *highlander*

'Someone once said to me they were thinking about having kids and what would I say to persuade them, so I told them that before my son was born I could go for months without feeling really happy, but since I had my son I had at least one moment of pure happiness and joy every single day and that is still true.' *Viggoswife*

Mumsnetters' 17-step new baby survival guide (stick this on your fridge, if you are a sticking-things-on-your-fridge sort of person)

- If you were, ahem, very organised in late pregnancy, it is great to have lots of tasty and nutritious frozen meals you can simply heat up – but, 'Survive on pot noodles if you have to,' advises one mum. Try to ensure there are lots of easy-to-eat things in your fridge – do an internet shop and stock up. One new mother's partner rather touchingly made her a packed lunch before going off to work. And remember, desperate times lead to opportunistic measures:

'If people offer to help, ask them to bring you cooked meals.' *legophobe*

- Don't worry about implementing any sort of routine (Gina Ford followers block your ears). But see Chapter Two for some more detailed thoughts on routines.
- If you watch lots of cruddy daytime TV or read trashy magazines during this period, IT DOESN'T COUNT! You will not suffer brain-cell loss and no one is allowed to hold it against you.
- Relax about housework, if you can. It really doesn't matter. But if you can't relax, don't stress Woody Allen-style about not being relaxed. If you can leave the chaos to accrue around you, great, but if you can't, try to work out a strategy for dealing with it:

'If at all possible get a cleaner for the first three months. I found I got really stressed about the state of the house (which was stupid, by the way, but I can't change me).' *whatdayisit*

Or make the visitors do the housework. Or your partner. Or frankly, if that's what you need, do it yourself with your baby in a sling (the Hoover makes lovely soothing white noise).

- It doesn't matter if you stay in your pyjamas all day, unless it matters to you. If you are in the stay-in-bed camp and you can afford to, have some nice new pyjamas and bedding at the ready for this period and barricade yourself in.
- On the other hand, some of us go mad if we can't be up and about. And that's OK too. 'Personally, I did like to get showered and dressed. My partner can have the baby for 15 minutes and I do feel better when refreshed,' admits one mother, while another says, 'I also put on make-up every day at some point, just to keep me in touch with my former self.'

- Sleep as much as you can (but don't beat yourself up if you can't).
- Get out of the house to fight the feelings of isolation and lack of adult company. Some people find mother-and-baby groups are the answer:

'Getting out and meeting other mums will really help – find a group to go to if you aren't already a member of one. Your local NCT will run coffee mornings, and you don't have to be a member to go. Or your health visitor can help you find somewhere.'
NorthernLurker

Also try Mumsnet local (www.mumsnet.com/local), local health centres and children's centres for information about local groups. After all, where else can you go and find people who are as 'tired and boring' as you are and prepared to discuss, nay apparently fascinated by, the dull minutiae of your baby's feeding routine? Mother-and-baby groups are useful even if your baby is a colicky screamer; as one mother puts it: 'Go out and meet other mums because your baby is screaming. Those other mums were a godsend for me. They took him off me for five to ten minutes (screaming of course), just so that I could get a little relief.' Remember, there's no shame in enjoying the comfort of strangers – and the fact that the only thing that has brought you together in the first place is the coincidence of simultaneous reproduction doesn't mean that some of them won't end up as real mates. And even if they don't, you may find that just getting out of the house and being given tea that somebody else has brewed is good for your mental health.
- If mother-and-baby groups give you the heeby-jeebies, don't feel you have to go to them:

'I know that everyone tells you to get out of the house, but baby groups are definitely not the cure for anything much, other than how to kill the long and fractious afternoons. You meet a whole load of women who you don't necessarily have much in common with other than child-rearing, and are forced to exchange banalities in case you say something controversial. Then you go home and tell your partner either that a) they are dull or b) they are weird because they prop books up on the playmat around their baby even though he is only three months old.' *twocatsonthebed*

Baby groups – even baby massage and increase-your-baby's-IQ-by-listening-to-classical-music groups – exist primarily for the benefit of parents. Your newborn is not going to be a social misfit or dim-witted if he hasn't been to baby yoga. But don't be too full of preconceptions either – some may indeed turn out to be cliquey and full of Stepford Wives, while others may be more to your taste. Not going to mother-and-baby groups can be a bit like that Groucho Marx line about not joining any club which would have you as a member. If you don't like one group, try another.

- There are other ways to get out and about:

'Go out when you feel physically well. Have lunch with friends and take the baby. Go to galleries or whatever you like to do. Your baby will never be so sleepy or so portable!' *aloha*

Sometimes just walking, walking, walking is the answer – it is likely to send a grizzling baby to sleep and salvage your mental health.

- Some mothers recommend taking a sleeping newborn out for dinner in a sling or car seat; it may be your last chance to do so without getting babysitters before he hits puberty (but put a napkin over the top of his head while you are eating if he's in a sling; it is shaming to carry around an infant with gravy in his hair).
- There are other ways to battle loneliness:

'I used to have a radio on very low during night/early-morning feeds; for me it was the World Service – that way, I kept up with what was going on in the world and didn't feel lonely thinking everyone else was fast asleep and I was the only one awake.' *glassofwine*

- Stash reading material, snacks, bottles of water, remote controls and telephones within easy reach of places you are likely to be marooned, feeding or just cradling a snoozing baby.
- Find someone else who will look after the baby, even for a few hours a week, so you can sleep or read or have a haircut or hang out on the internet (or stare into space, pondering your ruined life). If you can afford to pay for childcare, a mother's help, childminder, or even a part-time nanny may be an option. But unless you have organised this prior to the birth, be realistic about whether you are up to the job now of recruiting. If you are blessed with a competent and willing grandparent or other relative or friend, exploit him or her ruthlessly.

- Look to the future:

  'Nothing is for ever. No baby has ever cried for ever. You will get to sleep again; your house will get straight again ...' *fiestabelle*

- Eat cake.
- Finally, bear in mind that as one mother observed about this turbulent period: 'Husbands (and other partners) are your allies. Sometimes they don't know they are acting like assholes.'

What the Hell Do I Do With This Baby Now?

This is the bit where you put aside that fond dream of writing a novel/setting up a cupcake business/getting your PhD while on maternity leave (during all those hours when the baby is sleeping – yeah, right), because some babies love you so much, they don't want to be anywhere but in your arms. The following advice is for anyone who has been attacked by a cling-on or just needs to know how to distract a not-particularly-clingy small baby:

'You know the constipated stage after you've had a baby? Well couple that with a cling-on, a perineal tear and really bad piles and you have a recipe for disaster. When my daughter was a couple of weeks old, I sat on the loo with her in a sling, trying to go for an *hour*, as there was no way I could concentrate on the job in hand with her crying the house down!' MarmaladeSun

Surviving a Klingon

First, remember that most cling-on babies outgrow this stage within a matter of a few months, and that they are no more clingy at a later stage than any other baby. Next, consider survival tactics:

- Try a baby gym with appropriate dangly bits, a mobile or even wind chimes – something that can be batted at and/or which makes a noise, 'with some annoying plinky-plink nursery rhyme music going as well', adds one mum. Some parents rig up their own dangly contraptions for particular areas of the house, such as 'soft cubes or balls hung up while you are in the bathroom on a clothes horse', recommends a creative Mumsnetter. Be aware, however, that many babies don't really get interested in the dangly stuff until about five or six weeks, when they gain the ability to track the movement of objects with their eyes.
- Consider carrying a bouncy chair around to be placed wherever you need it. For some that means putting it in the bathroom, as they shower, while others find they can manage a bit of cooking by simultaneously wiggling a strategically positioned bouncy chair with one foot.
- 'OK, here's one that just happened to work for me: big bold Lamaze-type geometric designs printed out on squares of paper and stuck on the wall. My baby used to stare at them for minutes, rather than seconds.' *suzywong*
- You could try letting her cry for a bit, with or without the Hoover on, even if it's just long enough for you to go to the loo or make yourself a cup of tea. Be sure though that your baby is not crying through hunger, because his nappy is dirty or because he is in pain. If this crying thing is not something you are comfortable with, don't do it, but some mothers swear by it as a sanity-saver.
- Some swear by those automated swingy-chair-type things – particularly suitable if you've a living room the size of Japan to accommodate it.

But probably the most popular solution for Mumsnetters with very clingy small babies is to just ride with it and wear your baby. As one mum puts it, 'Get a sling; then you will have your arms back and she gets to be close to you.' She, like many others, found this is the only answer in the end; and, 'You can really do almost anything once you get used to it,' attests another mum. (Hygiene warning: if you have a leggy infant and a sling that straps baby vertically on your front, some careful positioning is needed when weeing.)

'If she wants to be held, then hold her. Yes, it takes up your whole day but it's not for ever, and

if it makes you feel less stressed because you're not always thinking that you *should* be able to put her down, then it can only be for the good.'

MarmaladeSun

And finally, a word of comfort from an old hand:

'Clingy baby fast becomes loveable toddler, and you will have forgotten all this.' secur

(See also Chapter Seven: Parenting – or What to Do With Babies All Day.)

Clingy baby plus toddler: time to get a new life?

There is much rumination on the Mumsnet talkboards on how to cope when you have betrayed your beloved toddler by bringing home a new baby. A new, tiny, helpless baby which you are cuddling *all the time*, and which cannot even play trains or do anything remotely interesting or amusing *at all*.

Some parents feel the solution can be summarised in one word: CBeebies. Others find there is only so much *Big Cook, Little Cook* they can be doing with. Here are some slightly fancier strategies devised by these neurasthenic types:

'The best bit of advice I ever got on this subject was: let the baby cry, deal with the older one. The baby doesn't know any different, and as long as he/she is somewhere safe, won't come to any harm being left to cry for a little while. The older one, on the other hand, seeing that you always see to the baby first and ignore him/her *will* suffer.' *Squonk*

'I involve my first daughter in caring for her baby sister as much as possible – helping me change her nappies, passing me muslins and generally supervising.' *Bakewell Tarts*

'These work for me: going out to toddler groups in the morning, where toddler can play happily with the other children, while I can sit and breastfeed and have some adult conversation; getting a sling that I can carry/breastfeed baby and still play with my toddler; when people came to see the new baby, we told them to make a fuss of my older daughter as well, so she didn't get left out.' *chloejessmeg*

'Perfect the art of entertaining from the sofa. While you sit feeding baby, have some music on and encourage your toddler to dance or jump or generally use up energy.' *mumwhensdinnerready*

After trying every tip available, you may just have to accept that the best you can do is to muddle through in a more or less inadequate way, until your baby is bigger and things improve of their own accord.

'Have to say, I am sinking. I can't leave baby to cry – it stresses me out beyond belief. Have had some success swinging the baby to sleep; I managed to get about half an hour to spend cooking with my son this morning ... It is really rough, and there's a lot of CBeebies watched and a lot of guilt felt here. Am assured it will pass though, and am strangely heartened to see other people in exactly the same boat.' *bohemianbint*

U-G-L-Y – That Baby's Got No Alibi

For some women, there is no such thing as an ugly baby; for others, there is no such thing as their own ugly baby. Some of us, however, may feel a painful identification with Grendel's mother, at least when it comes to the newborn period. One of the greatest consolations of the mother-and-baby group may be comparing your baby's level of bald pimpliness with that of the baby next to you (internal monologue: 'OK, my baby has a head shaped like a television, but at least you can see his eyes ...').

Beauties and beasts

'When I look back at my daughter's first few months, I could die of shame. I was quite convinced that no one would have seen such a cute baby, and insisted on showing photos at every opportunity when I returned to work. Cringe! Now, when I look at photos of my daughter from birth, she looks like a crumpled-up baby bird (not a cute fluffy one – a wide-mouthed, scrawny one with its eyes closed)! Of course, now she's the toddler equivalent of a super-model ...' *Moomin*

'My daughter was born with amazingly hairy ears! She had lots of hair on her head, but I actually trimmed the ear hair after my partner said that she reminded him of a werewolf.' *Jenie*

'I honestly was struck dumb by the sheer beauty of my son. I sat in bed seriously wondering what I was going to do when the baby model scouts saw him and I had to regretfully turn them down. Also, I strongly suspected I would be mobbed in the street if I took him out. I genuinely pitied anyone who didn't have as beautiful a baby as mine (i.e. everyone). Yes, I was quite, quite mad. However, I don't think my reaction was that different from most people's. You are not objective with your own child, but see them through a fuzzy soft-focus of love.' *aloha*

'Ha ... my baby was ugly ... really, really ugly! People still laugh at the photos of him when he was a few hours old. He looked like one of those pug dogs! I couldn't believe that I had given birth to such an ugly baby! He began to smooth out by the time he was a few weeks old and got better looking every day and, sorry to say this everyone, but he is now definitely the best-looking child on the planet ... there is no child better-looking than him ... honest!' *Ghosty*

'When my son was a baby he had severe eczema all over his face – really bad, bleeding, scabby eczema. People used to stop to look in the pram and say, "Oh, what a beautiful ... pram". But he was still the yummiest baby in the world to me.' *themildmanneredjanitor*

So, it's perfectly normal to think your ugly baby is beautiful or that your ugly baby is ugly (or to fall into the substantial minority of women who have actually given birth to the most beautiful infant in the history of the world). Don't worry about it. The anecdotal consensus is that ugly ducklings often become swans and most people would rather have a happy ugly duckling anyway (enough with the bird metaphors already).

Bear in mind that a lot of the odder aspects of being a newborn settle relatively rapidly – the swollen genitals and breasts, the body hair (more common in slightly premature babies), the misshapen and bruised heads. And, hey you'll probably miss those kissable wolfish tufts on his shoulder blades, particularly when the hair on his head also falls out, possibly in a fetching tonsure style.

Spotty babies

Many babies turn rapidly from newborn peaches to two-week-old pustule-monsters. This can be distressing, particularly if you are feeling postnatally somewhat unstrung.

'The standard "bad skin" of young babies is the reason that newborn babies are not used in advertising and why they use three-month-olds instead.' Twiglett

Generally speaking, your beloved's plukes will clear up by themselves, usually by about three months. Remind yourself of your mother's advice to you in adolescence: you *must not* squeeze your baby's spots, however tempted you are.

'Don't put any creams or lotions on them. Just wash with water and pat dry. Baby acne is very common at this age – my daughter had it from six to eight weeks – and it looks worse when hot/angry or agitated. My health visitor said

that it could occasionally get infected if they scratched at it, so keep an eye out, and if it does, they may prescribe a steroid, but this is unlikely.'
ShowofHands

And do not blame yourself. You cannot give your baby spots by existing yourself on an acne-inducing diet of chips and chocolate.

'Spots are hormonal within the baby, nothing to do with your milk at all. And these spots invariably appear the very minute you want to get out there and show off your baby or book a photo session.' aloha

Occasionally, spots are more serious or persistent and you should take medical advice.

'It's normal to get little milk spots, but they should clear fairly quickly. If they are angry red, spreading, and perhaps oozing, then do see your GP. It could be a condition known as seborrhoeic dermatitis (aka cradle cap), and will clear up quickly with a waft of hydrocortisone.' ScienceTeacher

Stork marks

These are reddish patches, usually found on your baby's eyelids or at the nape of her neck, caused by dilated blood vessels. They tend to get darker and more prominent if your baby is hot or cross, but grow fainter over time. They can seem very obvious and even alarming when your baby is new, then they fade away almost without you noticing them going.

'I was told varying timescales for when the stork marks would fade – from one to four years. Looking back at photos, I am amazed I wasn't more worried about my daughter's – she had quite a lot of her face covered at birth – but I knew I'd had them too and have no marks now. I found a photo yesterday of my daughter when she was about a year and a half and it had improved quite a bit, and was hardly noticeable at all a year later. She is now ten and you would never know she had them. It does vary by child and how "badly" they have them. All my three have had them, but my daughter's were definitely the worst, so seemed to take longer to fade.' KTeePee

Whatever Love Means

In the strange hallucinatory, sleep-deprived world that is many women's postnatal experience, it is easy to get stressed, not only about things like your baby's acne or whether you've ruined his life by calling him Percival, but also about the exact nature of your feelings for this new, helpless, dependent, cuddly/fierce, oddly familiar stranger who is occupying your bed and your whole life.

Remember that not all women bond instantly with their babies. While some are smitten immediately, many others find it is months before they feel anything they would identify as 'love'. Retrospectively, some mothers say that they are not that keen on the tiny-baby stage, although they love toddlers/seven-year-olds/teenagers (OK, maybe not teenagers). But most find that as the baby becomes more responsive and active, their feelings of affection and of having a relationship with the baby grow. Similarly, a lot of fathers, who do not have the early physical links with the new baby, also report a more gradual bonding process.

It is all a little unpredictable. You may have been a hard-living singleton, looking on your friends' offspring as dribbling, boneless horrors one year, only to become besotted with your own dribbler the next. Or you may have spent your entire adolescence selecting the names of your six lovely future children and drawing their hairstyles on the back of your geography notebook, but find yourself, none the less, baffled by your ambivalent feelings for your firstborn.

Having a difficult birth, poor postnatal care, difficulty establishing breastfeeding or developing PND are all factors which may defer the mother–baby romance. Allow yourself and your baby time to get to know and like each other. Don't give yourself a hard time about your feelings; your baby needs to be warm, fed and held. She cannot hear your evil thoughts when she wakes you for the fourth time between midnight and 6 a.m., and even if those evil thoughts occasionally escape the barrier of your lips, she will not understand them.

And looking on the positive side, if it turns out that you really are not one of nature's new-baby lovers, one great advantage of not being a neonatophile is that you are less likely to be plagued by random and inappropriate broodiness when you encounter newborns in the future. Feelings of horror and pity on encountering a new mother with child can, after all, have a very useful contraceptive effect.

Emotionally weird – how you might feel about your newborn

'Oh, but let's face it – babies are pretty unlikeable at that age: cry, shit, cry, shit, cry, shit, don't sleep, etc., etc.' *icod*

'It didn't happen at once to me (I was in so much pain for weeks after my daughter's birth that, frankly, I couldn't be bothered with her), but that great big heart-wrenching love happened in time. When she was several months old, whenever my husband asked me, "How much do you love our daughter?" I would cry. Literally. Tears coming down my face.' *CoteDAzur*

'I loved my son and was very protective when he was born, but not all-consumingly in the way I had expected. That crept up on me when he was around seven months – I was suddenly overwhelmed with how much I loved him and how amazing my life was now. With my daughter, it came much quicker –the moment I saw her, actually. I did have a horrible birth experience with my son though, and it was much more straightforward with my daughter.' *Viggoswife*

Chapter Two

Boarding the Milk Train

In this chapter ...

Whatever else happens to you along your breastfeeding journey, you probably won't be the Mumsnetter mum afflicted with new-baby vagueness of mind who carefully showed the blushing Sainsbury's delivery man where to put the bags in her kitchen. Only to notice, as he hurried off, that one of her breasts had been poking its nose, like a curious puppy, out of her 'nursing' top. Or then again, maybe you will. But you probably won't care that much. Motherhood – it's a great leveller ...

For something so very basic, the feeding business gives rise to some surprisingly tough decisions. Breast or formula-feeding? Demand-feeding or routine? There is probably no touchier topic on Mumsnet Talk than 'Breast and Bottle-feeding'. And yet there is probably no forum where more detailed, thoughtful and nuanced advice and support are proffered.

Because these choices touch our newly discovered, achingly raw maternal nerves. When everyone is telling you that breast is best, and you can't pick up a newspaper without reading yet another story about how breastfed babies are healthier, slimmer and brainier, but you are struggling to breastfeed, you can feel like a failure as a mother when you've barely begun. On the other hand, many women who would like to breastfeed still encounter the attitude that breastfeeding is 'a martyrdom for loony hippies'; or they have mothers, other family members or mates who regard the activity with unconcealed distaste; or they secretly worry that if they breastfeed they will end up reeling their breasts into their bras like old pantyhose.

We live in a society with *layers* of screwed-up attitudes to breastfeeding and to breasts. And sometimes, in trying to redress those attitudes, we manage to make women who don't breastfeed (for whatever reason) feel pretty rubbish too. Plus, we have a health service that tells women they ought to breastfeed, yet all too often offers very little to help them do so.

'All over the hospital there are posters saying that breastfeeding is so much better for your baby than bottle; maybe they should try and think for a moment about the message that puts across to those who can't breastfeed: you are

a bad mother; you are not doing the best for your baby; you should be taken outside, lined up against a wall and shot. I had more than one midwife come into my room and tut at me when they saw me with a bottle. I ended up shouting, "Read my f*cking notes," at one of them. I felt *really* sorry for the mums who didn't breastfeed but had no medical reason; they probably beat them on the bottom of their feet with a bedpan.'
CountessDracula

'Women are badly let down by the prevalent culture, which expects them to breastfeed, but often leaves them alone, vulnerable, without any proper support either from professionals, society or family.' harpsichordcarrier

'Breastfeeding is not best when you can't breastfeed for health reasons (traumatic birth, etc.). It is not best when you have PND and can barely look after yourself, let alone get up every two hours without any help. And it is not best when you are in such pain that breastfeeding actually destroys any pleasure that you could get from holding your baby, feeding him and cuddling him.' Pitchounette

Similarly, the choice between demand-feeding and various off-the-peg routines can feel horribly over-laden with significance. Some routines seem to promise that they will make your baby happy and healthy, that they will set her up for a life of success and wellbeing, *that they will make her sleep through the night.* And so you squint at the book, which may be full of pseudoscientific charts and tables, convinced in your heart that you are ruining your baby's life because you cannot make her sleep for an hour in a darkened room at mid-morning. Alternatively, you and your baby may find that a routine liberates you from the formlessness of demand-feeding in a way that suits you both. Until someone at baby-massage group tells you that you should be 'attachment parenting' and responding minute by minute to his needs ...

But, believe it or not, the day will come when you can laugh at all of this.

'I am currently writing a book on the new method of baby-led rearing. This is where you rear your child according to their wants and needs. So, for example, if baby wants to put their head in the dog's bowl, we allow it, as they need to find out what is acceptable or not for themselves. We, as parents, are just the observers in this scenario that is life. Baby finds out what is good and not so good by exploring for themselves. They decide when to eat and when to sleep and we are led by their decisions.' Rhubarb

'My babies have led my rear to be huge. Does that count?' ledodgy

And, of course, there are the practicalities. For some women, breastfeeding is deeply enjoyable, for others it is a tolerable routine, and for the unfortunate few it can be a cracked-nipple-inducing, mastitis-causing vale of tears (although for most of us it doesn't have to be that way in the long term). Sometimes, you will have to do it when you are out and about – where should you do it, how should you do it, what should you wear? If you are bottle-feeding, what kit do you need and what do you do with it all? If you are breastfeeding, is it OK to introduce a bottle? And what about expressing? Can you carry on breastfeeding when you return to work?

This chapter is not about telling you what is best for you and your baby (there are enough people doing that already), but about helping you find your own way and working with the choices you have made or that life and your baby make for you.

How to Get Breastfeeding Support (and We Don't Mean Bras)

It's worth saying at the outset that for some women, it all comes pretty easily. The baby learns to latch on quite quickly (especially if he's a fat, full-term guzzler with no health problems). There will be some soreness and the inevitable boulder-like mammaries when the milk comes in, but basically it all goes to plan.

But some babies and mothers just can't seem to get the party started without some help – sometimes a lot of help. There are all kinds of things that can mess up breastfeeding: a difficult birth, medication, lack of support at the right moment . . . Maybe the fact that we all get booted out of hospital into our ordinary lives these days with no 'lying-in' period has a part to play too:

'So many early problems of breastfeeding are solved by just taking the baby to bed and feeding for a couple of days. Presumably, that's what happened in the past, and many problems would have been sorted out quickly without a need for breastfeeding helplines, etc.' tiktok

It can be hard to find the support you need. Most midwives, health visitors and GPs are not breastfeeding experts. Sadly, a lot of mothers find there simply aren't the resources in the NHS to provide them with useful breastfeeding advice before they leave hospital and that, like one mother, they just encounter 'untrained nursing auxiliaries (not even midwives, I think) forcing baby on to the nipple with no idea what they were doing'. Literally hundreds of Mumsnetters have posted about poor, or frankly bizarre, experiences while trying to get started on breastfeeding. One mother, who was struggling to breastfeed in hospital, was grateful to be assisted by a cleaner who happened to be an experienced mother herself!

'I do remember one of the best midwives I ever met saying to me: "Mrs Caligula, I'm only a midwife – I can't support you to breastfeed. You really need a proper breastfeeding counsellor. Don't hang about here in the hospital; go home and phone the breastfeeding counsellor immediately."' Caligula

'When I had both my daughters, it was the middle of the night by the time I got on to the ward, and the midwife on duty made me feel like a total pain in the arse for asking for help with the first feed. It also didn't help having a different midwife helping with each feed; they all showed me different things, and most of them just shoved my nips in and said, "There you go, that's a good latch." The fact that it was agony to feed from start to finish was just because they needed to "toughen up". It would be wonderful if each ward had a breastfeeding counsellor on duty all the time, who could help (more than one mum at a time if necessary) and stay throughout the feed, but I think I may be being a little optimistic!' hazeyjane

Unfortunately, for many women breastfeeding is shortlived simply because they aren't given the right support. As one Mumsnetter who is also a breastfeeding counsellor puts it, 'Ramming heads on to breasts is known (from research) to be more likely to lead to a shorter time breastfeeding – and, I can tell you, we breastfeeding counsellors recognise it as a factor in turning babies *off* breastfeeding, as well as making their mothers feel like crap, to be honest. It's disempowering and intrusive.'

You may get lucky in hospital and receive skilled support, or you may be fortunate enough not to need it. But if you do leave hospital with sore nipples and a baby who is not latching on properly, your next port of call should probably be a breastfeeding counsellor. There are a variety of organisations which provide breastfeeding helplines (see box below). Bear in mind though that there is a limit to what can be done over the phone, and generally the volunteers on the helplines do not do home visits.

For actual face-to-face support from both other mothers and breastfeeding counsellors, try breastfeeding support groups (including 'baby cafés') and clinics. These may be run by Sure Start at a local children's centre, La Leche League, the NCT, other charities or your local clinic or hospital. You can approach the NCT for help even if you have not joined an antenatal NCT group.

If you are really stuck for local resources, any number of mums have been talked through the process on the Mumsnet breastfeeding forum, and there are some excellent breastfeeding books (see Resources, p. 434).

Breastfeeding support

National Breastfeeding Helpline: 0844 20 909 20

Association of Breastfeeding Mothers helpline: 08444 122 949. The website also gives details of email counselling and listings of breastfeeding groups by region: www.abm.me.uk.

Breastfeeding Network Supporterline: 0844 412 4664. The website also has some details of breastfeeding centres by region: www.breastfeedingnetwork.org.uk.

Breastfeeding Network Drugline: 0844 412 4665

La Leche League Telephone Helpline: 0845 120 2918. The website gives details of local groups; there is an online help form and an online shop whichs sells breastfeeding books and videos: www.laleche.org.uk.

National Childbirth Trust Breastfeeding line: 0870 444 8708. The site also provides details of both antenatal and postnatal courses: www.national-childbirth-trust.co.uk.

Mumsnet's breastfeeding forum: www.mumsnet.com/Talk/breast_and_bottle_feeding.

Milk, Sweat and Tears – Things That Mumsnetters Wish They'd Been Told About Breastfeeding

A little colostrum goes a long way

Colostrum is the thick yellow or clear liquid you will produce for the first few days before your milk 'comes in'. It is full of antibodies and other good stuff that your baby needs, but there will only be a very small amount of it. That's OK.

Open all hours

Once the milk comes in, many newborns have a kind of feeding frenzy for a few days. This can be disconcerting and you may feel you have been reduced to a pair of rather well-used udders during this period. Be assured that it all settles down. As, for most women, do issues of over- or under-supply arising from the constant consumption.

You ate all the pies

You may well find that you yourself are gripped by the most astonishing and urgent hunger. Eat, eat, eat. You need an additional 500 calories a day to make milk according to some studies (although this doesn't translate into quite as many doughnuts as you might hope).

Forceful let-down

This is the bit when the milk comes out suddenly, usually after baby has been sucking for a little while:

'With both of mine, when they were tiny, my let-down was so forceful that the poor little things got a jet down the back of the throat – they used to pull away, burst into tears and, in the meantime, milk sprayed all over their poor little faces and beyond.' motherinferior

Mothers who gush suggest nursing uphill (i.e. lying down to feed with baby on top) and/or expressing the first let-down. Things tend to settle over time and the good thing is that forceful let-down often means a good supply and easy expressing.

Cluster feeding

This usually happens in the evening. Your baby has a number of feeds close together, with longer gaps at other times of day. Sometimes, these are just normal feeds very close together. Or your baby may be helping himself to small snacks and then grizzling about them. The flaps on your maternity bra may be up and down like pants on a childless single woman with a healthy libido, trying to keep up with his changing whims. Contrary to what crowds of helpful onlookers may be telling you, this is absolutely fine and normal while getting breastfeeding established. Hopefully, he is filling himself up for a longer sleep to come.

Growth spurts (or the return of the feeding frenzy)

You think you've got it all sorted it out, you no longer look like a rather saggy contestant in a wet T-shirt competition and you have some vague structure to your day. Then *it happens again*. The snacking becomes constant, the supply goes haywire. What can we say? It does settle down again. Honest.

Positioning

Some of the available advice may not be tailored to your body shape, as a more generously endowed Mumsnetter found: 'I laughed out loud at the idea of "baby lying on top of mum to feed". Mine have to breastcrawl right over the top and down the side again under the ol' armpit to get to my (saggy) nipples.' So shop around for positions that work for you and experiment:

"To be honest, the book I found most helpful is no longer in print but you can buy it off Amazon, anyway: Sheila Kitzinger, *Breastfeeding your Baby*. The many, many, many, many photographs of positioning alone are worth their weight in gold. For example, I didn't know that if you had big boobs you could actually hold baby between your knees! 'Twas a revelation (which really helped me).' Mossy

Atypical feeding behaviour

'I would have liked it to be mentioned *somewhere*, in *any* of the breastfeeding material I was presented with or read, that not all babies do the "brush-his-cheek-or-nose-or-lips-and-he-will-open-his-mouth" thing. Everything I read claimed that all babies did that as an automatic reflex, and as my son didn't, I had almost convinced myself that he had some weird kind of neurological damage.' lemonaid

Breast ennui

Some mothers find that their initially adept feeders become hopeless once they start becoming more alert. The wide world is suddenly far more fascinating than the breast, and they are too busy peering at the dog to remain latched on for long. If you really can't keep your baby interested, you may eventually have to express and let her have a bottle which doesn't block her view.

That hindmilk/foremilk thing

'There is so much confusion about foremilk and hindmilk. The breast does not make two different types of milk. It is all one. The creamier part and the watery part separate a bit – the watery part tends to trickle down the ducts and the creamier part sticks to the storage cells in the breast. When the baby starts to suck, the let-down pushes the creamier parts down the ducts, and yes, this is mixed with the watery parts already in the ducts. It is ludicrous to tell mothers they have to have their babies on for a certain number of minutes otherwise the baby "won't get the hindmilk", as if every mother and baby were the same, and behaved in the same way and had the same physiology. There is no "the" hindmilk and no "the" foremilk. It's all just milk; the emptier the breast, the creamier the milk, and the fuller the breast, the more watery the milk. This is why babies left to themselves do regulate their own intake and why at least one study has shown that they all get more or less the same amount of calories, even if their feeding length and frequency has been very different.' tiktok

Dummies

Dummies are fine, but some experts say they should not be introduced while breastfeeding is being established because the baby may get 'nipple confusion' (i.e. get used to sucking one type of thing and not want to suck another). For more thoughts on dummies, see p.327.

Weird and weirder: things that people have said to breastfeeding women

'A midwife on the postnatal ward when my son was born used to equate all his feeds to whatever food he might have been having had he been fully weaned. So when she came to see me in the morning she'd say, "Ahh, just had his cornflakes has he?' and if he went for the other boob too, she would say, "Oh, now he wants a piece of toast and marmalade too; he's hungry this morning!" When she came round in the afternoon to discharge me she said, "Hungry again? Well you just give him a bun and I'll be back with your paperwork in a minute..." It was very odd.' *BroccoliSpears*

'We are going through security at the airport, on our way to my parents (a five-hour flight away). My nappy bag is going through the scanner. The security guard (who looks about twelve) rummages through it, appears puzzled and asks (pointing to my son), "Where is his food?"

Me: I'm nursing him.
Guard: So what does he eat?
Me: Breast milk ... ?!
(*Pause*)
Guard: Sooooo ... where is it?
Me (*Very slowly and distinctly*): In ... my ... breasts ... you freakin' moron!

Guard looks horrified, as he waves me through security.'
Jacksmama

What to Eat/Drink While Lactating (Ooops, There Goes Another Bag of Fun-size Chocolate Bars)

OK, here are the basics:

- Do drink lots of water.
- Do check any drugs you are taking, and seek medical advice if you are uncertain. Ibuprofen and paracetamol are the painkillers of choice. Do not take aspirin without medical advice.
- Do eat what makes *you* feel well; your milk will be fine. Many breastfeeding women find they get very hungry:

'I ate lots of cake and party rings to prepare myself for breastfeeding, and both boys seem perfectly scrumptious as a result, thank you very much.' *Hunkermunker*

'Beware all those old wives' tales about the numerous foods you shouldn't eat because they'll upset your baby. Breast milk from someone living solely on McDs is barely any different from that of someone eating a perfect organic diet.' *Geekgrrrl*

'I breastfed my son for 14 months, and *had* to eat well – if I didn't, I found myself totally drained of energy.' *HRHQueenofQuotes*

'I don't think it's a madly good idea to go on and on about a healthy diet to women who've just given birth. One gets through the first few weeks as best one can, fuelled on chocolate, while simultaneously feeling faintly suicidal about one's obdurate enormity.' *motherinferior*

'In preparation for and during breastfeeding, it is important that everyone must be very nice to you and bring you lots of nice, yummy things (including, *but not limited to* organic champagne, etc.) to eat, and tell you how lovely you are, and goodness me you have hardly put any weight on at all have you? That should get the bloody milk flowing. *harpsichordcarrier*

A raining-on-parade-type NB: organic champagne to be drunk in very modest quantities only (see also box, opposite).

The demon drink: what you need to know about alcohol and caffeine

Alcohol will make its way into your breast milk. The general consensus at the moment is that a few units a week are OK, but no more than one unit in a day. And have your glass of organic champagne just after a feed so that your body has a chance to metabolise the alcohol before the next feed.

Caffeine: one or two lattes, Cokes, cups of tea per day are fine, but much more and you may make your baby (more) sleepless. Caffeine consumption can also contribute to reflux in some babies.

How to Feed – Routine Vs Demand

Over thousands of years of human history, the feeding of infants has taken place in one of two ways: letting the baby eat whenever he wants (demand-feeding) or programming the baby to eat at regular intervals (routine-feeding).

'If you're looking at the clock, saying, "It's not feeding time yet", it's scheduled. If you're looking at the clock, saying, 'Surely you're not hungry already?' then offering the breast, it's on demand. If you're not looking at the clock, you've already had about fifty children and are too busy to check the time.' VictorianSqualor

We ponder the merits of these alternatives ...

The breast-laid plans of mice and mums: going for a routine

There is something profoundly scary about many baby books. Look, they seem to say, follow these principles and you will have a lovely, chubby (but not too chubby), happy baby who will ultimately win a Nobel Peace prize and bring up her own six lovely, appropriately chubby babies. Don't follow these principles, and you and your baby will be miserable for ever, never sleep again and, just possibly, become an awful mother–son serial-killing duo whose story will be given a double-page spread in the *Daily Mail* to demonstrate to the world the pernicious effects of bad parenting. Look, says the guru, I have trained 400,000 babies in this routine and it's worked *every* time! And every single one of these babies attended the Oxbridge college of his/her choice or an international institution of similar repute. The secret real title of many baby books is: *YOU HAVE RUINED YOUR BABY'S LIFE, YOU BAD WOMAN!*

Although the books do not actually use these words, to the postnatal mind in particular, that often seems to be the subtext. And many of us who have passed much of our adulthood in the world of work do like to have an instruction manual. We are desperate for targets to achieve, possibly a PowerPoint presentation, a spreadsheet, an appraisal of our performance, an away day. The fuzzy-edged surviving-each-day world of life with a newborn does not compute.

But bear this in mind: many (not all) parenting manuals are actually just the equivalent of *Men are Hamsters, Woman are Canaries* or *Ten Steps to Being the Most Popular and Successful Person in the Universe*. So tread as carefully in the Parenting section as you would in Self-help.

The boiled-down wisdom of the many Mumsnetters who have, over the years, pondered the routine issue is this:

- It really is horses for courses. Most mums and babies will eventually find that their own particular chaos coheres into a 'routine' of some sort that suits them, but you need to be patient. Try to relax if you can.
- Some mums and/or their babies can't be doing with that approach, and are happier with a routine that has been developed by someone else. What makes you both happy has got to be the best choice.
- Parents who get routines from books almost invariably adapt them significantly to fit their own circumstances, even when the books themselves are pretty prescriptive. If drinking a glass of orange juice at 9.25 a.m. is not your thing, don't do it, even if you and your baby are otherwise happy with the book.

- Bear in mind that the routine guru you choose may well not be an expert on breastfeeding. For really good advice on the mechanics and physiology of breastfeeding, consider the sources of support on p. 60 or read a good book all about breastfeeding by a breastfeeding expert.
- Routines are not for newborns:

'If someone really wants a feeding routine, and really thinks their life will be easier with one (and they are often disappointed in that!), then it's very important they do not risk compromising breastfeeding. Baby needs to be gaining weight well, consistently, Mum needs to have confidence in her milk supply ... you can't really be sure of this before several weeks have passed.' *tiktok*

- 'Most babies end up on a routine, but I think it is a misunderstanding to think you can find the whole answer in a book, and it can be painful to get hung up on there being a "right" answer. But if you do want a bit of advice, then you can read any book really – Gina Ford, Miriam Stoppard, Penelope Leach, talk to your mum, read the Mumsnet boards. Then pick and choose and find your own way.' *harpsichordcarrier*

The two most widely known routine gurus in a couple of nutshells

Gina Ford: *The New Contented Little Baby Book*

Gina Ford is an experienced maternity nurse. Her book was a big retro hit at the end of the last millennium and continues to sell well. Here are some of the main features of her approach:

a) Baby sleeps in own cot from birth.
b) Bottles of either expressed milk or formula are introduced in the first week, if possible.
c) Expressing milk in the early days helps mothers to establish breastfeeding and deal with growth spurts while following a routine.
d) Baby should not be cuddled to sleep while feeding.
e) Very structured eating and sleeping routines are set out for babies of different ages. The routines change ten times in the first year of the baby's life, covering pretty much every aspect of baby and carer's day: sleeping and eating, playing, changing and bathing.

Mumsnetters on Gina Ford

It is fair to say that Ford polarises opinion on Mumsnet. So here are some views from the front:

Gina babes unite
'I found I needed to know when I could have a rest or could have a window to cook or something after a while, and I went the Gina Ford route. It worked for me, and my daughter is very happy on it at four and a half months.' *XenaWP*

'If you like routines, then I would look at Gina Ford's books. In the first few weeks I sort of followed her routines, but fed "on demand" and also made sure that I fed at least every three hours – some babies will sleep for very long periods to start with, and so waiting for them to "demand" a feed means they don't get enough. With both of mine I found that this start led us automatically into the Gina Ford routines after a few weeks, but I did go off routine and give extra feeds if I felt my children really needed them.' *prufrock*

'Ha, well get your head round this. I fed my son on demand purely because I had never heard of Gina Ford, and the midwife had told me that that is what you do. So I did. Within two weeks, the little blighter had put himself into a Gina Ford routine. I don't know how, and I don't know why. Actually, an airy, floaty easy-going baby would have suited me better. My point? None at all. My conclusion? Babies do whatever the hell they want to do, and if you don't let them, they make your life miserable until you do.' *colditz*

The anti-Gina-routine-ites
'I don't like the Gina Ford routines, but that doesn't mean I'm anti-routine. My daughter had a routine, but it was her own routine, and I was only able to help her find it by demand-feeding to start with. She would never have found her own rhythm and routine if I had tried to make Gina Ford's fit her, and given that

for the first four months she fed every couple of hours, and for four hours at night time, she wouldn't have been happy to be restricted to three-hourly feeds, and neither would I. Isn't that what's important? We do what makes our babies happy and keeps us sane. The trouble is, the babies have never read the books, and don't know (nor do they care) that they are only meant to be hungry every three hours.' *WigWamBam*

'I hear this tale so often: a mother comparing her baby's day with one in A Certain Book, and judging it according to how close it is to it. She then wonders if there is something wrong with what she's doing if the baby's day strays too far away from This Certain Book. It's a good day if it approaches what This Book decrees. Crazy, crackers, mad, and it can ruin the early, magical weeks. There is bags of time to help a baby into a routine later, if that floats your boat.' *tiktok*

'I get concerned when breastfeeding mums are asking for advice on Gina routines. Quite often it is clear they are struggling to produce enough milk because they do not allow the baby to increase milk production when needed by feeding more frequently. I do agree that there are mums who need a structure and that scheduled feeds work for them. For breastfeeding mums who produce a lot of milk regardless, that is not a problem. Some mums need the stimulation of feeding and they do not realise the impact scheduled feeds are having on their supply. Often they are introducing formula when they didn't want to. That is when I will advise chucking the routine for now.' *mears*

Tracy Hogg: *Secrets of the Baby Whisperer*

(Note for addled mums: this has nothing to do with that Robert Redford film involving horses.)

Tracy Hogg was also an experienced maternity nurse and not a fan of demand-feeding. *The Baby Whisperer* routines are based on a system Hogg calls 'E.A.S.Y' (Eating, Activity, Sleeping, You) and which she describes as a middle ground between strict schedules and demand-feeding:

a) Essentially the day falls into patterns of eating, activity and sleep on the baby's part and time for 'you' when the baby sleeps. These are 2½ –3 hour cycles.
b) Work towards these routines should start from the first week.
c) Babies should not fall asleep on the breast, but evening cluster-feeding and dream-feeding (breast- or bottle-feeding a sleeping/semi-asleep baby at your own bedtime) is OK.
d) There is a lot of material on interpreting babies' body language; this is the 'whispering' bit. There is also a quiz to take to categorise your baby into one of five 'broad temperamental types'.
e) It is fairly easy to get your baby into 'bad habits' from which she must be rescued by EASY. Ideally you 'start as you mean to go on' in relation to eating and sleeping habits.

Mumsnetters on Tracy Hogg

The EASY fans

'I must admit to being a fan of *The Baby Whisperer*, but that may be because my son seemed to fall into her Eat, Activity, Sleep routine without much encouragement from me and he was generally an easy baby to deal with. In my opinion, her ideas are a middle ground for those who need some kind of routine and guidance, but who want to follow their baby's cues too. From memory, none of her advice (on feeding or anything else) was particularly controversial and, with hindsight, much of it appears to be common sense.' *jelliebelly*

'I swear by *The Baby Whisperer*. There is a routine, but it's not fixed times. You always follow the order: Eat, Activity, Sleep. In the early weeks, the activity bit may simply be a nappy change, but it's all about separating eating and sleeping. I know it's not everyone's priority, but I really wanted a routine that never involved leaving baby to cry – *Baby Whisperer* achieved that for me.' *SquiffyHock*

'Thanks to that stupid book, I got up at 7 a.m. when my baby was a week old, dragged him downstairs and tried to get him to wake up and do some "activity". Complete lunacy – should have been asleep!' *bohemianbint*

'Sometimes babies will fall asleep on the breast and that is OK and normal (despite what the Baby Whisperer says – she is dead against this, for some reason). Sometimes they need a bit of rocking. A very young baby is still getting used to this world. Most of her conscious experience has been in utero. Rocking, or whatever is needed, is a kind, gentle, loving way for your baby to ease her transition from waking to sleeping. She won't do it for ever. You are not teaching 'bad habits'. She can learn, later, if she has to, different ways of getting to sleep. Comparison: she is in nappies now. You don't think: "Oh my God, we are teaching her it is OK to wet her knickers!" She is in nappies because at present she is not able to control bladder and bowels, and she wees and poos rather a lot. In time, she will do this less often (that's physiology) and she will learn to do it in the "right" place and in the "right" way. Same with feeding and sleeping.' *tiktok*

Demand-feeding: the proverbial bloody rod for your own back?

The name itself can be alarming – if I feed my baby every time he demands it, will he become 'demanding'? Will he be 'spoilt'? The notion may appal not just your 'put-them-out-to-cry-in-the-garden;-the-fresh-air-is-good-for-them' granny, but your own internal control freak too. The phrase 'bad habits' may haunt you if you have been reading some routine guru literature. Try telling your external and internal control freaks you are 'cue-feeding' instead. Or make up your own name for it, blind granny with science, it matters not. Cue-feeding is basically about feeding when your baby appears to need to be fed.

The tricky bit may be in interpreting the cues; it is likely to be no fun if you assume that every time your baby cries she is after food. She might just be windy, sleepy or grumpy (but probably not any of the other dwarves). As one mother who gave up cue-feeding puts it, 'I also think that I would be a bit pissed off if someone shoved a sandwich in my mouth every time I was a bit grumpy – I'd probably have a nibble and then not eat dinner properly later on.' But then, 'The thing that is worth remembering about demand-feeding is that it means feeding the baby when it's hungry, which is not necessarily the same as plugging it on to your boob every time it squeaks,' says a cue-feeder who stuck with it. So check your baby's nappy, burp her and see if a cuddle or a little play is what is wanted before flapping your chest at her.

Some babies are not demanding enough. Placid or sleepy (or ill) babies may not cry for food, and there are other subtler signs of hunger in all babies.

'You need to learn to recognise when the baby is signalling the need to be held and fed, and this may start with mouthing movements, waving hands, turning the head. Placid babies may do this for a while, and then drop off to sleep again when the cues are not responded to; they don't bother crying. Other babies wake up and start yelling for food immediately! The "good" baby who "sleeps for hours" can end up not getting the food he needs.' tiktok

A lot of mums reckon that, after the newborn period, you can assume a baby who has had a good feed is unlikely to be hungry for about three hours, but you do need to assess your own baby. Some are naturally more frequent feeders and all babies tend to have hungry growth spurts. So look out for proper rooting signs and learn to read your own baby's cues.

Those 'wanting-a-feed-now' signs in full

Your baby will probably have his own specially tailored repertoire, but here are the basic ones:

- Cycling with arms and legs and wriggling
- Lip-smacking
- Rooting and nuzzling at the breast – or whatever is near by and might be a breast
- Sucking fingers
- Making feeding movements with the mouth
- Pushing the tongue in and out
- And finally: a hungry cry (this is often short, and rises and falls rhythmically – think 'Ulah, ulah, ulah')

The early weeks may feel like a purgatory of non-stop feeding. But remember the following:

- As your baby gets bigger, his feeding pattern will tend to become more regular, and your supply will too; many mothers find that feeding gradually settles into a two- or three-hourly pattern, with lengthening times between feeds.
- 'Don't worry about him being on a long time, as long as you aren't getting sore nipples and the baby is happy – staying on a long time can be a sign that he isn't positioned correctly and isn't getting enough milk, but it can also be, and often is, just a sign that little babies love to suck and be cuddled by their mothers!' *aloha*
- You can actually have a more flexible sort of day with a non-routine baby who does not have to eat and sleep by the clock (and, in some routines, only in designated locations).
- The truth is it is much easier to relax about all this when you have done it once. By the second or third baby, some mums and their infants are living a life of blissful hoggishness.

Public Convenience: How to Be One for Your Baby Without Feeding in One

Unsurprisingly, there is a spectrum of opinion among Mumsnetters as to just how out-and-proud they want to be about public breastfeeding. Some hanker for a society where it's never a problem for a woman to be breastfeeding and at the same time revealing some breast.

'I'm tempted to go for a third child, *just* so I can sit in someone else's sitting room entirely topless. I didn't cover up when my babies pulled away – it's only a bleedin' nipple that's been feeding a bleedin' baby!' onebatmother

Others favour a more discreet approach:

'I have breastfed all mine and don't know why you *wouldn't* want to cover up.' UniversallyChallenged

'I think that you have to do what makes you comfortable; but of course, remember that what makes you comfortable may not be the same for everyone, and it is always worth being considerate if people are very uncomfortable. I would not want to breastfeed openly in front of a hormonal teenage boy if that was the very first time in his living memory he had seen it done. I would consider it my job to feed my baby, but not my job to "re-educate" a teenager at a very complicated time in his life.' rantmum

Although it is usually feasible to breastfeed publicly without displaying anything you don't want to, total discretion is not always possible or desirable: 'I was discreet to the point of not getting a good latch, as I didn't want to "flaunt" my breasts,' laments one baby-up-the-jumper mum.

When you are establishing feeding, it can be well-nigh impossible to get a baby with latch issues to feed properly without your nipple seeing some fresh air. Worst-case scenario is small baby having a giant paddy while engorged breast spurts merrily at aghast onlookers. Fortunately, these are issues which tend not to arise after the early days, but some older babies and toddlers enjoy playing a kind of peekaboo with breast and shirt, which can be less than enchanting to a self-conscious mum.

When out and about, many women feel happier feeding in a private place. If you are self-conscious, try to scope out places which have breastfeeding facilities before setting off on an outing. Although these are rarely anything better than a hard chair in a baby-changing room, sometimes the fact that you have privacy is good enough. Or head for a venue where you know there will be lots of mums and prams. Most neighbourhoods will have breastfeeding hotspots.

Do, however, bear in mind that much of the time when women are breastfeeding, no one is actually noticing what is happening. Once your baby is actually latched on, there should be nothing to see.

'I have to say, I have rarely glimpsed even a flash of nipple, let alone full boobage, and I spend more time in places where breastfeeding is happening than your average punter.' MrsJohnCusack

Although there can be unusual ratios ...

'My nipples are so big and my baby so tiny that you can still see a crescent moon of areola above her head.' Enid

Mumsnet Breastiquette: How not to frighten people with your nipples (unless you feel like it ... mwahaha)

- In a busy café or other public venue, sit with your back to the room, if possible, or in a quiet corner.
- Try breastfeeding in front of a mirror before you go out; it will give you a good idea of how much or little is actually on display.
- Check out other mums breastfeeding for further reassurance. Smile innocuously, while gesturing vigorously at your bump or baby, so they know you are not perving at them.
- Use a ring sling (a sling that sits like a sort of hammock across your chest). As one mum raves: 'Discreet feeding in the sling is an absolute breeze. You can even walk around at the same time.

I swear, the only way anyone would know I was feeding would be the slurping noises and my smug expression.'

- Don't ask for permission. If you just get on with it, no one is likely to object. Very few Mumsnetters report ever being on the receiving end of negative comments about breastfeeding in public:

'People really don't notice; the only times I got comments were when my son was really little – older ladies came up and said how lovely it was to see and how much they wished they had been able to feed in public when their babies were small. If anyone is looking at you, that's probably what they're thinking – the very few people who are bothered by it look away quickly and pretend it's not happening!' *systemsaddict*

- Feed with a friend: 'If you know any other breastfeeding mums, then going for coffee or something and both of you feeding together does wonders for your confidence. I had two friends who were supremely unbothered about feeding in public, and being around them was what helped me the most,' says one mum. And, of course, if there is a mob of you, you can violently quash anyone who looks at you funny.
- Try the patented Mumsnet minimal-exposure feeding outfit. This consists of two vest tops: one goes up and one comes down around the feeding breast. This is particularly good for avoiding abdominal exposure for those who, in one mum's words, 'have an enormous white, crêpey belly you would rather not display'. 'At least the view of my huge exposed breasts was quite nice, nicer than my huge exposed belly,' explains another. Other less widely road-tested variants include using a boob tube to cover your midriff area under your shirt.
- If you don't get on with the patented outfit as above (and users find it does not suit all babies and body types), there is always that old favourite – the long, loose, floppy shirt or the pashmina or wrap. 'I used to use a very lightweight scarf, so that baby could breathe and I wouldn't get too hot when I had to breastfeed in company,' says one mum. Others drape a cellular blanket over baby and breast. Some babies get (perhaps understandably) a bit annoyed by effectively being fed in a tent; some find it quite cosy.

(continued)

There are many special breastfeeding clothes out there, but approach them with a critical eye. So-called breastfeeding capes are thought by many Mumsnetters to actively draw attention to what they're doing, leaving aside questions of aesthetic absurdity. Some Mumsnetters have found joy with an apron-like affair once winningly marketed as a 'hooter hider', but rebranded, Hyacinth Bouquet-style, as the 'bébé-au-lait nursing cover'; others have remarked that when in action, it creates the impression that you are storing your baby in a (floral) shopping bag ... Lovers of bad puns will also enjoy the 'mamaflage'. Tops with slits for nipples to poke through can look a bit porno and don't find favour with many – as one mum recalls: 'I could never line my nipple up with the slot and ended up with the baby rooting like crazy at the fabric and me getting the giggles.'

But take heart. Many a Mumsnetter has lost all her inhibitions along the way. Says an ambidextrous old stager:

'Before you know it, you'll be feeding with gay abandon everywhere – I once fed my son one-handed while loading my trolley in Sainsbury's with the other.' seeker

And an even more flexible mum recalls:

'I have dangled my boob from the front seat of the car into my daughter's car seat in the back of the car in a traffic jam; not my finest hour. I think the lorry driver in the next lane is still having counselling.' greedygoose

'I used to whip my baps out any old place. Other people's goose bumps are bigger than my boobs, so it was never a big deal.' filthymindedSixSixSixen

'I suppose the truth is, I quite like getting my norks out.' motherinferior

Tea for Two: Yes, You Can Breastfeed Twins

There are three basic principles you should follow if you want to breastfeed twins: eat more breakfasts; eat more snacks; lie down more.

As well as doing all this eating and lying down, try to get as much support as you can in the early days. While you are establishing breastfeeding, you are likely to have your breasts out almost constantly.

'You need people to help; it is a two- or three-person job in the early days.' swanriver

Ignore the buckets of advice which will rain down upon you:

'Loads of people don't believe it's possible, but IT IS! You have TWO – count them – TWO breasts. People are fond of saying, "Oh you poor thing, you must be so tired; why don't you just give them a bottle and have a little rest?" But it's having twins that's knackering, not breastfeeding! At least when you breastfeed you get to sit down!' madlentileater

Don't feel you have to feed both babies together right from the start:

'My sister ran into difficulties breastfeeding twins (first babies) because she ended up with painful nipples. I think one of the reasons for that is that she was insisting on feeding them together and, as a result, one twin was often uninterested and the latch was poor. In hindsight, I think it would have been far better for her to become confident feeding one baby at a time, till she got used to handling them and ensuring they were fixed properly. Another problem was wanting to be in a routine – not possible in the early days and should not be strived for!' mears

Expert advice, possibly from a breastfeeding counsellor, can be crucial for some mothers of twins. As one Mumsnetter says, 'I know, as a midwife, that it is possible to breastfeed twins successfully, but you need to be armed with good information and support.'

Once you feel that you and your babies have mastered the basics, you can begin to try to synchronise their feeds, so that you can 'tandem-feed'. This is likely to involve waking the baby who is happily snoozing and thrusting a breast at her, while her hungry twin angrily pummels the other breast. Tandem-fed twins are often propped up on pillows with their heads facing towards each other, and one of your hands cradling each head (in what is described as a clutch or rugby hold). V-shaped breastfeeding pillows are useful for this kind of feeding. Plus extra pillows to support your arms and back and all the other tired parts of you.

You may well find that you develop your own preferred positioning:

'I find it easier to feed them both pointing the same way, rather than both round my back. I have one on my right breast in the normal position, across my body, and the second lays on my left breast, in the rugby hold, with his head above the first one's feet, going on to the arm of the sofa (or a fat cushion, if I'm in bed).

This way, I can hold them both with one hand/ arm and have the other free.' Kelly1978

If there is no one around to hand you babies, you may have to work out cunning ways to get the three of you together for a tandem-feed:

'If I was on my own, I would have a Moses basket on a stand next to the chair, put one baby in it, sit down with the other, then reach over and get the first out the basket.' theslownorris

Some mothers just don't get on with tandem-feeding and carry on feeding each baby separately:

'I have to say that even though I was an experienced breastfeeder, I struggled with the tandem-feeding. I often fed them one by one. There were some major disadvantages to this: it takes more time and you often have to listen to one baby crying while you feed the other if you mistime.

The upside was that I could carry on breastfeeding. I might have had to give up otherwise, and it ensured that I had some quality one-on-one time with the twins.' Overrun

Expressing milk may be the key to getting a bit more sleep:

'If you are anything like me, your twins will probably be keeping you up all night. That means you are VERY tired, and that will be affecting your supply. So you need to sleep as much as possible, and eat and drink lots.

Also, if you can express 3fl oz-ish (75ml) in the mornings that should be enough to give one twin one bottle of expressed breast milk a day (whether that be evenings, night time, whenever you need) or you can save the expressed milk and have someone come once a week and give the twins two feeds of expressed breast milk so you can get five to six hours' sleep.' Neenztwinz

But expressing is not for everyone:

'A lot of people find expressing tremendously hard work.' TheProvinicalLady

For further information and support, contact the NCT, La Leche League or theBreastfeeding Network; the Twins and Multiple Birth Association (TAMBA) also produces some useful fact sheets on feedings multiples (see Resources p. 439).

Hitting the Bottle: the Practical Stuff for Formula-feeding

By its very nature, bottle-feeding is a more equipment-laden business than breastfeeding. And there are more bits to wash. So it's worth doing a little preparing and practising in advance, if you get the chance.

If you know you are going to be bottle-feeding from the start, check with your hospital whether you will be expected to bring in your own bottles and formula. Do a trial run with your bottles and sterilising equipment, so you know what you are doing before you have to do it in 'real time'. Experienced bottle-feeders suggest you take four to six pre-sterilised bottles to the hospital and a similar number of cartons of prepared formula, two spare sterilised teats and some sterilising tablets.

But don't let the equipment get between you and your baby. Bottle-feeding should not mean you miss out on bonding:

'You can give the first feed straight away after the birth if you want – and there is no reason for your baby to miss out on skin to skin contact and cuddles.' tiktok

Bottle bits and bobs

Bottles

There are many to choose from, and no consensus as to which is best. A new baby will probably get used to whichever one he starts off with, so pick one you like the look of and which seems easy to clean. Buy a few 120ml (4oz) bottles for the early weeks and some of the larger 240ml (8oz) bottles for when he gets hungrier.

Teats

These come in different shapes, materials and flow rates. You will want to experiment to see what suits, but generally speaking, a newborn will be on a slow-flow teat and will want to move on to faster teats as he gets bigger. Some Mumsnetters find that switching to a softer teat works for small babies who are struggling.

Bottle brush

This is very useful for cleaning – especially after a manky, lost-bottle-behind-the-sofa incident.

Sterilisers

The microwave steriliser is thought by many to be the easiest gadget, but you can also use a bucket with chemical sterilising solution or a freestanding electric steriliser. The low-tech option is to boil bottles and teats in a large covered pot of water for ten minutes, and then allow them to cool while still covered.

Cracking the formula: which one to buy

Formulas are much of a muchness in terms of quality. They all have to conform to government standards on the basic mix of nutrients. Some will have extras, which may or may not be beneficial to your baby, although there is no hard evidence on this.

'Some have probiotics and EFAs (essential fatty acids) in the mix, which may be helpful to the developing baby. I gave my baby formula alongside breastfeeding and I tended to choose those ones.' aloha

'There are some studies which show that babies at certain ages seem to have slightly more developed skills if they have had a formula with EFAs compared to those whose formula was without EFAs. But that is a long way from saying these formulas are "better" – maybe the EFAs have another effect, a negative one, that wasn't looked for! I don't know of any independent study showing that probiotics make any difference.' tiktok

Finding a formula which suits your baby is a question of trial and error – some babies seem to strongly prefer the flavour of one to that of another. You can always do your own taste test – some mums themselves express surprisingly strong preferences. Many parents find that particular formulas are less likely to cause sickiness, windiness or constipation for their baby. You can even chop and change formulas until you find one you both like – *nothing bad will happen*. There are also now a number of organic options on the market, if that floats your boat. Remember that you should not use a soya formula without seeking medical advice.

'I bought the brand I did because it was familiar to me (here's a long-term ad – my mum used to have a biscuit tin that was an old formula milk tin, and so I grew up with that name branded into me).' SueW

It is obviously cheaper to make up formula from powder, but many parents find it useful to have some cartons of ready-made for when they are out and about, or if they are only giving the occasional bottle of formula. Or if they are improvident. Or just damned tired.

Preparing formula feeds

There is much advice on Mumsnet and elsewhere on the internet about convenient ways of making up formula in advance and keeping it at the ready: disregard that advice. There is a very small risk of infection from contaminated formula, so the most up-to-date recommendations are pretty strict. There is an excellent leaflet on the safe preparation of formula feeds at www.babyfriendly.org.uk. Be aware that guidelines on safe preparation and storage of formula do change, so be careful when looking at older books, or out-of-date advice on the internet. Some Mumsnetters have found the instructions on some formula tins themselves unclear or misleading.

Essentially, formula feeds should always be:

- made up using freshly boiled water (not stuff that's been hanging around in your kettle getting reboiled, or unboiled bottled water)
- mixed while the water is at no less than 70°C (so no longer than half an hour after boiling)
- stored for as short a time as possible and used within two hours.

You may well need to cool your bottle down very quickly if someone small is shouting angrily at you. Well-prepared parents suggest keeping a cup of ice-cold water in the fridge for this purpose.

The preparation guidelines may sound like they will make bottle-feeding a nightmare if you are out and about, but:

'It's easy enough to get a teapot full of boiling water from a café and bring your own cold pre-boiled water. You take the powder in a tub, mix with less boiling water than you need to make the whole bottle, shake, and then add cold to taste. Or fill the bottle with boiling water if you know your baby will be drinking it within half an hour of leaving the house.' Aitch

Similarly, you can apply the same principle at night – you do not have to let your baby scream the house down while waiting for a bottle to cool.

Your other (if pricier) option is to use cartons of ready-made-up formula which are sterile, if only for those desperate middle-of-the-night feeds when the neighbours are ringing Social Services.

Some bottle basics

- You *can* cue-feed with formula; don't feel that bottle-feeding means you have to have a rigid routine (unless you want one).
- Be rigorous about measuring the quantities of powdered formula; too much formula to water can lead to dehydration.
- Don't encourage your baby to finish the bottle if he's had enough. But 'had enough' in infant terms may mean 'had enough for a moment or two, while the cat is doing that funny thing with his tail', so don't hurry the bottle away. It is easier to overfeed a bottle-fed baby (whether the feed is formula or expressed breast milk).
- Chuck out the remains of the bottle when your baby has genuinely finished a feed.
- 'Hungry-baby formula is a gimmick. The main protein in it is casein, which is harder to digest than the whey which makes up so-called first-stage formula. Why give a tiny baby something that

is harder to digest when their digestive tract is not ready for it?'
knifewieldingtoddler

- Many parents say their babies are very happy to consume formula at room temperature. Some even enjoy it chilly from the fridge, but a few Mumsnetters report increased windiness in babies who drink cold milk:

'If you have a windy baby, make sure their bottles are very warm, and remember to swirl the bottle to dissolve the powder, rather than shaking it vigorously, filling it full of bubbles!'
PrincessPeaHead

- If you are heating bottles, don't do it in the microwave – although some parents swear it's OK as long as you shake the bottle, there is a risk of hot spots. Stand the bottle in a pan of hot water and then squirt a little on your wrist to check the temperature in the time-honoured fashion. It's safer, and will make you feel like you're in an old film. Especially if you hang a folded muslin over your arm while doing it.
- Never prop the bottle and leave baby alone during a feed. Apart from the choking risk, he wants to be with you.
- If anyone gives you funny looks because you are bottle-feeding in an otherwise breastcentric neighbourhood, follow the advice above for funny looks while breastfeeding (mob violence, etc.).

Mixed Blessings: Breast Plus Formula

Mixed feeding can take different forms. It might be 'topping up' a hungry baby with the odd bottle of formula or it might be regular formula-feeding of an otherwise breastfed baby by a father or other carer when the mother is away from the baby. If you are happy to breastfeed exclusively, you may still have to fight off unhelpful health visitors, midwives or family members who try to insist your baby is hungry or skinny. The vast majority of women can produce enough breast milk to nourish one or even two babies, so mixed feed if it suits you, but don't feel you have to, unless you have proper medical advice to that effect.

Mixed feeding can cause problems with breastfeeding if introduced too early:

'"Topping up" a newborn is the fastest way to end breastfeeding. Those first few weeks are building your milk supply to meet your baby's needs. You need to feed as often and as long as your baby wants. If you introduce bottles, your body won't get the messages from your baby about how much milk to make.' edam

'Many women (not all) can "get away" with a bedtime bottle for a young baby, as long as the baby continues to wake in the night. Many women can appear to get away with reduced breastfeeding, only for the supply to hit a crisis point weeks later when the baby wants more. It is absolutely not a question of being "determined". Generally speaking, you risk your milk dwindling to a crisis point where it can be hard to retrieve it without a lot of work and motivation, if you limit breastfeeding in whatever way when the baby is very young.' tiktok

None the less, many Mumsnetters say that if introducing a bottle of formula while you are having breastfeeding problems enables you to continue breastfeeding while you ride out your troubles, then the risks of affecting supply or of the baby preferring the bottle are worth running:

'In the end, it's what you feel most comfortable with. I mixed fed because the sluglet was in hospital for a while after she was born, fed by a nose tube. I never established a good supply, no matter how hard I tried. Expressing resulted in a few dribbles, an ounce at best. The result was a well-fed baby, with all the closeness of breastfeeding, as many of the antibodies as I could give and an opportunity for her dad to be involved as well.' slug

Other mums find they can take action to combat the decline in supply:

'I did mixed feeding, but I think it worked because I would have feeding frenzies with my son on weekends and days off if I felt my supply was declining.' aloha

Don't beat yourself up, if you decide mixed feeding is your best option. A baby who has been fed some formula does not get all of the benefits a baby who is purely breastfed does, but he will get many of them. And if leaving baby and dad to battle it out together the odd night with a bottle is what maintains your health and sanity, it may be the answer.

'Antibodies are still there in breast milk, and giving formula alongside breastfeeding does not reduce the nutritional benefits of breast milk.' tiktok

All Glands to the Pump: Expressing Yourself

There are lots of reasons to express breast milk. You may want to express so that someone else can feed it to your baby from a bottle, enabling you to get a break when your baby is small, or in order to keep providing your baby with breast milk when you return to work. Expressing enough so that your partner can do some night feeds during the early weeks may save your sanity. Expressing can also be used simply to relieve engorgement. And some mothers have to do pretty heavy-duty expressing for premature babies in hospital.

Old Mum River: tips for successful expressing

- Don't expect a particular amount the first time you try; keep giving it a go and experimenting.
- Some mums find the way to open the floodgates is to express from one breast while feeding baby from the other.
- Swapping the pump from breast to breast as the flow from one breast slows can produce the best results because milk comes in spurts. Alternatively, invest in a double pump for super-efficient expressing.
- Get in the mood. We've said it before and it sounds unrealistic, but do try to relax. The conventional wisdom is to think about your baby, but one mum found that 'if you think about sex, it works better'. Others suggest reading a magazine or watching television, having a hot bath or thinking about Daniel Craig. (This may sound positively milk-curdling, if your libido has lain down and died postnatally.) Timing is everything. Many mums find that there is more to be had in the morning, while others get better results with a night-time slot. Experiment.
- Devices called breast shells work for some. They collect what comes out of its own accord (particularly when feeding), and you can then freeze even small amounts in an ice-cube tray (or, as one Mumsnetter did, in successive layers in a bottle, 'like one of those rocket lollies – but all white'). If you do not need vast amounts of expressed breast milk, this may be an easy solution.

Expressing kit

Pump

Some people are very happy with hand pumps but they can be hard on the wrist, particularly if you are finding it difficult to get milk out at all. Most models seem to survive being thrown angrily at the wall. At least the first time.

There are some one-handed pumps (which require quite a lot of wrist strength), but most manual pumps will not leave you with a free hand while expressing. Manual pumps need to be dismantled and sterilised after each use, which can be taxing when you are tired and fumble-fingered. If you have a forceful and dependable let-down, a manual pump may be your best bet. They are also the cheapest pump option, so an obvious choice if you are only planning to do occasional expressing.

Other mums prefer the speed of extraction they get from an electric pump. If you are only expressing one breast at a time, you should end up with at least one hand free, although some nimble Mumsnetters can manage a free hand even while double-pumping (depending on the pump). Electric pumps vary widely in terms of noise, bulk and cost and whether they do one breast or two at a time.

'I did feel a bit like a dairy cow when hooked up to my "industrial" double pump.' mummypig

Another mum found a particular model was 'like sitting on top of a small asthmatic vacuum cleaner'. Many electric pumps are small enough to be portable, which is useful if you are expressing at work. However, if you are self-conscious about the noise, you may wish to use a manual pump instead.

Some mothers find that larger hospital-grade pumps are best of all, particularly if they are having difficulties getting supply going, or are having to express large amounts for an infant in hospital. This is one to rent rather than buy.

Finally, there is the super-low-tech option:

'I hand-expressed last time round which has no cost attached to it and I found was actually

quicker than using a pump. Once you get the knack, it is so easy.' mears

You can hand-express straight into a wide-necked bottle.

Storage

Freezer bags – there are special, pre-sterilised bags for breast milk, and some which fit on to a device which attaches to the pump, so you do not need an interim container. Remember to date the bag. You can top up a bag of frozen milk, but chill the milk to be added first.

Steriliser

For bottles and pump components. The ever-popular microwave steriliser may be your best choice, but see the range of options on p.85.

Storing and using expressed breast milk

The La Leche League International website has comprehensive guidelines. Basically:

- Storing at room temperature (up to 26°C) for no more than four hours is ideal, while six hours is acceptable.
- Storing in the fridge (below 4°C) for 72 hours is ideal, while up to eight days is acceptable.
- Storing in the deep freeze for up to six months is ideal, while up to 12 months is acceptable. If you have a freezer compartment in a fridge, the advice is to store for up to two weeks, but if you have a freezer compartment with a separate door, then the guideline is up to three to four months.
- Frozen milk should be thawed in the fridge overnight, or under cool running water, gradually increasing the temperature. Thawed milk can be kept in the fridge for up to 24 hours. Do not refreeze thawed breast milk.

The mother of all battles: getting a breastfed baby to take a bottle

You might get lucky and have a baby who takes readily to the bottle. Or you might find yourself locked in a strange extended period of psychological warfare with a baby who: a) simply ignores the offending bottle, as if politely overlooking the parental faux pas you have made in seeking to introduce him to it; b) equally politely investigates it, chews it and then shoves it aside in favour of a more interesting toy; or c) shouts indignantly at you for your effrontery in trying to place this truly horrible item in his mouth – what were you thinking of, you *terrible* woman?

Here are some thoughts on how to proceed:

- Wait a few weeks and try again. If, however, you are trying to get this sorted out in the frantic run-up to returning to work, clearly this is not the advice for you.
- Persist. Try introducing a small bottle of expressed breast milk every day, at a time when she is in a good mood. However, 'Persist, but don't insist,' advises one mum. Stop before she gets upset. Stay calm (but don't let your partner say, 'Calm down, calm down' in your presence – unless you have a large stick to hand).
- An older baby may gradually get the idea through play:

  'I said to my partner, "Let's just let her play with the bottle," and she played with it. Then chewed on it. Then sucked it. Then, before we knew it, the milk was gone!' *EdieMcredie*

- Experiment with bottles and teats. Bottles and teats which mimic breasts may be the answer for many (Nuk teats and Playtex bottles get a lot of mentions on the Mumsnet boards) and have the advantage that baby can use the same latch, so won't get into bad habits on the breast. A slow-flow teat is likely to be better during the transitional period because she won't get a sudden horrifying gush just when she's working it all out.

  'It took me a month (and six different types of bottle) to persuade him to take a bottle.' *jaz2*

- Squeezing a little milk from the teat into baby's mouth may tempt her and give her the idea that that is what the bottle is for. Because, let's face it, even the breastiest bottles don't look or feel that much like breasts.

- Some people find that getting their partner or another person to give the bottle helps because there is no distracting breast alternative; others, however, find that this increases the levels of outraged screaming.
- Some babies are lulled by being held in the breastfeeding position, particularly if the mother takes her top off. Some mums find slipping the bottle in when baby is nearly full of breast milk helps to make the transition. But babies are all different – some may be confused or infuriated by being held suggestively near a breast, while being offered some annoying bit of latex to suck.
- With some babies, you can overcome their objections by slipping the bottle in when they are very sleepy. 'I started to feed her while she was still asleep and that seemed to work. By the time she realised she had a bottle in her mouth she was sucking and realised she was getting milk out, so continued,' says one crafty mum.
- Straight to cup is the only answer for some.

'Try the lid of a bottle first. Turn it upside down and let him lap the milk up.' *Greedygirl*

Experiment with different varieties of cup; some babies only like an open cup. Others will prefer a spouted cup which they can manhandle freely. Non-spill cups are appealing from a housework point of view, but some babies find they require too much hard sucking to be worth bothering with.

- 'What helped us was strapping the little fella into his sling, facing outwards (so he was distracted), then walking around the house, feeding him with a bottle.' *Champagnesupernova*

Wet T-Shirts and Wearing Vegetables: the Fabulous World of Sore Nipples

Don't assume before you start breastfeeding that you are going to get sore nipples. As one Mumsnetter commented cheerfully, she must have 'nipples like shoe leather' because she never felt a thing. Another blushingly pointed out that having, ahem, sensitive nipples did not mean she suffered from any nipple pain while breastfeeding. Being red-haired or fair-skinned is apparently not an indicator of likely nipple ills, either. Like much else in the world of parenting, it's all a bit random.

Many nipples will, however, suffer some painful wear and tear while being toughened up by the sucking process. Worse problems (significant soreness, cracking, bleeding) are 'almost always caused by positioning and attachment issues' says a Mumsnetter who is also a breastfeeding counsellor. Cracked-nipple veterans suggest not letting baby feed until you are sure she has a good latch; 'the big mouthful seems to be the key – don't let them sip on the end at any cost,' cautions one mum. Remember, both of your baby's lips should be everted (thrust outwards like a cartoon fish) and pressure should be on the areola, not the nipple. Seek breastfeeding support if you are struggling to get the latch right.

Mumsnetters' favourite home remedies for when your nips have really been in the wars

- Rub in a little breast milk and do some nipple massage. Let nipples air dry, but never use a hairdryer, as you could make things worse by drying out the skin. If you take no other advice from this book, at least take this piece: **never hairdry your nipples**.
- Change breast pads frequently, or walk around topless. Maybe stay at home, if you are doing the latter ...
- Use Lansinoh/Purelan cream: pure lanolin which moisturises, promotes healing, 'sticks them back together' and does not need to be cleaned off before feeding.
- Try nipple shields. These are rubber or latex shields which cover the nipple and areola and 'sort of stick on while the baby feeds over them', as one mum describes the technology. They can help 'to reduce some of the sensation when really sore. They might just be enough to help you keep going until you can heal a bit.' Some experts don't recommend them for anything but a brief period while nipples recover, because the baby may become accustomed to latching on to the nipple shield and not learn how to cope with the real thing. They can also cause supply difficulties.

(continued)

- Savoy cabbage leaves in the bra – traditionally soothing for engorged breasts, these can also help with cracked nipples:

'My nipples kept scabbing on to my bra or breast pads, and the scab would break when I removed the clothing. Cabbage leaves helped prevent this.' *alexsmummy*

- Some Mumsnetters swear by devices (such as Silverette) – they are worn under the bra, to allow the nipple to air dry and, apparently, use silver to promote healing.
- If you are really desperate, you can express milk very carefully and feed via cup or syringe while nipples heal. This is obviously not one to try unless you are confident you can get enough milk into your baby this way. Seek advice from a breastfeeding counsellor and/or your GP or health visitor.

And finally:

- Total immersion: one Mumsnetter's nipple recovery plan

'I found that I was in so much pain I couldn't wear bras, so what I did was to wear an old T-shirt with no bra and, although this sounds so unpleasant, I just leaked on to the T-shirt and therefore my nipples were soaked in breast milk. This worked for me. I looked a right sight, but only had to do this for about five days. If a visitor came, I just put on a dressing gown.' *Meid*

Fungus the Boobyman: Thrush

Sore nipples which do not respond to any of the above blandishments may be victims of thrush. The pains may extend right into the breasts and the ducts themselves can be affected:

'It's agony. It really stings during the feed, and then there are stabbing pains through the breast and in the shoulders after feeds.' spidermama

Thrush on your nipples tends to be something you and baby share. He may have white spots in his mouth and a dark red rash on his nethers, or he may have no visible signs. Whether or not your baby also has symptoms, you both need to be treated with antifungals or you will be merrily passing thrush back and forth indefinitely.

Quite a few Mumsnetters report a lack of awareness of nipple/duct thrush on the part of GPs; they suggest that, if you are not getting the help you need, you print out the Breastfeeding Network pamphlet from the internet (which has up-to-date treatment advice) and tactfully thrust it under your GP's nose.

In order to prevent re-infection, you need to pretty much sterilise anything that goes in your baby's mouth (or your mouth) or touches any part of you where fungus might lurk, and chuck out old make-up and deodorants which may be contaminated. Also dispose of expressed breast milk which may be contaminated, including frozen milk. 'Put vinegar in the laundry when washing bras, sheets and towels, to kill off fungus and spores', suggests one sufferer. Think laterally about where fungus might lurk. 'How hot a bath can teddy survive do you think?' wondered one mum with a soft-toy-gnawing infant.

And If You Thought Scabs Welding Your Nipples to Your Bra Were Bad ... Welcome to Blocked Ducts and Mastitis

First the science bit: a blocked duct is what it says on the tin – a blocked milk duct which feels like a lump in your breast. Mastitis is an infection of the ducts which can be caused by blocked ducts or unrelieved engorgement. As well as breast pain and inflammation, signs of mastitis can include fever and other flu-like symptoms. Afflicted Mumsnetters agree it is pretty vile.

To prevent and deal with blocked ducts and stave off mastitis, try these tips:

- Wear a soft, well-fitting bra. Now is not the time for your frillies and underwires.
- Drink lots and lots and lots of water.

- Massage the blockage towards the nipple. As one mum describes:

    'Not by rubbing the skin, but by pressing the heel of my hand quite firmly into the breast, starting at the outside of the breast blockage. I hold this for a few seconds, or as long as I can bear, and then repeat, moving inwards towards the nipple with each press. The idea is that the pressure forces the blockage along. This can be quite sore and I have to grit my teeth to do it.' *scarylittlecarrot*

- Expressing while massaging, and doing both at once in a hot shower, works for some.
- Find the plug. Some mothers find little plugs of old milk get stuck in the nipple and need to be pinched or rolled out (think of squeezing a blackhead). There can be several such plugs in one blocked duct. When you get one 'bit' out, 'take advantage of it quickly, and use the heel of hand pressure and hand expressing to get as much milk out as possible,' recommends one seasoned pro.
- Comb your breast towards the nipple with a wide-toothed comb. Like massage, this may be less painful in a shower and with lubricant.
- Apply warm flannels or similar:

    'I've got a couple of microwaveable hotties that are fab. I can heat them up to more than is recommended and they sit nicely on me poor mammary.' *Pagan*

- 'If you get mastitis and blocked ducts repeatedly in the same place, there may be some kind of "kink" in your milk ducts that keeps the milk from being drained properly, even if your breasts feel empty after a feed. So after feeding, try to massage out the remaining milk (worked for me, there was always a bit left in the tissue next to my armpits).' *Homsa*
- Breastfeed with baby's chin pointing towards the blockage. This can end up looking a bit like a game of mum and baby Twister. One mum explains, 'I did read that recent research suggested the plumbing in the breast wasn't that straightforward and ducts tended to wander around a bit. That would make it harder to predict where to position baby for maximum benefit, but if you nearly always feed holding the baby the same way, it might be worth trying something different.'

- Breastfeed on all fours if practicable (don't laugh bitterly at this point; it will only hurt more).

If you do get mastitis, there are different schools of thought among Mumsnetters. Some repeat sufferers head pretty sharpish for the antibiotics, but others say try treating it with ibuprofen (which is an anti-inflammatory) first:

> 'Take ibuprofen first; it clears 80 per cent of mastitis. The issue with antibiotics is that it increases your risk of thrush, passes through your milk and can affect your baby and your gut flora.' pupuce

Other mums suggest alternating paracetamol and ibuprofen because 'you will feel much better if you can get the temperature down'.

You also need to carry on breastfeeding and/or expressing, so the milk keeps flowing (and try the tips above for blocked ducts to relieve pain). Also, get someone else to look after the baby, so you can get a good kip.

Obviously, if things worsen, you can't get your temperature down, you get blood or pus in your milk, or you are just plain worried and miserable, get yourself to the doctor.

Fangs for the Mammaries: Biting

Sticking a sensitive part of your body between a set of teeth is a potentially hazardous activity. Lots of mothers find their babies don't even wait until teeth come in before having a practice chew. Many an enquiring infant will hold on to the nipple firmly with her hard little gums, while twisting her head to see who has just entered the room. This is, frankly, excruciating.

Perhaps the oldest and most widespread method of deterrence is the short, sharp(ish) shock:

'As soon as I saw his mouth shape change in an "I'm-just-about-to-bite-you" fashion, I grabbed hold of his chin, pulled it down, pushed him away from my boob, tapped him gently on the nose and said, "No!"' Hunkermunker

Sadly, some babies think being told 'No' or having a finger waggled at them is quite funny, and worth provoking multiple times. Other sensitive souls will go on nursing strike. Neither is a good result, so try something else instead:

- She has to unlatch to bite – watch out for this happening and remove her immediately you see her getting the notion.
- Biting is more likely to happen when your baby is full and getting a bit bored with feeding; if she is biting because she is bored or distracted, watch for the signs and terminate the feed before it is too late.
- 'Draw her in to your ample bosom next time, so her nose is smothered by it and she has to open *her mouth to breathe – counterintuitive, but it worked both times for me.' Swampster*
- Some babies bite because they are just trying to get a firm hold on the milk supply. Make sure she is adequately supported while feeding.
- Sometimes babies bite because they are teething. Give her something to teethe on other than your breast. Some mothers find putting some teething powder or gel on the gums before feeding helps. The biting tends to settle down when the relevant tooth comes through (so that's only 20-something to go ...).
- Babies who bite, pinch or fiddle idly with bits of your body while they feed may be distracted by a nursing necklace (a necklace with big interesting beads to fiddle with). There are various enterprising souls making these and selling them via the internet; or you could string your own – just make sure the beads can't come unstrung easily or break.

The Breast of Times, the Worst of Times: Breastfeeding and Returning to Work

If you want to continue feeding your baby breast milk exclusively when you get back to the coalface/restful-clean-office-with-no-one-crying-or-biting-you, transferring to bottle-feeding, if this is something your baby is not au fait with, may present a challenge, and you will need to get used to expressing too. Both of these potentially tricky subjects are dealt with above (see pp. 95 and 92).

What you will need to think about in addition, however, is how you are going to express at work. The Health and Safety Executive (HSE) advises employers that it is good practice to provide breastfeeding mothers with somewhere appropriate, safe and private (and *not* a loo) where they may express and somewhere to store expressed breast milk, but you have no absolute legal right to such a provision. If your employer is being an arse, you might want to get hold of the HSE's *Guide for New and Expectant Mothers Who Work* and wave the relevant passages under their nose. Also check with your HR department (if any) as to whether they have a written policy relating to breastfeeding mothers. A first-aid room may be a good option for expressing in, preferably one with a lock on the door or, failing that, a sign; it can be a challenge to achieve let-down, if you are fearful of being burst in upon by the acned adolescent from the postroom while hooked up to your industrial grade milking machine.

If you are worried that your co-workers may be rendered blind by the sight of actual human milk in a communal fridge, parcel it up in a lunch box or bag.

Try to build some expressing breaks into your work day, so you don't have to eat your lunch one-handed, while fretting about how many millilitres you are getting. The 'rest' will do you good, particularly when you are newly back to work.

Do dress to express. 'I usually wore tops that I pulled down over most of my breasts while pumping, so that there was nothing to see – I also kept my back to the door,' says a mum with an eye to the postroom lads.

'You need to make yourself a pumping bra – get an old sports bra and cut little holes where your nipples are, then put the breast shield thingies inside, so they poke out through the holes.' sallyforth

Some mothers recommend expressing every day the quantity of breast milk you will need for a day's feeding, so that you do not run into supply problems; obviously if there are hiccups, however, you should have a stash in the freezer to fall back on.

Even if you cannot face all this faff (and most mums find it's not so bad), you do not have to give up breastfeeding altogether when you go back to work:

'You can still feed first thing and when you get home. I did that for yonks. It also makes stopping much easier for both of you if you drop feeds gradually. And it is a lovely way of reconnecting when you get home from work. And you can get back to fully breastfeeding at weekends, if you like, and not bother with bottles. I found breastfeeding very, very flexible.' aloha

'When I went back to work and my daughter went to nursery I started expressing at work, but gave up after three days as it was just too much trouble. I then managed to express 400ml/14fl oz for during the day by pumping morning and evening. Eventually, this got too much as well, as I constantly had either a baby or a pump attached to my boobs, and my daughter went on to formula at nursery. We still breastfeed once in the morning and once when I get back from work, and it is a lovely relaxing time for both of us. It is also a wonderful way to force my husband into making our dinner while I'm "making" hers. I actually find this easier than bottle-feeding at home – no need to worry about making up feeds and sterilising. But because my daughter is used to a bottle, it means that I can go out occasionally and leave bottles for her, and I've found that my supply now isn't so much as to cause leakage if I don't feed.' prufrock

An older baby who is already weaned may be able to get through the day happily on solid food and water, and take breast milk morning and evening. Babies are generally happy to tank themselves up at night. You may be less happy to deal with what may be more frequent wakings, but some mums find a bit more nocturnal togetherness helps to compensate for lack of contact in the daytime (if, of course, they don't go completely mad due to sleep deprivation).

Goodbye to All That: Stopping Breastfeeding

When it comes to calling a halt to breastfeeding there are two things to be avoided: a) recriminations from your infant b) recriminations from your breasts. Many mothers who choose extended breastfeeding say that there comes a stage when a child decides to give up the breast. But if you do not find extended breastfeeding feasible or desirable, you can still make the transition a gentle one for both your body and your baby.

How difficult all this is has much to do with timing. A baby or toddler who is eating large quantities of solid food may not miss breastfeeding terribly. With a younger baby who still needs a significant quantity of expressed breast milk or formula, you may need to check out the section on introducing a bottle (see pp. 95–6).

Thinking about baby

A 'don't-offer-don't-refuse' system of gradual weaning from the breast may work if you are under no particular time pressure. In other words, don't refuse a feed, but don't offer one if baby doesn't demand it.

If you have a baby who still wakes to snack, but is no longer at an age where night-time nourishment is essential, you may need to substitute a regime of cuddling her back to sleep, with or without a cup of water. This can be difficult and upsetting, particularly because you are trying to do it when you, yourself, are tired and befuddled. It can be more practical to get your partner to do this because then temptation isn't put in either your way or your baby's (internal monologue: 'God I'm tired. Oh, just have the bloody thing then ... ZZZZ'). Also, put yourself in your baby's booties a minute. Imagine you are being cuddled by a large, soft person *reeking* of chocolate (substitute sushi/gin/sausage rolls as applicable), which you know they have stashed about their person. And they won't let you have any. You can see the problem.

If you are co-sleeping with a night-time snacker, consider wearing a big no-nonsense bra to bed for a while.

Of course, you may not need any of this advice; some babies are almost insultingly happy to pack it in.

Thinking about you

Cutting down by one feed per week is recommended to minimise the risk of mastitis. This can be tricky if you are a bit vague about how often your baby is feeding, so try to keep track, perhaps in a diary, for a period before you start cutting back. Dropping daytime feeds first seems to work best, leaving the morning and evening feeds until last.

If you experience pain and engorgement as you drop feeds, express a bit to relieve the pressure (but not so much that you are not curbing the demand).

If you have to give up breastfeeding very rapidly for some reason, you will definitely need to express.

Some women find stopping breastfeeding a very emotional time. Partly, this is hormonal – you are no longer getting 'all that lovely oxytocin', as one mum puts it; and partly it is, frankly, another one of those end-of-an-era things. 'Have a pint or two of vodka and a large bag of sweets,' advises a philosophical mum.

Chapter Three

You, Yourself and You

In this chapter ...

Your postnatal body is likely to be a rather Gothic affair – lots of gore and drama, with your vagina and labia starring as Frankenstein's Monster, your perineum as Edward Scissorhands and your belly as the Blob. You will have to swap the roles around a bit if you have had a Caesarean. So as well as caring for a baby, you will have to care for yourself. And you may not feel so happy about the bits that have expanded, stretched and drooped.

If you are unlucky, your postnatal mind may also be a disturbing place. For everyone, there is a whole range of new responsibilities to confront. There are new stresses and anxieties, as well as new bonds of affection. But for some women, the lows get really low and they develop postnatal depression (PND); while others may experience post-traumatic stress disorder (PTSD) as a result of their experiences during birth.

This chapter is about dealing with the changes to your body: the short-term ones (like bleeding and constipation) and the ones which may take more time and effort to resolve, like your waistline. And this chapter is also about where you may find yourself mentally and what you might do about it.

You will still be receiving medical attention for the first little while. In the period immediately after the birth, you will have visits from a midwife (up until day ten), although their frequency will depend on how much support you and your baby need. After that, you are at the tender mercies of the health visitor. The advice of random other mothers is grand as far as it goes, but remember to raise any significant concerns about your health or your baby's with medical professionals.

One Becomes Two: On Being Without Your Bump (or Not)

This is a strange transition and one about which women have different feelings. Some are so busy with their babies and their undercarriage that the bump issue gets little attention. Others report feeling oddly alone in their own bodies. The lack of weight out front may make you feel like your balance is off for a few days, but there is very great joy to be had from being able to sleep on your front again:

'You can roll over on to your tummy and just wallow about on the bed. Your hips and back will instantly forgive you for the pounding you gave them for three months.' colditz

And then there is the sudden freedom from heartburn or nausea which may lead you to eat – 'like a maniac, with a kind of crazed glee', as one mum puts it.

Other women are just delighted at being able to pee normally – only having urgency when there is actually a lot of urine there and then being able to produce 'reassuringly vast amounts' at one sitting. You don't know what you've got till it's gone and come back again.

Many women report that they still feel phantom movements, although in a few cases this proves to be something else:

'I had such bad wind after my C-section, I felt like my baby was still in my tummy.' Olissa

Others don't always remember the bump is gone and still reach down to stroke it. Or try to balance a plate on it. The bump, as repository of any number of potential babies, can seem conceptually very distinct from the actual baby in your arms.

Home alone: how Mumsnetters felt without their bumps

'I felt really weird and couldn't quite relate my bump to the baby that was in my arms; they were kind of separate things. One day I had a bump, the next day I had a baby, but they weren't related.' McCadburysDreamyegg

'I missed my bump. Really I did.' AitchYouBerk

'It just seemed totally normal; I didn't notice it. It was weird because when the baby is in your tummy you can't imagine anything else, but when the baby is out of your tummy you can't imagine anything else.' *morningpaper*

'I remember lying on my back and wobbling my weird jelly belly. Strange empty-bag sort of feeling.' *themoon66*

'Seven weeks on, I try and imagine my daughter inside and the feel of my bump under my hands – but I can't, it feels like some very distant past life.' *cathcart*

'I know it's a strong word, but I felt I was grieving for my bump, despite having a beautiful daughter in my arms. The two relationships were very separate, and the one with the bump had come to such an abrupt end after months of total intimacy.' *WillyWonkasEgghunt*

As to the appearance of the 'ex'-bump, a surprising number of people will ask a mother with a tiny baby in her arms/strapped to her front/otherwise dangling in their face, 'When's it due?'

'Some bag in Tesco asked me when I was due – *four months* afterwards!' bohemianbint

Be prepared with your snappy rejoinders well in advance:

'I don't think I'm going to suffer in silence though. I think I will just give them a Paddington Bear (hard stare), then lay it on the line and say, "I had my baby X months ago, and what you have said is incredibly demoralising." I will feel better and they won't ever do it again.' LadyThompson

And remember you are *entitled* to look like this:

'Get a balloon. Blow it up really big and let the air out. Look at it again. *That* is why your belly is so big.' SoupDragon

Some women look really pregnant for a number of weeks or even months. Others of us sport a soft belly which hangs over the top of our pants (like those Salvador Dali pictures of melting clocks) and has the texture of warm pizza dough. The ooziness of your belly before muscle tone returns may actually make you feel quite slim, because, as one mother reports, 'you can tuck it down your trousers with ease'. The amount of further excess you find layered about your hips and bottom depends a lot on your genes and a bit on your greediness.

What to wear before it all ... you know ... magically springs back into place

The key here is not to wind yourself up too much. It's tempting to get out your skinny jeans/best work suit/anything at all fetching to wear and do some horrible stitch-busting contortions to try to funnel your postnatal body into the desired garment. Don't go there. Remember, in the early weeks you are still losing a lot of the baby weight in lochia (see p. 116), your womb is contracting down, you are *transitional*.

'After my third child, I still had to wear some maternity clothes for a couple of months (i.e. long, floaty skirts with stretchy waists, not smock dresses which shout "I Am Pregnant And Still Think It's 1974").' *OldGregg*

'I walked into Slimming World six months after I had my son still wearing maternity trousers!' *IndigoMoon*

'After two weeks, I was sick of wearing stretchy clothes and my mum suggested I just go and buy a couple of cheap outfits in my "interim" size, so at least I felt human again.' *pinchypants*

> 'I only had a stone to lose after my daughter, and was really fit – back at the gym as soon as she was six weeks old, doing pretty tough workouts. However, it wasn't until she was eight or nine months old that I actually looked like my pre-preg self and could wear my loveliest jeans again.' *pistachio*

It Ain't Over Till It's Over: After-pains

After-pains are one of a plethora of things about childbirth which somehow do not seem to have entered general consciousness. You never see women in films holding the fake baby in the little pink hat saying, 'What fresh hell is this?' as they are assaulted by after-pains – basically, pains caused by the contraction of the uterus as it struggles back to its original size.

The good news is that some women do not get any after-pains at all, particularly with first babies. When they do occur, however, after-pains tend to strike during breastfeeding, although initially they may be more constant. They may last for as little as hours and generally go on for a few days at most, but some Mumsnetters report them going on for up to about two weeks.

They also vary hugely in intensity. Some women find theirs are really nothing much to write home about – 'a bit like a period pain in waves', says one mum; while a very small minority say theirs were worse than the labour itself.

Generally speaking, things that work for bad period pains tend to work for after-pains. A big hot-water bottle can be soothing, as can a nice, hot bath.

'It helps to feed in a rocking chair, as the rocking motion helps with the pain.' Spacecadet

Some Mumsnetters with bad after-pains suggest the use of visualisation techniques when starting a session of breastfeeding (imagining yourself away to a tropical beach, for example, possibly with the assistance of a CD). If you need painkillers, try ibuprofen and paracetamol or get something stronger on prescription if you are really suffering. Co-codamol gets lots of endorsements.

The ugly news is that after-pains do seem to get worse with each child. 'My midwife told me your womb has to contract down harder with every child,' explains a mum. But at least that knowledge gives you the opportunity to be prepared:

'I know someone who has eleven children and she bought a canister of gas and air to cope with the after-pains after the last one.' RosiePosie

Lochia Mess Monster

Lochia is the reason they invented those maternity pads which look like loaves of poor-quality white bread and feel like you are wearing a small soft toy in your pants. Lochia is like a giant period in which all the thickened-up lining of your uterus gradually falls out, so expect blood and fleshy bits. It will usually be much lighter and not last so long if you have had a C-section because they tidy a lot of it up during the op, but it does depend on how much tidying they manage.

Your midwife will probably tell you to report any clot bigger than a fifty-pence piece, and this is advice you should follow. It is, however, not at all uncommon to extrude what appear to be offcuts from an butcher's shop:

'I passed what seemed like huge lumps of liver after my son was born. The midwife said to keep them so she could see them. She examined them and they were just bits from the wall of the womb.' harktheheraldfoxessing

'I passed what felt like a small child after I got home from hospital, but was told this was normal.' jampots

'I produced a huge clot – the size of my hand – a few days after my son was born and called the hospital in a panic thinking something was very wrong. My midwife told me it was probably OK because I had been feeding my son (which obviously stimulates the uterus) and sitting down so that the blood "pooled" for want of a better description.' Coolmama

Although most sizeable bits are just big old clots or large lumps of lining, some large clots and lumps may indicate that there are retained bits of placenta, so do not take any chances. Get the big ones looked at. If you have headaches, a temperature, vomiting or flu-like symptoms, you may have an infection due to retained placenta and again should seek medical advice. Changes in clot colour should also be reported to your midwife.

Lochia after a vaginal birth tends to linger for up to about six weeks but it might be over after just two or three. Women who do too much on their feet tend to bleed for longer. And bouts of exertion can cause a sudden gush too. The really heavy stage tends to last for a period of between a few days and about three weeks, and some women are still having light bleeding at about nine weeks. The colour tends to change along the way too – from red to brown to yellowish or light pink. If it gets heavier again, there is suddenly lots of heavy, fresh bleeding after a few weeks or there is a smelly discharge, you should get in touch with your midwife or doctor.

Many Mumsnetters recommend purchasing cheap black pants and leggings to minimise the horror of leaks should they happen (wear the leggings under skirts or dresses for a less demoralising look). You cannot use tampons or, indeed, Mooncups, during this period (even if you think you could keep one in) because they can cause infection.

The truth about pads and bogs

Maternity pads can be a horror: they are bulky, they are mobile because they don't have wings and other fancy fasteners to keep them in place and they can be leaky. There are good reasons to wear them, rather than heavy-duty sanitary towels, however: the plasticky parts of sanitary towels can interfere with healing, the area can stay too wet (which is bad news if you have stitches) and it is harder to see how much blood loss is going on with those soak-it-all-away style sanitary towels:

'If you have stitches due to an episiotomy, then I can recommend maternity pads. They're so thick it's like sitting on cushions. I tried ultra sanitary towels shortly after the birth and found it really painful to sit down as they were so thin. Also, my stitches felt like they were forever catching on the absorbent covering. My tip for straight after the birth is to put an ultra pad in your pants, then put a maternity pad on top of it. You'll look like you've laid an egg in your pants, but you'll be comfy and won't leak everywhere.' *EagleBird*

'I found the heavy-duty sanitary pads far better, but I had a C-section and no stitching. I've been told by people that have had stitches, that the maternity pads are a lot softer on the fadge!' *PussInJimmyChoos*

Or try layering:

'Horrible even to think about, but if you buy paper pants a size up, you can get two of the maternity pads in side by side ... I did this for the first 36 hours or so.' *tassisss*

'I used adult nappies; didn't have a C-section, but had stitches – not sure if I was supposed to, but I didn't get an infection and it meant I could get rid of the catheter.' *QueenGina*

'Tip: make sure your partner knows what towels to get you, should you need to send them out desperately having used your stash up – checking I had enough towels was the last thing on my mind, having just given birth. So my husband popped to Tesco. Came back with super-slim ones!' *biscuitsmustbedunkedintea*

Another tip: do not even think about putting maternity pads down the loo. It is about as sensible as putting soft furnishings into your waste disposal.

What Your Bits Look and Feel Like After a Vaginal Birth – Bruising, Labial Grazing, Stitches, Tears and More

Well, it's pretty common, possibly universal, to have a general heavy sensation below the pantyline and a feeling like your innards are going to drop out when you are walking. Hence the last-gunslinger-in-the-west amble of the woman with a new baby (also attributable to needing to keep your legs wide enough apart to straddle a maternity pad the size of a small futon).

It is important to say at the outset that *things will improve down there.* They really will. Some women resolutely refuse to look in their pants during the early days after giving birth, even while attending to hygiene and other matters: 'It's best not to look, really,' asserts one Mumsnetter. Others, however, are inexorably drawn to inspect the damage: 'I had to contort myself, but managed to look with the aid of a mirror,' says another.

Visions of horror ... what some mums have found (disarrangement of the nethers – a great spur to metaphor)

- 'An open steak and kidney pie.' *spidermama*
- 'A baboon's bottom.' *notnowbernard*

(continued)

- 'Elephantiasis of the undercarriage.' *thankyouandgoodnight*
- 'Mine is a shadow of its former self. Well a shadow makes it somehow seem small and unnoticeable, so that's probably an inappropriate euphemism for what I mean. I recognise it, but not as I once knew it.' *Squarer*
- 'Imagine a nicely decorated lounge. Then a massive earthquake. Then the same lounge. That's my genitals.' *morningpaper*
- 'I had a vag that looked like an accident in the Channel Tunnel.' *HUNXXXX*

But the swollen-up baboon's bottom/elephantiasis thing is not for ever, and that which is torn and stitched will heal, so don't panic.

Here are some specific sore things which may be going on and some home remedies to try for them.

Bruising

Even if you don't tear or have an episiotomy, you are likely to find things pretty swollen and tender.

'I was told by the midwife it looked like I had a black eye down there.' TotalChaos

Some ideas for soothing the bruising:

- Arnica tablets or gel. Some says the tablets are 'quackery', but they still have many fans, and the gel is especially popular.
  Note: do not apply gel or cream to broken skin.
- Try lots of sea salt in your bath water and a bit of lavender oil.
- Sitting on sports ice packs wrapped in a towel can help to reduce swelling.

Or, if things are that bit more severe:

- 'I had some very helpful ultrasound therapy from a physiotherapist which reduced the swelling enough so I could sit down.' *TotalChaos*

- Anti-inflammatories can be a big help if you are too sore to sit. Speak to your midwife or GP; the stronger ones need to be prescribed.
- Consider acquiring a valley cushion to ease the pain of sitting (see also 'Stitches', p. 122).

Some happy news about bruising is that many mothers report less bruising and swelling with each birth. Other mothers of older children squint enigmatically when asked about the bruising, because it's all just a bit of a blur really.

Labial grazing

This doesn't sound so bad, a least when compared with 'tearing' and 'cutting' and 'stitches' (enough already), but can be very sore indeed.

'My graze was more painful than the wound that got stitched.' CarGirl

Some 'grazes' are, in fact, euphemisms for labial tears. Labial tears are not stitched as frequently as perineal ones because the stitches can be more painful in that area and labial tears apparently tend to heal OK on their own. You may also have vaginal grazing.
Give your wounded flaps some love and attention:

- Tea tree or lavender oil in the bath and sea-salt baths are all good.
- Witch hazel can be lovely:

'Put it in the fridge, then on a cotton wool pad – 'tis bliss for the nethers.' *Piffle*

- Try nappy cream:

'Our community midwives recommend Sudocrem for labial grazes – works wonders, I am led to believe.' *mears*

- 'The best thing I did was to put a capful of Dettol in my bath every other day. It healed it up almost immediately. It doesn't sting either when you go in the bath. I used to shower off afterwards, so that I didn't stink of it!' *lauraloola*

- 'Germolene (the ointment rather than the cream, if you can get it); it has local anaesthetic and it really does help. Will help with the sting when you wee.' *EarthwormFrittataBugEnchilada*
- Make your own soothing pads:

  'Get some comfrey tea (online or from Holland & Barrett). Make it nice and strong, add about a tablespoon of witch hazel to each cup. Put a couple of tablespoons on a maxi pad, wrap in clingfilm and put in the freezer. The comfrey tea is astringent and healing; the witch hazel stops the pad freezing hard.' *ajm200*

- Another lovely herbal option, described by an expert:

  'I have a big bag of mixed dried herbs that I usually give to clients postbirth for any kind of healing – perineum/section scar – and all have reported excellent results and trauma has healed well. You need equal quantities of lavender, comfrey, calendula and echinacea (you can buy either online or from herbalists). Take a handful and put it in a bowl and cover with boiling water. Leave to go cold and then put in a clean spray bottle and spray on the scar/stitches or put on a sanitary towel. You can also make a DIY bidet by placing a clean plastic bag over your toilet seat and pushing it down in the middle to form a dip, you can then place some of your herb liquid in the dip and use it to bathe your perineum. The other option is to place some of the herbs in a muslin, then put it in your bath.' *Howdie*

  For help with how to wee in a relatively pain-free way, see under 'Stitches', below.

Stitches

There is poetry in the pain:

'My fanny looked like a patchwork quilt after I had my son; and it felt like a crown of thorns.'

EagleBird

You may have stitches as a result of an episiotomy or because the area has torn. Stitching may be in your vagina, your perineum or elsewhere:

'Even my poor old clitoris had to be stitched.'

piratecat

Some women have internal stitches:

'They'd be the ones holding your vaginal wall together. There are a few different layers inside between the vagina and the anal passage, so the stitches could be anywhere.' avenanap

The upside of internal stitches, if you have these only, is that they don't sting when you wee. That makes you feel really fortunate now, doesn't it?

Stitches need to be looked after. Your midwife may check them every day during the period when she is visiting (cue hasty removal of visitors from living room, so you can get your bits out) or may simply tell you to watch out for signs of infection such as 'weepiness'. If you have concerns about infection, get your stitches looked at. You may need treatment with antibiotics and, in some cases, restitching.

Tea tree oil in the bath can help to ward off infection, and pouring water over the area after every trip to the loo will keep the stitches clean. Many Mumsnetters recommend sitting in a salt-water bath a couple of times a day. Some say you should then dry down below with a hairdryer, but you may find this too harsh on sensitive skin. Others suggest it is better to apply antiseptic dry powder spray or simply let it all air dry.

The intensity and duration of the pain from stitches will depend on many factors – how many, where, what else is going on down there. In the early days, it is sensible not to stand up too much or walk too far.

Do take painkillers if you need them. Try paracetamol or get stronger anti-inflammatories on prescription, if necessary. Many drugs are compatible with breastfeeding, but let your doctor know before anything is prescribed.

Wee in the shower or in the bath if that's the only way you can manage. 'Lots of us have done this, whether we admit it or not,' confides one mum. Alternatively, try keeping a jug or a sports bottle (one sophisticated Mumsnetter used a cafetière) by the loo, then sitting facing the cistern and throwing water on your bits from your container of choice during the process.

'I used an empty and well-cleaned-out tomato ketchup bottle in the bathroom. Whenever I needed a wee, I'd fill it with lukewarm water and squirt myself while weeing, so it didn't sting.'

VeniVidiVickiQV

It also helps if you drink lots of water, so that your urine is more dilute and less stingy.

'Sleep with no knickers. In fact, stay as knicker-free as you can and sit on a towel.' LadyofWaffle

Or simply wear a towel around your waist when you are at home alone – you want to keep things dry and aerated, but you are also likely to be battling with a messy lochia situation.

For topical pain relief, consider the suggestions under 'Labial grazing', above, and the following:

- 'Gel pads which you cool in the freezer and pop into disposable paper covers. Swap as frequently as you can hobble to the freezer.' *BabiesEverywhere*
- 'Call the NCT and hire a "valley cushion" which has a groove down the middle and a pump on each side to get just the amount of air you want under each cheek. It gives you maximum support and blood flow without your bits being pressed. You'll need to get someone to pick it up for you from a local NCT lady. They come with sealed clean covers each time, so are as new.' *Lotster*

It can be alarming to find, in the course of an exploratory fumble (by you, that is – unless you are really enjoying a quick recovery) some weeks after the birth, evidence that your allegedly dissolvable stitches are still there. One Mumsnetter found 'string hanging above the incision area about an inch long with a knot at the end!'

But don't panic, says a Mumsnetting midwife:

'The dissolving stitches are actually absorbed into the tissue and sometimes lengths of stitch material come away intact. It can take over 42 days for some stitches to be fully absorbed.' mears

Other mothers report that the stitches can become a bit more sore and tighter just before they disappear, but obviously if things get very sore or there is any sign of infection, you should get yourself to the GP.

Those Tears: What Do They Mean?

There are more precise and elaborate definitions of the possible tears to your perineum to be found on the internet, but the following is a reasonably good rough-and-ready layperson's guide:

'First-degree – skin only; second – skin and muscle; third – skin and muscle, up to the ring of muscle around the anus; fourth – the same as third, but also tearing of that ring of muscle.' MrsTittleMouse

Light at the end of the tunnel: some Mumsnetters' experiences of timescales for tears to heal

Here are some experiences of the less severe types of tear.

'I had a second-degree tear without stitches. It took about ten weeks to be completely healed, but was pretty much better after a few weeks.' *nappynuttynormabutty*

(continued)

'I too had a second-degree tear. I remember waking up every day feeling worse, not better. But I know that on day ten, I felt a huge amount better for the first time and after that things got much better quickly.' *Bky*

'I was pain-free after two days and healed in seven.' *vole3*

'I was sore for a couple of weeks.' *HeathersMummy*

Third-degree tears are where the really nasty risks like faecal incontinence tend to begin. But many, many women have third-degree tears and are absolutely fine. If you are 'lucky', you will be well repaired in hospital, but some women do have to return for more radical repairs and have ongoing issues. Read on for some thoughts from Mumsnetters about coping with these.

Sphincter damage, fistulae and other ongoing injuries

Many women have no idea that childbirth can lead to damage to the bits in between the vagina and anus and the anus itself, which may result in problems, such as faecal incontinence. And it's probably not surprising that they don't major on it in NCT classes. But if you are in the small minority of women with these problems, you can end up feeling horribly alone, unprepared and unsupported.

The fact that there has been a sphincter injury (which may not be an actual tear) is sometimes not spotted in the aftermath of labour, or the damage may be noted, but the repair carried out badly. Some doctors think referral to a physiotherapist for help with pelvic-floor exercises after a sphincter repair is helpful, but for many women this may not happen.

Bad sphincter damage can have very unpleasant and upsetting consequences:

'My problems – wind from vagina, urge incontinence (I believe that's what they call it – i.e. basically, that if I don't run to the toilet the minute I feel I have to go, I soil myself completely), small amount of leakage from back passage throughout the day. Lovely, eh? Really makes you feel like a woman. My episiotomy scar feels like it's pinching and my butt hurts still; sitting is so uncomfortable.' DMCT

As for fistulae, this stoical Mumsnetter's account is probably as good a layperson's explanation as any:

'You can get fistulas in other parts of your body, but basically, it's a "communication" between two parts of the body that aren't usually connected. In my case it was vagina–anus, but it can also be bladder, etc. It is essentially a weakness or breakdown in tissue that is a constant hole that doesn't/can't heal on its own. In my situation, it meant that wind and small amounts of stool could come through. If the fistula is large, then it can mean more material comes through. Fistulas are generally not just "stitched up" because the tissue is weak anyway and the repair may not hold. So I've read of "patches" being used or, in my case, the fistula was excised and the remaining tissue was overlapped and stitched back up.' Cyee

And it's not just sphincters that can suffer. Some labours – time to gird your loins – can so weaken the tissues supporting your uterus, that your uterus cannot stay in place and slips down, causing what's known as a prolapse. There are various degrees of prolapse, according to the degree of 'slippage', but the general sign that you have one is a feeling of 'something hanging out':

'Since very early on, I've had a feeling that something is hanging out of me – like I've got a tampon hanging out. I also need a wee almost as soon as I stand up, but it's OK when I sit down. And I have to go to the loo every 20 minutes, if I'm walking about.' GYo

Given that it is statistically unlikely that you are going to share your sphincter problem with anyone in your antenatal group, you can end up feeling like the only person in the world with a tiny baby and an inability to leave the vicinity of your own lavatory. Women going through the medical mill and waiting for treatment may find the internet a good place to find support and sympathy from fellow sufferers. There have been long, supportive threads on Mumsnet where women with sphincter problems even manage a little black humour:

'Oh yes, the unexpected fartlets at inopportune times: I did one the other day when I was giving a presentation; I quickly shuffled my papers and tapped them on the table to camouflage the (pretty small, but embarrassing) sound!'
Bluestocking

The message which comes through strongly from these discussions – and others, started by women with prolapses or whose vaginal or perineal repairs have resulted in long-lasting symptoms such as pain, itching and painful intercourse – is that you may have to insist on the medical care you need and deserve. Don't be embarrassed about discussing these problems with your doctor. Or, at least, not so embarrassed that you carry on suffering in silence. Keep pushing for a proper diagnosis and treatment. You may have a lovely GP who gets you the referrals you need right away or you may have to work harder:

'I've had postnatal problems after a difficult delivery, and I've had to push for treatment. I told the GP at the six-week check that I was in constant pain and was told to have lots of sex – "that'll stretch you out", they said. I felt like saying, "Didn't I just tell you that I was in *constant* pain??!?" I don't know what she thought I was supposed to do – have lots of agonising sex, then worry about the effect on our marriage later? I felt quite awkward about getting a second opinion – like I was being pushy and wasting NHS resources or something. But it was the best thing that I could have done, as I ended up with cortisone injections for enlarged scarring.' MrsTittleMouse

'Go to your GP and demand a referral to a gynaecologist; there is so much they can do these days to help with recovery like physio, injections for scarring, etc.' theautomatic

For sphincter injuries and fistulas, you may be seen by a colorectal surgeon. Some continence problems respond to physical therapy. For more serious issues, you may need reconstructive surgery:

The tunnel of love: getting an honest answer about postnatal vaginal circumference

'I will wake my partner at three in the morning, shine a torch in his eyes, scream, "HOW TIGHT AM I NOW COMPARED WITH HOW TIGHT I WAS BEFORE THE KIDS?" and report back tomorrow, shall I?' *policywonk*

'What if he says, "It's like throwing a sausage down Oxford Street"?' *morningpaper*

'Testicle shredding, of course.' *Flamesparrow*

And what one dad says:

'After two natural births, my wife is definitely looser. Sex is still very good too.

I count myself very fortunate that she still allows me to go near enough to find this out.

Of course, after witnessing two births, it's entirely possible that I've shrunk ...' *BarcodeZebra*

The Walking Wounded (in Big Pants): Looking After Yourself Post C-section

As with vaginal births, how sore you are, how much you can do in the aftermath and how quickly you recover depend on lots of factors. In particular, some C-sections are just much rougher than others. If you have an emergency section after a significant period of labour, you are likely to be pretty knackered, as well as having undergone major surgery. A general anaesthetic will also tend to leave you feeling crummy for a while.

Tips for coping post C-section

- Remember that it's normal to feel like your insides are sloshing about; it gets better.
- You will be given guidelines by the hospital for when you can perform heavy lifting, do the Hoovering (you'll be raring to get back to that one) and carry out other tasks that put stress on your abdominal muscles.

   'Listen to the recommended recovery times and stick to them. If you try to do too much too soon the recovery will take much longer.' *hippmummy*

- Don't be a hero. Take your painkillers regularly and take it as easy as you need to. As one wise mum says, 'There are no medals; all you can do is listen to your body.'
- If at all possible, do get help with physical tasks. Ideally, you would have someone who could help for up to six weeks or so, if you turned out to need it. But some women find themselves sending their partners back to work after a week or two if they are feeling sprier than expected.
- Have a look at the advice in the first chapter about how to cope in the first couple of weeks. Get help with the housework or leave it. Do your food shopping on the internet and make use of convenience foods.
- Stand tall when you can. You may just feel like slumping, but you will feel better sooner if you don't.
- Arnica tablets are popular with some Mumsnetters who have had C-sections. And try all the usual stuff in the bath – sea salt, tea tree oil and lavender oil.
- No driving during the initial period. Some insurance companies apparently say you can resume after six weeks; others will cover you sooner, if your GP says you are fit to drive.
- Pants are a big issue; you do need the giant, waist-high granny ones. And the disposable ones are condemned as uncomfortable by many:

(continued)

'Am now remembering all the tips, like putting a sanitary towel over the scar so your knickers don't rub it and instead of getting disposable knickers, get huge armpit-length ones from Matalan, which are probably cheaper, anyway.'
IAteRosemaryConleyForBreakfast

Or try this:

'I just took some of my husband's pants – big ones, those sort of fitted boxer ones. The waistband is very high, and they're a bit more modest than even giant women's pants. Oh, and the catheter went out through the fly. Very practical.'
NotQuiteCockney

- Postnatal wind (which can afflict vaginal birthers as well) is reputedly worse for C-section veterans: 'I remember after a section a terrible five minutes when it just carried on and on. And I was in the supermarket. Had to go into the pet food section (as it's largely empty and a bit smelly, anyway).' *gettingthere*

But if standing about in the pet food section isn't working for you as a lifestyle choice, Mumsnetters suggest that exercising those pelvic-floor muscles will help you to repress yourself. In the meantime, consider getting an elderly poodle who can be blamed for any inadvertent emissions.

What your scar looks like as time goes by will depend on various things: whether your operation was emergency or elective, the difficulty the doctor had getting your baby out, the skill of your surgeon, your genes.

Many scars dwindle to a tiny line, and they are generally below the bikini line, so will be disguised in due course by hair. A lot of women also seem to get a bit of overhang – loose skin or flesh which flops over the top of the scar and which is more intractable than the general postnatal muffintop. This floppy thing can afflict the fit as well as the unfit. And will apparently defy most everything bar surgery:

'God, perhaps we should all have tummy tucks? I've had three C-sections and when I lie on my side it's like having a small puppy rolled up next to me.' ahundredtimes

'A nurse friend told me that if your overhang hangs down so far that it covers your fanjo(!) you can have cosmetic surgery for it on the NHS, called an "apronectomy". <visions of MNers hanging little weights to their overhangs to meet the requirements>' snowleopard

Some Mumsnetters suggest that massaging the scar to loosen it will reduce the overhang, and some do respond to the usual blandishments: sit-ups, yoga, Pilates, reduction of fat intake, etc.

Pelvic Floor

Whether you have had a C-section or a vaginal birth, your pelvic floor will need help to get its groove back. It is pregnancy itself which puts much of the strain on the muscles, but pushing a baby out doesn't help either. It's important to sort out your pelvic floor because, well, you don't want to be an old lady who smells of wee; or a young one, for that matter. And those muscles are important for sex, however remote a prospect that might seem right now.

'Do pelvic-floor exercises every day for the rest of your life.' belgo

You can read about the mechanics of pelvic-floor exercises in any number of books or internet sites, but many Mumsnetters suggest getting someone to train you to do your exercises correctly: 'You could also ask for a referral to a physio. They are *amazingly* knowledgeable about pelvic muscles,' asserts a mum.

There are many tricks for reminding yourself to do your exercises: do them whenever you have gone to the loo and are still sitting there or do them every time you feed baby. Buy a sheet of red circle stickers and put one on the kettle, your toothbrush, your partner – then do pelvic-floors every time you see a red sticker.

As well as the conventional pelvic-floor exercises, one mother recommends 'a lot more masturbation because it will tone up your pelvic-floor muscles'.

Movements of the People: That First Poo After Childbirth

Keep repeating this mantra to yourself: the idea of the poo is worse than the poo itself, the idea of the poo is worse than the poo itself ... The thought of forcing anything out in the vicinity of all that bruised, extruded and possibly stitched flesh can be terrifying, but truly – no stitches will burst and no viscera will come flying out (although it may feel like they are about to).

'I maintain that the first poo was *way* more scary than labour, though not in front of blokes because it opens up – sorry, no pun intended – the possibility that their "morning manoeuvres" are the equivalent of childbirth ...' willywonka

Some mothers find it is a good few days before anything happens, but do try to make sure that you are not stopping it happening through, well, fear. Here are some tips for getting things moving and making sure you are not permanently caught between two stools.

- Drink lots of water and eats loads of fruit and vegetables. Try figs, prunes and apricots.
- Getting your GP to give you something like Lactulose is a more certain way of ensuring that everything is pretty soft. As one veteran advises: 'The softer you keep the poo, the less painful it

will be. If you can arrange it so the poo just falls out, rather than you having to strain at all, you will put far less pressure on your various sore bits.'

- 'I put glycerine tablets up my bott after every birth. A godsend I can tell you. I had to make sure that whatever was passing through me was total liquid.' *spidermama*
- If you are very worried about bursting your stitches, try having a look to reassure yourself. If you have no more than a second-degree tear, the stitches probably are not that close to your anus.
- 'A tip from midwife was to hold a pad/wad of tissue against your stitches when you go. This is psychologically reassuring if nothing else, because you feel like you are holding everything in your vagina, which feels like it might otherwise be popping out. Be careful how you wipe afterwards! Nice and easy does it!' *DumbledoresGirl*
- Or try the jug-of-water technique for sloshing the area clean or moist toilet tissue/baby wipes.

'You'll feel so fabulous afterwards and want to tell everyone you see. I think there should be First-Postnatal-Poo announcement cards.' *mrsdarcy*

Coming soon: Mumsnet Postnatal Poo announcement cards. (For charity naturally.)

The Grapes of Wrath, Great Balls of Fire and Other Abominable Puns: Postnatal Piles (and Fissures)

'I'm reminded of a sketch Victoria Wood did a few years ago. She said when she gave birth she asked her mother to knit two hats. One for the baby and the other one for the haemorrhoid.' karmamother

Piles are those dilated veins in your anus that cause swellings which may protrude out of your anal sphincter. External ones tend to be itchy and sore and sometimes bleed. You may have had the pleasure of making their acquaintance during pregnancy or they may be new friends caused by pushing a baby out and/or by postnatal constipation. The tips above for dealing with constipation and managing postnatal defecation are all relevant to piles. In addition, keep your piles clean and keep movements as regular as possible, sit on a valley cushion and do your pelvic-floor exercises.

Or discover some surprising new uses for condoms:

'My midwife suggested a condom filled with ice cubes wrapped in cloth and placed on the area concerned. Sounds awful, but it really helped to shrink and took the "heat" out of the buggers!' agalch

'I sat on a peeled frozen banana in a condom wrapped in a soft facecloth, as it softens and is more comfortable than ice cubes or peas.'
PrettyCandles

Get to your GP for a prescription for heavy-duty piles ointment, if things don't improve.

Bleeding when pooing when there is no obvious cluster of external piles may be caused by internal piles or an anal fissure. Again, your GP will be able to prescribe an appropriate cream and/or suppositories for a persistent fissure.

The Stunningly Anticlimactic Six-week Check

This sometimes happens in tandem with a six-week check of baby and is carried out by your GP.

'It normally goes like this:
Doctor: Cute baby; you feeling OK?
You: Thanks – he's lovely. Yes, I'm fine.
Doctor: Great, we'll send you a smear
appointment in due course.' whomovedmychocolate

You will then go home wondering why you put on clean pants and flossed your labia.

There are various other topics which may be broached though, depending on your GP. You may get a blood pressure test. You are likely to face the 'Have-you-thought-about-contraception?' chat (which can seem almost surreally inapposite). And you may be asked some questions to ascertain whether you might have PND.

You should definitely bring up any specific concerns you have and persist with them if your GP appears to be staring into space or blethering about Mirena coils inappropriately. You should also raise any queries you might have about whether it is safe to resume swimming or other types of exercise. If your GP is looking really bored, try cheering him/her up by asking about the feasibility of some really esoteric sexual practice.

Up and about or down and out

How soon after birth you feel physically well enough to get out of bed/resume normal activities/stop crying depends on a lot of things – your pregnancy, your labour, the drugs you had, the state of your body, etc.

'I felt pretty lively after all three births, but I think it was partly because for each pregnancy I'd spent nine months feeling relentlessly heavy and bulky and tired.' *Fennel*

'I had some weird adrenaline thing going on after my third son. I couldn't stay still, was up and about, packing all my stuff away. My husband sat holding the baby and laughing at me, telling me to sit down.' *dingdongMegaLegsonhigh*

(continued)

'I got some weird hormonal rush and was shopping and cooking for guests who were visiting, while sporting immaculately coiffed hair. You should have seen me ten days later when the high wore off – I was like some sort of hermit bag lady.' *ImBarryScott*

'I have never been OK enough to get out of bed within at least twelve hours really, let alone go out, do housework, etc.; and it makes me feel a bit inadequate, or that I must be doing something wrong, when I read other people saying they were getting on with things as usual shortly after giving birth.' *twinklyflightattendant*

'Blood loss and anaemia will certainly make you feel very weak for weeks or, as in my case, a couple of months.' *JingleBelgoHoHoHo*

'I have always been physically fit and exercised right the way through pregnancy and felt absolutely fine. However, the day after my delivery, I felt like I had been run over by a truck and could only hobble round the ward *very, very* slowly. I always remember feeling demoralised when a lady came up that day from the delivery suite, having just popped out the baby 30 minutes before, and jumped (yes, sprang) up on her bed and sat there cross-legged, holding her newborn. She left later that day, walking off like she had just attended a hearing test. I didn't walk like that for at least a fortnight.' *Notyummy*

Hair Today, Gone Tomorrow: Hair Loss

This is the flip side of the lustrous shampoo-advert locks (for which read Janis-Joplin-style fright wig) you develop during pregnancy. It all falls out again and sits in furry heaps, growling at you from the corners of your unhoovered living room. This is apparently because you do not lose hair in the usual way during pregnancy, so you have nine months' worth to fall out. The great hair exodus usually happens around three to four months after birth, but it can be earlier or later.

Most women just lose the excess, but some find their hair gets really thin, and some even develop bald patches. Happily, the majority can then expect pretty rapid regrowth:

'I currently have a lovely half-inch fringe all the way round my hairline (my daughter is six months).' e14mum

Some women find the new hair is different from the old: curlier, straighter, sometimes greyer – think of it as nature's free restyle.

Bear in mind that hair loss can be made worse by iron deficiency, so keep your iron levels up with iron-rich foods (dark, leafy vegetables, pulses, red meat) and consider getting your iron levels checked out.

Severe hair loss may be an indication of some other problem:

'I had this really badly after I finished breast-feeding. It really upset me, as I had always had lovely, thick, shiny hair and suddenly had thin, wispy bits, with a hairline that receded at least 5 centimetres (2 inches) and bald patches all over my head. It took about five months before my hair stopped falling out, and another year for it to be back to normal. Hair loss at this level is not "normal" – it's an extreme reaction to changing hormone levels. It can be caused by a misbehaving thyroid, so ask your doctor to check that, especially if you have other symptoms like extreme fatigue. (But then who hasn't with a five-month-old?)' prufrock

'The GP said that hair loss well after the baby is born is not hormonal, but most probably nutritional or stress-related. He suggested that I try multivitamins first of all. They helped a lot, and when my PND was diagnosed several months later and I began treatment for that as well, the hair loss reduced to what I would consider a normal amount.' wmf

There are various post-pregnancy 'thickening' shampoos and conditioners on the market, which some Mumsnetters rate. See what a hairdresser can do with your denuded scalp if you are feeling really demoralised by hair loss. A shorter style, layers and some colour to create what hairdressers call texture can all help.

Regrowth of hair may leave you with some short, fuzzy bits, described by one Mumsnetter as 'the tennis ball effect', which is another reason you may want to think about a restyle.

'The regrowth at the front was really obvious and drove me insane! Until it grew long enough to brush/blend in with the rest of my hair it looked as though I'd accidentally cut a mini fringe that was a couple of centimetres long!'
BettySpaghetti

Or you could just try a paradigm shift and learn to love your new fuzzy hair:

'You will notice, on you and other new mums, a "halo" of new hair around your face. It grows straight up until it's heavy enough to fall in with the rest of your hair (style depending). I think it looks rather sweet.' MalmoMum

And a couple of practical considerations for heavy shedders:

'I lost so much hair my husband made me buy a new Hoover without a roller because my hair kept breaking the old one.' liquidclocks

'My husband has just pointed out that checking the nappies for hair is vital for those of us with long hair – apparently a hair wrapped around the goolies is a major cause for complaint! mines

Getting in Shape/Getting Your Tummy Back

Some women find the weight 'falls off' when they are breastfeeding. Others find they are so hungry and tired, they seem to pack on the bits that have fallen off those other women. It is, after all, easier to eat a bag of buns than to cook up a wholesome feast. And breastfeeding cravings do seem to focus on refined sugar in its many marvellous forms.

There is much debate on Mumsnet about how you might 'get your tummy back' or, preferably, acquire someone else's flatter model. There is, occasionally, wild talk of stomach binding, but more sensibly:

You will probably be given a leaflet in hospital about what excerises you can do before your abdominal muscles recover. Stick to these exercises and as much walking as is comfortable for the first six weeks. Then, after six weeks, if all is well and any scars are healed, swimming is wonderful for your mental as well as your physical health. Pilates and yoga are popular for targeting the muscles which have seen the most service.

'Get your trainers on and get pushing the pram round the park. Walk as fast as you can for at least 20–30 minutes every other day, or more if you can manage it.' freshprincess

But remember to choose low-cal destinations for your walks or you will undo all your good work:

'In the year I was breastfeeding, I gained well over two stone. In my case, it was due to going for pram walks which led to trips to the baker's for cream cakes, preferably with chocolate too; obviously, if I'd gone for a walk I "needed" to maintain my strength ... I was also told that eating lots of carbs following pregnancy could help to stave off PND – hence all those "medicinal" cheese sandwiches.' twink

If you are not blessed with lots of lovely free childcare or bags of money to buy childcare to enable you to go to the gym, consider exercise DVDs for use while baby naps. You will know in yourself whether you are the kind of person who might possibly cavort about your living room to Davina. Or conversely, the kind of person who will be overcome by existential angst after rolling painfully on to a dummy during a stomach curl or crunch or whatnot.

There are different views on sit-ups. From the spectators' gallery:

'Do you do sit-ups? That is the way back to a flatter tum (so I am told).' CountessDracula

And from a more expert perspective:

'Obviously, sit-ups will help you regain muscle and tone if that is what you are after. However, if you want to lose fat off your stomach sit-ups will do nothing to help you; the muscle will simply build up underneath the fat, pushing it out and actually making you look bigger. Cardio and a diet low in refined carbohydrates is the only way to lose weight from your stomach.' kama

'Sit-ups as well as swimming helped me. Still took me nearly four months to get my pre-pregnancy stomach back, but I am sure it helped. I did 50 every morning (when I remembered).' FairyMum

And here are some other figure-reclaiming ideas:

- Fun and practical:

  'I started belly dancing, which is great crack and you do feel it working if you practise!' *Bethron*

- Resigned:

  'My intestines are being kept in by a layer of Green & Blacks-sponsored fat.' *NoviceKnitter*

So far as diets are concerned, you don't want to crash diet while breastfeeding (or at any other time for that matter) and many Mumsnetters take the view that you should just try to eat normally during this period. Those who carry a lot of extra pounds or who are more depressed by those pounds disagree. And healthcare professionals say gradual weight loss is fine:

'Eating a healthy diet (lots of fruit/salads/ veggies/protein) is perfectly OK when breastfeeding. Cutting out high fat food is perfectly OK.' prufrock

'It is perfectly safe to try actively to lose weight at a sensible pace when breastfeeding.' mears

If you find you are gaining weight and/or your post-baby body makes you unhappy, you need to find a sensible eating plan that allows for a modest rate of weight loss. Diets which involve cutting out entire food groups are a *bad thing*.

Some organisations, like WeightWatchers, have special programmes for breastfeeding mothers. You can also do some programmes online, but actually going somewhere and being weighed or otherwise supported by other real-life persons can be a needful kick up the arse for some.

If you are not a public weigh-in sort of person, here are some Mumsnetters' sensible-eating tips:

'I just cut out all the junk – chocolate, crisps, etc. I can't be doing with cooking and preparing special diet meals and just ate normally with the family, but I switched to skimmed milk for tea/cereal, fat-free yogs and salad dressings.' Jodee

'My advice, if you don't want to go to a slimming club is:

1. Cut out all the high fat snacks (crisps, chocolate, etc.).
2. Drink loads of water (I switched from Diet Coke to water and I am sure it has helped; tap water is fine).
3. Eat three sensible meals (I have cereal or toast for breakfast, jacket potato and beans and salad for lunch, and pasta and low-fat sauce or rice and stir-fry veg for dinner).
4. Fill up your fruit bowl (take advantage of the lovely fruit in season, apples, grapes, cherries, strawberries, kiwi fruit, melon, etc.).' crunchie

'It takes the body 20 minutes to realise you're full, so the slower you eat, the less likely you are to overeat. Doing stuff like not eating in front of the TV, not eating standing up, starting with a small amount, but with the proviso that you can go back for seconds in 15 minutes if you really want it, etc., will help.' Joanne

Red Badges of Courage: Stretch Marks

The bad news is that stretch marks (those red road-map lines which snake across not only bellies, but also bottoms, breasts and thighs, before becoming silvery road-map lines) are permanent, but the better news is that a lot of mothers find they fade considerably.

"They will fade in time. Mine looked like I'd been attacked by Freddy Krueger. My legs, stomach and breasts had thick, red, deep stretch marks. Thirteen months post-birth they're silver instead of red. I found losing the weight slowly, moisturising daily and toning up has helped enormously.' ShowofHands

Return of Periods

Here's the deal:

- Your periods can come back even if you are breastfeeding.
- You might be ovulating even if you are breastfeeding and haven't had a period.

So don't be a numpty and get pregnant accidentally. You will probably get this advice at the six-week check and go off muttering, 'I can't believe my GP thinks I'm such a numpty ...' Periods may return quite quickly (within weeks) or may take months. Some lucky breastfeeding Mumsnetters report gaps of up to two years before periods return. They may take some time to settle down into whatever was your pre-birth pattern (or lack thereof):

'It is very common that the first few periods after childbirth are weird – they can be light, heavy, a mix of both and irregular too.' whomovedmychocolate

Postnatal Depression: You Are Not the Madwoman in the Attic

For many women, this is the big fear. Especially if you've had any history of depression, whether formally diagnosed and treated or not. And it is common – many estimates suggest that 10–15 per cent of women suffer from PND. Some people think it's a lot more than that, but that many women just suffer in silence.

It's not easy to predict who will get PND. Some predisposing factors are a personal or family history of depression and also difficult life circumstances: stress, social isolation, an unsupportive partner, a difficult birth or pregnancy, medical problems with the baby. Yet some women with many of these factors are fine, while other women with apparently satisfactory home circumstances who have just had desperately wanted and planned babies find themselves suffering:

'There's no reason for me to feel like this. I'm blessed with a baby who sleeps, and a husband who works from home and is a fantastic support, so I feel as though I have no excuse at all. And to all appearances, I'm coping fine: getting

dressed every day, cooking dinner, talking to people, getting out and about and so on.'
twocatsonthebed

Some women suffering from PND find it difficult to discuss the problem with their mothers or other older relatives, because for earlier generations postnatal depression was not clinically well-recognised or necessarily very sympathetically dealt with:

'When I was first diagnosed, my mother was horrified. She said things like, "No one told you it would be a walk in the park," or, "In my day we just got on with it," and, "Do you realise you will have this on your record for ever? That you have a mental illness. The stigma stays with you for ever." It was only later that she admitted that she remembered the feelings of hopelessness and that perhaps she had had PND herself.' Ghosty

Similarly, some partners may be alarmed by the thought of you having PND or indeed seeking treatment:

'Show them some Mumsnet threads where perfectly wonderful, intelligent devoted mothers have taken antidepressants and say they changed their lives and helped them get better.' wickedwaterwitch

Realising that you may be suffering from PND can take some time, particularly if no one around you is au fait with the various possible symptoms. These may include what most people think of as the classic symptoms of depression: feeling very down, sometimes particularly at certain times of day, inability to feel pleasure, insomnia, loss of appetite and libido. But PND can also cause symptoms such as extreme anxiety and panic attacks, worries about harming baby and obsessive concerns about health – extreme versions of the inevitable angst that having a new baby brings. Mumsnetters also mention 'morbid thoughts'.

What you need to know about PND

PND can start at any time after the birth, but a lot of Mumsnetters have found that they start to crash around the four- to five-month mark 'when the euphoria wears off'. It's important to know that it is not your fault; you are not a failure/weak/inadequate for feeling like this. It's worth getting help as early as you can; although PND does tend to resolve eventually by itself, why suffer so long? There is no shame in seeking professional help.

'Identifying what was wrong with me felt almost like a benediction.' adrift

Even mild or borderline cases of PND still need attention:

'I had mild PND after my first child and my doctor prescribed St John's Wort, which helped a little. I was a bit tired and stuff, but a lot of the time felt I was going through the motions – I wasn't that interested in anything. There's a school of thought that mild depression is a perfectly rational response to being a new parent if you are inadequately supported/ prepared for being one. I had never even held a baby before having my own, so it was all a huge shock to me, and I really think it contributed to my depression.' wickedwaterwitch

For some women, counselling and/or antidepressants will lead to a swifter recovery. Speak to your GP or your health visitor, if you've got a good one. As with all things medical, you may get lucky with the first doctor you see or you may have to persevere to find someone really helpful – maybe a different doctor in your existing practice. Your doctor can prescribe antidepressants which are suitable for use while breastfeeding.

Cognitive behavioural therapy can also help and is a godsend for many women, but getting an NHS referral can be a sadly slow business. In addition, there are many 'self-help' techniques worth trying. A Mumsnetter who has been there shares what she has learnt:

'Sometimes, just taking control of small things when all else around feels chaotic is a very positive thing to do. I cannot stress enough how important it is to get plenty of rest – exhaustion is a proven contributing factor to depression – and eat regularly too (even if it's just small amounts). Regular exercise has also proved very beneficial. This can be formal (i.e. a gym or class) or informal (walking briskly with pram or going swimming), but try and fit something in each week – the endorphins released will help you feel better. Try and have time for yourself, and some relaxation – even ten minutes focusing on your breathing can be useful. Or a hot bath. Talking to other people helps. Find out if there are any support groups near you or come on Mumsnet and let rip. Finally, take baby steps. Be kind to yourself, lower your standards a little. Don't worry about tomorrow, just getting through the next hour and the hour after that. You *will* get better.' Filthymindedvixen

'Friends, HELP, SUPPORT (even if you think you don't need it!), exercise, good food, no alcohol, plenty of water, vitamins – this is what I do, and it usually gets me through.' Enid

'Anyone who tells you to "just pull yourself together" or "snap out of it" is an ignorant arse. No one would choose to feel what you are feeling. People's ignorance of PND can be summed up when they say, "But he's such a good baby!" Yes, I know but I still want to hang myself.' colditz

Finding other mothers you can speak to honestly about how you are feeling, rather than comparing notes on poo colours really can help. Even if you have to find them on the internet.

If you feel dispirited about your physical self, try a little grooming – even if that is just a hot shower, clean clothes you feel reasonably yourself in and maybe a decent haircut.

For some women, eventually working their way through the life changes that having a baby has caused or been the catalyst for will assist recovery. For others, starting to retrieve some features of their old life helps:

'I recall that my daughter was about four months when I started to lose the plot a bit – was too introverted, spending too much time alone, too much time worrying about things that don't matter, etc. I couldn't do the meeting-other-mothers thing – am in London and there are lots of others about, but I never had anything in common with them, other than having had babies, and it made those meetings rather awkward. And I am the first of my friends to have a baby. Also it was November and getting dark and miserable; I felt trapped too. When that happened, I got my daughter started at nursery one day a week to give me some time to myself (my husband works away and otherwise I would never have left the house alone) and arranged to go back to work (from a few months later, but at least my return date was agreed). It may not be the cure for you, but it was really helpful for me to know that I was going to have some outside interests again from a set date.' Plibble

> Women with PND often worry about harming their babies, although they almost never actually do. Most new mothers probably worry about harming their babies at some time; it is no doubt an evolutionary trick to make you take extra care when near steep places and open fires. And make you finally put the baby down and have a cup of tea when you are near breaking point.
> It gets better, gradually:

'The healing process was this: I began to get a few good days in between the bad days. Then I had more good days than bad days. Then I would maybe get a bad day a week. Eventually, but I didn't notice until I was off antidepressants completely, I realised that I hadn't had a bad day for a month or so ... and then by the time my son was two, I had not had a bad day for three months.' Ghosty

Many women do not get PND again with subsequent babies. 'I know how to reduce the risk and deal with it,' says one mother who avoided PND with subsequent babies.

'A mixture of antidepressants if you need them, therapy and just knowing you won't be dropped like a hot potato whenever you are discharged from hospital really can help.' Toothache

Birth Trauma/Post-traumatic Stress Disorder

Some women suffer from post-traumatic stress disorder caused by birth trauma. This may be associated with PND or it may not. And it can happen after a birth which is not, in the view of the medical folk who are around, very difficult or medically concerning.

'There is no degree of birth trauma. It is not predicated on how many hours you laboured, whether you tore, had an episiotomy, forceps or whatever. I know a couple of women who have been really traumatised by incredibly quick births, the sort that are 30 minutes long or quicker, and they get the response of, "At least you didn't have to be in pain for hours", or, "At least you didn't have to hang around the hospital for ages". But a quick birth can be really traumatic, as you have not got the time to get into the mindset and "other place" of labour.' Lulumama

Women with PTSD connected with childbirth experience some or all of the following:

- feelings of intense fear, horror and helplessness when thinking about the birth
- panic attacks
- flashbacks, intrusive thoughts about the birth, nightmares
- avoidance of things connected with the birth
- sometimes an obsessive need to discuss the birth
- problems with mood, sleep, concentration

It is important that PTSD is not misdiagnosed as PND because treatment for the two conditions is not the same and some antidepressants can make PTSD worse. Postnatal PTSD is not yet well researched or widely understood. Once again, you or someone on your behalf may have to push for you to get appropriate treatment.

'It's normal to feel anxious about birth and labour, it's normal for it to be painful, but not everyone ends up traumatised. In fact, some women go through far worse than I went through and are able to process their experiences and get on with their lives. Others, for whatever reason, can't let it go so easily, and I think that includes me. There are plenty of things that happened in my past that sensitised me to feeling particularly vulnerable while in labour, so the things that happened during my labour affected me on many, many different levels. Trauma is about not being able to integrate memories of an event coherently and weave them into the memory web that makes up your own personal history. I guess right now I don't fully understand why my labour was so utterly bleak, frightening and lonely, and I am working hard to understand it.' coveredinsnot

The Birth Trauma Association website has a great deal of useful information and links to other websites that offer information and support (see Resources, p. 436 for details).

Postnatal Psychosis

This is pretty rare fortunately, affecting about one in 500 women. It can come on very suddenly and is characterised by symptoms which include some of the following: delusions and hallucinations, rapid mood swings, bizarre beliefs, manic symptoms, restlessness, excitability, inability to sleep, confusion and disorientation. It is treatable, sometimes by way of hospitalisation, but it is vital that treatment is sought.

Postnatal psychosis – one very brave Mumsnetter's story

'I was convinced something serious was wrong with me. I thought that the afterbirth was still inside me. It culminated with me yelling at the nursing staff and ringing my husband at 2 a.m. to come and get me. I was breastfeeding, but my son seemed to be fitting after each feed and no one would listen to me. Coupled with this, I hadn't slept in five days and was beginning to get delirious through lack of sleep. I ended up in hospital again two days later as I still thought there was afterbirth left inside. I had passed a huge clot and was shaking all over; I had begun to avoid food and was trying to sleep all the time and still feed my son.

Mum was concerned. My husband was concerned. Everyone told me I could pass the debris left inside me naturally. I wasn't so sure and thought I was dying. I had also begun to think that God was punishing me and that my husband was in league with the Devil. Not natural, happy birth thoughts. They sent me home with a sedative. A day later and I was trying to "exorcise" my husband. He had to forcibly carry me inside and call the GP who immediately diagnosed me as schizophrenic and sent me to a psychiatric hospital for assessment. I had begun to think I was possessed as well.

I was diagnosed as having puerperal psychosis. I could barely function. I was a mess. I was sedated for two days in the hospital, and at one point thought the radiator was giving me messages! I was allowed home visits from the second week. In total, I was in hospital for four weeks until my section was lifted. When I came home, I was like a child. Mum moved in for two months and I had to start to learn to function again. I was on high doses of medication to keep my thoughts and sleeping in check. A mental-health nurse came and saw me every week.

Things got better though. Slowly, I became myself again. I continued my degree. Things with my husband improved as well. I no longer thought he was against me and we became closer than ever. My medication was reduced. The mental-health nurse was fantastic – she had another two puerperal psychosis cases on her books, which is highly unusual considering the statistics.

I have now landed my dream job and my medication has finished. I truly feel myself again. I have put on four stone due to the medication, but at least I'm alive and eating. I've started going to the gym to get back to being a size 12. My son is happy and thriving and developing normally. My husband is relieved to have me back and functioning normally (I can clean the house again without freaking out). I just wanted people to know about it. It's rarely talked about and there is still such a stigma attached to mental illness.' *tinytoessizefour*

And Finally ... Anti Tips for the Broody

Astonishingly, you may find yourself, despite the exhaustion, physical discomfort and relationship turmoil, already longing for another baby. Broodiness can hit you in the delivery room, while you are holding your new baby (internal monologue: 'This is so great. I should do this again!'); it can strike anywhere and at any time. For some women, giving birth is a kind of emotional crack cocaine. So try some of these simple practical manoeuvres for outwitting broodiness:

- 'Invest in an entire wardrobe of clothes three sizes too small for you.' *hoxtonchick*
- 'Get a horse to kick you in the fanny. Start reading a fascinating book. Then stop and leave it for four years.' *wickedwaterwitch*
- 'Ask everyone you meet if they could give you some unsolicited advice designed to make you feel like a bad person and a complete failure. Write to national newspapers, magazines and broadcasters with the same request.' *eddm*
- 'Spend not less than twelve months practising the parental version of tantric sex as follows: lie in bed (for full effect, sheets should need changing so badly that you have to cling on with your toes to stop yourself sliding out); ensure that you are both wearing greyed, baggy, mismatched pyjamas, liberally sprayed with bodily effluent; hold hands; say in unison, "F*ck, I'm tired" ZZZZ.' *Issymum*
- 'Go to your favourite clothes/interiors shop, accompanied by a restless baboon and a wheelbarrow. See how the assistants rush to greet you! Now try to get into the changing room with the baboon and the wheelbarrow and carefully select a flattering and elegant outfit without having to rush out and recapture the baboon in your bra and knickers.' *aloha*
- '<sneaks in, sabotages thread> Ah, but just think of their little floppy soft heads. That lovely clean baby smell; the little meepy noises. Their little milky trusting faces. Little snuggly bodies ... <sneaks off, amid shower of well-filled nappy sacks>' *frogs*

Chapter Four

The Sleep of the Damned

In this chapter ...

It's a funny thing. A peculiar thing. People chortle happily at new parents about how little sleep they must be getting. The same bit of small talk is hardwired into everyone's brain and triggered by the sight of a red-eyed parent and a new baby. 'Getting much sleep?' asks your neighbour/colleague/the postal delivery officer, chuckling mildly. These are people who, in most cases, would not make low-key sympathetic noises if they noticed your leg had just fallen off. And they would probably be most surprised if you shouted in response to their enquiry: 'Well NO, actually, I am not getting any sleep; I think I may be hallucinating and I feel quite insane.'

Ah, well.

So in this chapter, we are not going to pretend that there is anything very funny about the sleep thing. We are just going to look in a serious and cold-eyed fashion at the different ways Mumsnetters have struggled through the various sleep issues that have afflicted their infants, pausing to reflect soberly and judiciously on what general lessons might be drawn from these experiences for the novice parent. We will consider some general facts and figures about sleep, which should give the struggling parent some cause for mild optimism. We will have a look at some of the sleep experts, who promise to solve all children's sleep problems, consider whether their prescriptions work for all parents and all infants and whether they might possibly work for you. We will scrutinise carefully anything that purports to be science and reject anything purporting to be expertise which is actually nonsense. We will try very hard to remember that everyone gets to sleep in the end. They really do. And we may laugh just a little, morosely, along the way.

'I know a very annoying woman who says both her sons slept through from birth. She does exhibit signs of madness though ...' GhostofNatt

'She is either lying or delusional or she drugged them.' motherinferior

In the Beginning: the How and the Why of Baby Sleep

There's a bit in Genesis when God is creating the world where one almost feels a bit sorry for Him. There He is, grappling with the onerous task of creating light, then dividing it from darkness, working out the whole night-and-day thing (not to mention all that land, sea, firmament stuff). Well, being a parent of a newborn is a bit like this on a smaller scale.

You are in charge of a very small chaotic being, who has no idea about night and day. And instead of being able to sort it all out in under a week, like the Almighty, you have to very gradually coax your small piece of chaos towards a more adult sleeping pattern (or, depending on your parenting philosophy, just wait – possibly for quite a long time).

Babies are different from us. They sleep a lot more than we do, but they do it in much smaller chunks. They have shorter sleep cycles, so they pass more frequently from light sleep to dream or REM sleep, to deep sleep and back again. The whole cycle takes about an hour in a young baby. They need to wake up a lot because, quite frankly, they need to eat frequently. And when we lived in caves, they also needed to remain alert in case something dangerous happened, like a woolly mammoth or a blocked nose.

Babies who wake during the light sleep phase do not have an adult's ability to resettle themselves and may need soothing back to sleep. Overall, babies have about twice as much 'light sleep' as adults, so they have longer periods when they are vulnerable to waking.

For the first few weeks, unless you are going with one of the more regimented parenting routines (and succeeding), you will just have to go with it. By about six to eight weeks, there is usually some improvement in a baby's ability to differentiate between night and day but he will still be having small, frequent naps. Some babies get a bit mixed up and start having a longer sleep in the daytime rather than at night. Generally though, things continue to settle as he approaches the three-month mark, and some time between three and six months he may be getting a good tranche of sleep at night with some discreet daytime naps.

These are not universal truths, however, as some of the more desperate posts on the Mumsnet 'sleep' talkboard attest.

Try to bear in mind that all babies are different. Some are just lousy sleepers for a long time. All you can do is try to play the hand you are dealt with as much grace and fortitude as you can muster. There are also more or less predictable wobbles along the path to a more adult sleeping pattern: developmental surges, growth spurts, teething and illness are all sleep disruptors in the first 12 months:

'Four months is an absolutely classic sleep regression time – combination of developmental changes and growth spurts and teething leads to crappy sleep.' IAteRosemaryConleyForBreakfast

'Five months is an awful time for many babies (my son was a nightmare at this age as well). It is so wearing, isn't it? I just dreaded night time, as I knew I would be battling all night, and even if he did have a better night, I would be awake worrying about whether he would wake up … It *is* a phase though, and it will get better. I honestly don't think there's a lot you can do at this stage to change anything, so go for whatever works for you.' EffiePerrine

Sleep requirements at different ages

There are no absolute rules here. These are averages. No doubt there are some Margaret Thatcher-style infants who only need the baby equivalent of four hours per night.

Birth to three months: baby sleeps approximately 14–18 hours out of 24

(continued)

Three to six months: 14–16 hours

Six to 12 months: 12–14 hours

After a year, sleep tends to settle around the 12-hour mark during the pre-school years.

Generally speaking, as time goes on, a greater proportion of this snoozing should be going on at night, but be a little wary of tables of figures which give you an exact split.

Imposing a Little Order: Settling a Newborn

You can help even very small babies to settle into sleep or sleep a little longer. Here are some Mumsnetters' favourite methods.

Temperature control

Make sure her environment is not too hot or too cold, bearing in mind what clothing or other coverings she has on. Roughly speaking, they need to be wearing one more layer than you, but no hats indoors.

The art of noise

'One thing I have to say we have found absolutely *invaluable* is white noise – following a tip on Mumsnet, we noticed one day when my son (15 weeks) was grumpy and I was drying my hair, that he just chilled out and went to sleep with the sound of the hairdryer! Since then my husband (gadget freak) has recorded the noise of the hairdryer on to a CD for me and it really helps him to drift off.' pumpkin2

Other parents find actual or recorded Hoover sounds useful for luring the sandman. There are also commercially available white-noise CDs to try.

Laying on hands

A little gentle stroking or patting may well encourage a baby to make the transition into sleep or send a rousing infant back into slumber. Or try this surprising old trick:

'Gently stroke your baby's nose in little downwards movements. This encourages them to close their eyes and fall asleep.' Sexgoddess

Taking time

'An important thing to realise is that it can take 20 to 30 minutes to settle a newborn to sleep. It's normal. Try settling him in the place you want him to sleep. I used to lay my son down and just stroke him, slowly, steadily, for as long as it took. When he seemed asleep, I would make the stroking lighter and slower until I wasn't touching him at all. My daughter seemed to like me humming or buzzing while I settled her. Try also always doing the same things before settling him to sleep – maybe a little song, rocking, swaddling him or wrapping him in a blanket or muslin, so that eventually he has cues to remind him that he will soon fall asleep.' PrettyCandles

Hands off

There appears to be a subset of babies (often very alert, attentive babies) who find any stimulation interferes with them getting to sleep. This type of baby will not settle by being held on a lap or in a sling, being gently stroked or patted to sleep, and may just need to fuss a bit in a cot or Moses basket or other place of repose in order to doze off. You need to learn the difference between a cry of distress and a little pre-sleep grizzling and fussing. Remember:

'A good rule of thumb is that a newborn can't stay awake more than two hours at a time. So if yours has been wide awake for two hours, retreat to a quiet room with little stimulation and see if you can get them to sleep.' Amber1

Make a cosy sleeping environment

'Our baby wouldn't sleep in her Moses basket until our midwife suggested rolling a towel (bath towel) up into a long snake shape and laying it in the Moses basket in an upside down U shape. Baby then sleeps inside the U shape and should feel more secure. It worked like a dream for us.' Nooney

'My two slept on lambskins for years and they're so easy to take everywhere – I just put it on the floor and they'd settle straight away.' Alibubbles

'Babies don't seem to like cold sheets. Use a hot-water bottle to gently warm the bottom sheet of your Moses basket for a minute or two before putting your newborn down to sleep.' KJ

Or try placing a blanket over a baby who is falling asleep in lap or sling and transferring him with his body-warmed blanket to Moses basket or cot.

Swaddling a thrashy baby can work well for some babies who literally wake themselves up by accidentally giving themselves a good clout, and even those without jittery arms may welcome being cosily restrained.

'Swaddling saved my sanity. My daughter was far more settled when we wrapped her – you just have to be careful to make sure that they don't overheat. We used a cotton cellular blanket, but when it was really hot, we used a sheet.' Sass

Babies grow out of swaddling at different ages, but you'll know when he's ready to stop because he will wriggle free.

Never cover baby's head during sleep, don't overdress him and remember the advice from the Foundation for the Study of Infant Deaths (FSID) that swaddling is instead of, rather than in addition to, a blanket.

'I fully swaddled my baby until she began to struggle and get her arms out at around ten weeks. Then I swaddled her under her arms until about six months. Then she went into a baby sleeping bag.' Ghosty

(Visit www.babycentre.co.uk for a step-by-step photo guide on how to swaddle.)

Not in my lap

There is a whole panoply of solutions for encouraging babies who only want to sleep in your lap during the day to sleep somewhere else, many of which depend on finding a motion that your baby finds congenial. This might be a bouncy or rocking chair, a swing or a buggy (although if you find yourself pushing it round your kitchen, while making realistic traffic noises to persuade him he's actually out on a walk, you might reconsider the lap option). Some parents swear by swinging hammock-style baby beds. Or there is that old fallback the sling (discussed more fully on p. 10 and a central feature of 'attachment parenting' methods considered on pp. 43 and 186). Providing a muslin or T-shirt that smells a bit milky and Mummyish can also help some babies to feel at home in a non-Mummy environment.

Cuddle/feed/whatever she needs

'The fact remains that there is nothing at all wrong with feeding or cuddling a tiny baby to sleep. They change so much and so quickly – they will be different people in a couple of weeks. Lie down with them, sleep when they sleep. It's only a tiny phase, even though it feels as if it's going on for ever. People put a lot of stress on themselves by trying to impose routines on what are basically random little animals. They settle into their own routine once they realise that they aren't still part of you.' seeker

'Make the most of it. I remember how frustrating it is when you spend all day with a baby snuggled on your chest, but the newborn bit flies by, and it will be over all too soon. I miss those lovely snuggly times.' Olihan

(This is, of course, easy to say when it is all over.)

'Is It Bedtime Yet?'

In those fuzzy, early weeks, the closest you get to the clean-fluffy-haired-sweet-scented-cosy-sleepsuit-clad-infant-being-sung-to-sleep-in-white-broderie-anglaise-nursery-splendour Disney ideal may be the propped-on-sofa-with-perpetually-suckling-infant-watching-crap-TV-on-obscure-digital-channels-surrounded-by-greasy-takeaway-boxes-at-midnight cinéma vérité alternative. But fear not. The sweet-scented infant can be yours eventually, as can the evening in which you do Other Things – things you cannot do with a baby about your person.

Opinions vary as to when you might first start working towards a Proper Bedtime. Some think you can get going pretty much from the off, but most Mumsnetters think six weeks is as early as you can realistically get started, while others would wait until nearer the 12-week mark. Even proponents of the gentlest approaches to sleep issues suggest that a structured bedtime is ultimately a desirable goal. And remember, the things you may well be doing anyway to help settle your baby to sleep are part of what will eventually, hopefully, be a fully-fledged bedtime routine.

> **'I'm a chronic Type A and have to have a plan. Even if it doesn't work every day. From about four weeks, I start writing down what I think baby should be doing, based on what they have been doing the last four weeks. If it doesn't happen, it doesn't happen. By three months they often have a good, consistent routine.'** nannynz

The actual details of the routine may be unimportant – what seems to work is doing at least roughly the same things in at least roughly the same order every night. In the jargon, this is 'creating sleep associations'. Babies are, in the main, conservative souls and feel secure if things happen in a predictable way.

Generally speaking, the component parts of your bedtime should be soothing, so if he is unbearably excited by Pingu DVDs, these have no place in your bedtime routine. Some babies flake completely after a little massage; others are stimulated to wiggling, gurning super-awakeness.

If you have been tripping the light fantastic and/or slumped with baby in front of a DVD until all hours during the early weeks, you may need to move 'bedtime' gradually back towards your target, probably no earlier than, say, 6.30 or later than, say, 8.30, if you are aiming for a vaguely normal eventual morning waking time.

Mumsnetiquette: And so to bed

'With both of mine I had a "routine", as such, within about a week or so. I always did bath, last feed and then bed. It doesn't need to be at exactly the same time every night, just within an hour or so. I then did everything at night time different to daytime, hushed tones, low lighting, little eye contact, etc. But this wasn't to get them to sleep through. Babies do that when they're ready. It just created a difference in their heads. They knew daytime was when it was busy and loud and bright and happy and night time was when everyone was sleepy and boring and quiet.'
TinyTimLivesinVictorianSqualour

'Try to do the bedtime routine very, very slowly, so he doesn't get frazzled, feel rushed or overexcited. Allow twice as long as you think it might take to bath, dress and feed him. You could even try reading him a story in a soothing, monotone voice. Investing in a CD of light classical music can help settle fractious babies – you can leave it on constant repeat. You might also want to try burning a lavender candle somewhere the aroma can waft through the house around bedtime. Don't leave it unattended in his room though.' *bookwormmum*

And once you have got your baby to doze off for what you are trying to persuade her is night time, remember to minimise excitement during night wakings:

'Feeding during the "long" sleep must be as stimulus-free as possible – no talking/singing. No need to change little one either, unless the nappy is particularly full/smelly!' *StarlightMcKenzie*

Where to Sleep

There are a surprising number of options here. Cot, Moses basket or your bed are nocturnal possibilities. Bouncy chair, lap, beanbag, sling and pram are all likely to be pressed into service for daytime napping. Moses baskets and carrycots have a limited lifespan and are annoying to some thrashy, mobile babies in particular, but score highly with those infants who like a cosy womb-like environment and can't bear the vast open spaces of a full-sized cot or cot bed. Travel cots are not recommended for more than occasional use, because the mattresses are not very well padded and can, therefore, increase the plagiocephaly (flat head) risk; many also carry warnings that they do not soak up fluid or vomit so can be a choking hazard. However, some Mumsnetters suggest that if you are looking for a compromise between a Moses basket and a full-sized cot, you can kit out a travel cot with a proper mattress.

If you are going for a traditional cot, remember that you will need a firm, clean mattress. The advice from the Foundation for the Study of Infant Deaths is still that this ideally should be a new mattress for each new baby. Mothers of more than one baby tend to take a pragmatic view as to whether a mattress with one careful owner of known habits is acceptable for a new tenant:

'I think if my first had been a very sicky baby and the mattress was heavily puked on, I might have considered buying a new one.' Bugsy2

Duvets and quilts are not recommended for small babies. There are basically two safe ways to go with bedding:

The first is to layer sheets and thin blankets (how many depends on the room temperature, which should ideally be between 16 and 20°C) and tuck them tightly around baby. She should be sleeping on her back in the 'feet-to-foot' position at the bottom end of her cot, so that there is no expanse of blanket for her to wiggle under. If she is sweating or her tummy feels hot, remove some layers.

Cot bumpers are the work of the Devil. Little babies can get tangled up in them and big babies can use them to vault out of the cot. And they attract dust.

The second option is to use a baby sleeping bag with the appropriate tog rating (although not until she has reached the manufacturer's recommended size for the smallest one). There are summer and winter varieties, and some manufacturers also produce travel bags, so you can transfer a sleeping baby seamlessly from car seat or pushchair to bed. Make sure her sleeping bag fits properly, so that her head cannot slip down and get covered by the bag.

'With the Grobag make of sleeping bag, you get a room thermometer which tells you which Grobag to use, and how many layers to put underneath it.' Xena

Note: remember the cot death prevention advice that baby should not wear anything covering her head at night and should not sleep near a radiator or fire.

Voulez-vous Coucher Avec Moi? – Co-sleeping

Co-sleeping is yet another issue which divides some parenting gurus and parents into sometimes surprisingly crabby camps.

The advocates of co-sleeping (in particular, Dr William Sears and Deborah Jackson of *Three in a Bed* fame) point to the fact that co-sleeping has been the norm for most babies in most cultures throughout history. They say that co-sleeping improves bonding between parents and infant, can reduce or eliminate sleep problems and makes night-time feeds as easy as snuggling a snoozy baby closer to an adjacent breast.

Other parenting experts point to our different cultural context, which encourages independence and personal privacy, and the fact that at least some parents and babies don't seem to get much sleep in the family bed. Some experts think that babies need to learn to sleep independently and get into bad habits as a result of co-sleeping. Other experts and parents want to dance on the bones of people who think that small babies are capable of having bad habits.

Mumsnetters on co-sleeping

The many, many co-sleeping stories on the Mumsnet talkboards suggest that:

a) co-sleeping works brilliantly for some people, fits in with their overall parenting philosophy and generally makes them happy
b) co-sleeping does not work at all for some parents and some babies and instead renders them grumpy and mad, causing them wisely to abandon the attempt
c) co-sleeping can be a useful interim or occasional solution for some families – either when a baby is tiny and breastfeeding is being established or when, at a later stage, she is unsettled.

Sleeping beauties and waking nightmares – Mumsnetters' co-sleeping experiences

There are the beautiful dreamers:

'I love it when I wake up and have a "sleeping beauty" on both sides of me – those little faces all relaxed and gorgeous, without doubt the nicest thing you can see early in the morning.' *GreenMonkies*

'I co-slept with my son. It was magic. My daughter? No way. She wants her own space, always has.' *Piffleoffagus*

'I am more disturbed by hubby snoring than wee babby night-time bleats.' *butwhatdoiknow*

'It seems like so many people see co-sleeping as a negative thing. Before having my son I probably would have said the same thing. I didn't let my son into my bed in the first place, but learnt after a while that that was the best thing for all of us. It still is the best thing for us, but that's not to say it is easy. But living with a

(continued)

demanding toddler isn't always easy. Sometimes I wish my son would sleep all night in his own bed. Sometimes I wish he could eat his dinner without getting food everywhere. I could probably make him do the things I want him to do, but at what cost? It's missing the point, in my opinion. If your baby sleeps through with a little gentle encouragement, great, but some *do* need comfort at night, and there is nothing wrong with that; you haven't done anything wrong.' *tatties*

'We are in Japan and almost everyone co-sleeps here – usually until the kids start school (aged six). It is easier because most people (including us) sleep on futons on the floor, so there is no danger of falling out of bed and, because futons tend to be firmer than beds/mattresses, not much danger of suffocation. Everyone tends to have their own futon too, all lined up in the room.' *sakurarose39*

And there are the parents who are sleeping with the enemy:

'My kids sleep *horizontally*, leaving me miserably clinging to the edge of our king-size bed. They chase me round the bed, kicking me rhythmically.' *misdemeanour*

'I read Dr Sears' book and I loved the idea of a family bed. But for me, co-sleeping was not a good experience. When she was in bed with me, my daughter wished to suck all the time. Not really feeding, just sucking. It was quite uncomfortable, but if I gently detached her she would scream. I could not sleep well at all with her constantly sucking. She also squirmed a lot and woke much more with us than she ever did in her own cot.' *artichokes*

'My sister read the Deborah Jackson book when she was pregnant. She was *enchanted*, being a full-on lentil weaver. Fast forward about 12 months and she rang me in tears saying, 'I could kill that **** who wrote "Three in a Bed".' *moondog*

'I've got nothing against Sears, except I do personally think he's a bit obsessive and dogmatic about bed-sharing, etc. Believe me,

I would have done anything to get my son to sleep, including sleeping with him every night, but it didn't work for us. It's not magic.' *aloha*

'I don't think one method of sleeping is any better than the other – it's what suits you and your child more than anything – and I *really* don't believe that I am going to have a better relationship with my first daughter and my son and not my second daughter, simply because I co-slept with them for a few months and not her! Relationships are FAR more complex than that.' *Slinky*

'Can't stand wriggling kids in bed.' *codswallop*

'I wouldn't co-sleep because I like spontaneous sex – and love my own space. But if it floats your boat, well, good for you, is what I say.' *custardo*

It'll be all right in the night: one Mumsnetter's co-sleeping story

'I do not like being vomited on in the night. Or weed on (under). Or sleeping next to a smelly, milk-sodden pillow that then has to be thrown away. Or kicked by a horizontal child. Or falling off the side because my two lovely children are sprawled across the whole bed ... but on the other hand ... I have had much better sleep with them in the bed. I have not often had to get up to deal with stuff at night. I know where they are, and if they are safe, happy, healthy. Lastly, and I feel most importantly, it is good for us as a family. My children have disadvantageous circumstances, being with a depressed, single mother. I am often occupied in the day and unable to direct too much attention towards them, as I am doing the stuff nobody else will – like decorating, gardening, housework, shopping, etc.

And I've found that despite the emotional insecurity this scenario was potentially engendering, things were Not That Bad,

(continued)

simply because at the end of the day, Mummy was still very much a physical presence. I was there in the night, even if I'd hardly played all day. It was the one time they "got" me. I really believe that this made the difference between rather wild, scruffy, slightly cross little boys and children who were pretty disturbed and very unhappy. Just in our case, of course.' *Flightattendant*

How safe is co-sleeping?

The jury remains out as to the relative safety of the cot versus the family bed. It is very rare indeed for a baby to be accidentally suffocated as a result of co-sleeping. The horror stories you do hear tend to be about sofas or to involve alcohol or drug consumption.

None the less, the Foundation for the Study of Infant Deaths advises that the safest place for a baby is in his own cot in the parental bedroom. FSID particularly advises against co-sleeping in the cases of low-birthweight or premature babies or where one parent smokes or has been consuming alcohol or sedative drugs. However, some studies point to the fact that co-sleeping infants breastfeed better, and that breastfeeding itself cuts a baby's cot-death risk.

So it seems there is no clear-cut, right answer to the safety question. You need to have a look at the tips for safe co-sleeping below and decide whether it is likely to work for you. If you are going to lie awake all night worrying about squashing your baby, don't go for a family bed.

The boisterous bed: safe co-sleeping

There are two considerations here: the people in the bed and the bed itself.

The people
One big issue is whether your partner is a safe co-sleeping companion for a baby. If he is not, are you both happy for him to be evicted to a spare room/sofa/floor? You do not want him sharing

a bed with baby if he is a very heavy sleeper, if he smokes or if he likes to have a few tinnies/joints/sedative drugs of any kind before bed. Or you may feel he is just too fine a figure of a man:

'My husband is a fat bastard and would squash the kid.' *custardo*

Smoking daddies in particular will have to be banished to a tent in the back garden or perhaps a converted shed. However, if the problem is just one of husbandly deep sleeping or adiposity, you can adopt the baby-on-the-outside configuration; in fact, it is generally safest for baby not to sleep between her parents, in any case. Plus, fathers tend to be less well attuned to baby's presence in the bed, and it is harder to manage a safe arrangement of duvets and blankets if baby is the ham in the sandwich.

'We got a bedrail and it revolutionised our co-sleeping because my husband was no longer banished to the spare room. He didn't like sleeping next to our daughter and this was the answer for us. She slept on the outside then me, then him. Perfecto.' *gingerninja*

Another way to achieve the same result is to push the bed securely against the wall and have baby sleep on the wall side.

A bigger, rollier baby may roam about the bed and threaten to fall out the other side or end, in which case:

'You can put the mattress on the floor for a while. Or surround the bed with pillow/duvets so that she at least has a soft landing if she does fall out.' *policywonk*

Obviously, if you yourself are a smoking, boozing, deep-sleeping crack fiend, your baby should sleep in his own cot. Probably in someone else's house.

The bed
The bed and bedding themselves need to be suitable. First of all, size does matter. Some Mumsnetters with several co-sleepers (and in some cases multiple cats) have created their own family beds:

(continued)

'We have a super-king with a double joined on. As I am fond of boasting, that is ten and a half foot of bed. We found super-king size quite adequate until our son started really moving around, then we all ended up crammed into the same two foot with his head in my armpit.' *FrannytheGazelle*

'Not sure exactly how big our bed is, but my husband and my brother built it together and it's really big. It's especially built for co-sleeping.' *FairyMum*

A specially designed bedside cot which opens into the parents' bed may be the perfect compromise for some:

'The bedside cot has been really great for us. I've definitely slept more, it's given the baby his own space to wriggle without waking up, but we haven't lost the closeness of the family bed, which we all love so much. I can still feed him easy peasy at night, but I can also turn round and cuddle my husband occasionally.' *fluffsuptheduff*

The mattress itself should be firm and clean (banish that Austin Powers-style waterbed now). Baby should not be under a duvet with you because the likelihood is it will be too hot for him and he may wiggle too far down so his head is covered. And he certainly should not be in his own baby sleeping bag and under your covers as well.

Most parents work out an arrangement whereby baby has his own coverings and the parental duvet is kept well away. You may want to chuck all of the pillows out for a while as well, rather than fret about their whereabouts. If baby is still sleeping with you when he is a bouncy toddler, you can get a lot less precious about the exact disposition of the bedding.

'I sleep in a sleeping bag and she goes outside it, so there's no chance of her slipping under the covers.' *Rhiann*

'One thing I was worried about when I started co-sleeping was smothering him with a big fluffy, billowing duvet. So I changed to using a simple woollen blanket (in a duvet cover) with which he was unlikely to get covered by mistake.' *mumoflukas*

For daytime naps, some young co-sleepers are fed to sleep on the big bed; others may remain in their slings or prams or accept a snooze in pram, bouncy chair or carrycot. Many co-sleepers object to the removal of the warm, milky, sleep-inducing presence of Mummy. In which case, try this:

'Have a big pillow on the other side while you're feeding him. Then, when you move, quickly put the pillow beside him. It will be warm because you've been leaning on it and it will smell of you.' *thisisyesterday*

But *don't* leave him alone with the big pillow – he could wiggle under it.

Time to move on?

Do bear in mind that co-sleeping can be a long-term commitment. Some parents, having slumped into co-sleeping, find there comes a stage when they are desperate to move their sleep-boxing toddler to his own room. Young Cassius may have other ideas, of course, and moving him slowly and gently to his own bed or bedroom can be hard work. Co-sleeping babies often seem to be fed or comforted to sleep rather than being self-settling. Some parents are very happy with baby-filled beds and bedtimes and some mothers who go out to work full-time like the night-time closeness. Others find it difficult to get up and run a home/classroom/business/government after a night of wurgling.

'At about one year old, we moved our daughter on to an adult-sized mattress on the floor, pushed right up against my side of the bed. She was about 10cm (4in) lower than me and was an early walker, so she was able to wake up and climb into our bed between us when she needed to. We got her own room ready a couple of months later and put all her toys in and another mattress on the floor and that was her play room. At about 18 months, we started putting her to bed in her own room. We leave both bedroom doors open at night and she just wanders in if she needs to in the night. Sometimes she sleeps the whole night in her bed, other times she comes in in the middle of the night, other times she comes in at six or seven and will then sleep an extra hour or two.'

UpSinceCrapO'Clock

Dawn of the dad: co-sleeping and, er, sexual relations

The topic of how to get down to it when the bed is crammed with children inevitably comes up in Mumsnet threads on co-sleeping. Although, in theory, a very small baby won't notice what you are up to, many folk find it hard to get in the mood with another person squeaking, snorting and flapping about the love nest.

Picture the romantic postnatal scene: you've lit the smelly candles, propped your floppy bits up in some inventive lingerie, put the Barry White on low and are moving in for some sexual healing. Then, 'WAAAAAH!' Your own personal seal pup of love makes violent objection and interrupts the incipient coitus. The same deflating outcome can be achieved with the infant in his own cot, so it's not necessarily co-sleeping which has wrecked your love life – it's the fact you have reproduced.

Frolicsome Mumsnetters suggest that, in any event, there are many locations in which such activity can take place in an imaginative relationship or, indeed, other times of day when you might get it on. Others indulge in a little hollow laughter.

Mumsnetiquette: Co-sleeping and sex (warning: this may be too much information)

'Can I ask a rude question? How do co-sleepers, you know, have ummm "relations"?' *jollymum*

'Jollymum, on top of the fridge.' *FairyMum*

'Come now, jollymum, all it takes is a bit of imagination, a kettle and a teabag. And some water, of course. Milk would be a bonus, as would cups. That is what you meant by relations, yes?' *FillyjonktheSnibbet*

Do keep the sex issue under review; it may not be a big deal for the first three/six/45,000 months postnatally, when you really don't feel like it anyway. But if long-term co-sleeping is seriously interfering with the parental nocturnal relations, you may need to rethink.

Just When You Thought It Was Safe to Go Back to Bed: Changing Sleep Patterns

Throughout the first couple of years of your baby's life, his sleeping patterns will evolve and occasionally may just become, frankly, bizarre. Generally speaking, your baby will be awake more and more in the day and begin to have longer sleeps at night, consolidated eventually – hopefully – into one long sleep which gradually extends until it becomes something we would all recognise as 'sleeping through'. The timescales do vary enormously between babies and (look away now if you are of a sensitive disposition) there are plenty of Mumsnetters with babies who do not sleep through until well into their second year, sometimes beyond.

If, after the six-month mark, you are still unbearably sleep-deprived, you may begin to flirt with the sleep-training approaches discussed below. In the meantime, however, here are some Mumsnetters' tips for settling a bigger baby (lots of these are very similar to those for teaching babies about bedtime, but you may find that some ideas which didn't work earlier may start to work now). Remember, as ever, that you need to experiment to find the ones that suit you and your baby.

- 'I found singing the same songs and building an association really helped in the long term. We still use the same songs now he is two and a half.' *liger*
- Rotating lights which play music and project images on to the ceiling or wall are soothing to some babies. Other babies sleep best (and stay asleep longer) in darkness. Consider putting up blackout blinds.
- Some kind of soothing or comforting touch is still a useful prelude to sleep for many babies:

  'I start off patting their back or bum, then reduce speed and pressure (when rocking to sleep). You could reduce this to just the pressure of your hand on him, so he knows you're near.' *WanderingHolly*

- Take the swaddling off (what one mother of a wriggly baby calls 'controlled flapping') or adjust it so that baby has arms free. Some babies need to 'find their fingers' for teething purposes.
- Don't rush in with every peep. Baby may be just 'whingeing in light sleep'. Anxious listeners to baby monitors might want to turn the volume down a tad.
- If your dummy-using baby wakes serially because his dummy falls out, you may need to wean him off it, possibly on to a replacement muslin or soft toy; or, suggests one mum, 'Scatter dummies around the cot, so if he loses the one he's sucking he has a chance of grabbing another one.'
- Get him his own place:

  'What about putting him in his own room now (if that's a possibility)? Our son was a very light sleeper and would wake several times a night. Just rustling the duvet, or one of us coughing at night would stir him. He slept in our room until six months because we were in a small flat. As soon as we moved house and he had his own room his sleeping improved.' *hippmummy*

The twelfth of never

'OK, I keep reading that they all sleep through eventually, but exactly when is eventually?' *mawbroon*

'Eventually is when they're about 14 and you have to physically pull them out of bed in the morning to wake them up.' *Overmydeadbody*

Daydream Believers: Daytime Naps

Most weary veterans of the sleep wars seem to agree that gradually coaxing your baby towards some more regular diurnal sack time will also help to regularise the night sleeps. You'll be trying to round up those little bits of slumber he may be doing all throughout the day and gather them into two or three larger sessions. If this sounds a bit like trying to herd mercury or teach hamsters synchronised swimming, well, it can be.

A lot of babies will settle into a three-nap pattern (earlyish morning, midday-ish, late afternoon) then graduate eventually to two naps, then one. The order in which they disappear varies, but many parents find that the late afternoon nap goes first and that it is the post-lunch siesta which endures the longest. One Mumsnetter, demonstrating the fine art of selective use of parenting manuals, found that, 'Gina's schedules for naptimes were bang on the money', despite not otherwise being a *Contented Little Baby Book* fan.

Here are some ideas for regularising and extending the siestas:

- 'Try mimicking your bedtime routine at naptime.' *WanderingHolly*
- Putting a baby under six months down to sleep after two hours of waking time can catch them at the point when they are sleepy, but not overtired. But you need to observe you own baby's personal

habits and tiredness signs. Some have obvious regular signs: fussing, eyes rolling back in head, yawning, rubbing eyes, head lolling. Others become mildly, then increasingly, grumpy.

'I put him in his pushchair in the hall when he shows signs of being tired (rubbing his eyes, getting grumpy and sucking his thumb). I rock/push the pushchair for a few minutes and he falls asleep.' *EagleBird*

- If your baby sleeps in a cot, blackout blinds may help.
- 'What do I do? Put her cot mobile on and give her a dummy and leave her to cry for a few minutes at a time, returning to ssshh her and replace the dummy. Not a technique that some people like, but it works for me.' *PorridgeBrain*
- Some babies are what you might call sleep-walkers. They are horrified at being left in a darkened room, but slumber blissfully when out and about in their chosen mode of transport, be that sling, pram or car seat.

So some parents resign themselves to perpetual motion:

'My son is now two and I still have to take him out in his pram or in the car to get him to sleep during the day. Just think of the exercise and it's a great excuse not to get anything done in the house.' *Kevinsmother*

Others resort to cunning:

'None of mine would ever sleep in their cot in the day, so we just used the pushchair. We went from having to walk for the whole of naptime, then after a while we could just walk for part of it and then pop back home when they were asleep. Eventually, all we had to do was pop them in the pushchair and they'd drop straight off.' *Biza*

And there is always the pushchair-next-to-the-washing-machine trick.
- There is a fairly sizeable constituency of babies who will only nap at all if they know you are *working really hard* to help them.

'The first five months were the hardest of my life. I would have to jiggle my daughter, while blowing raspberries to get her to sleep. The sound seemed to calm her.' *cwtchy*

'Someone asked me how I'd lost all the baby weight so quickly. It's because I had to do 30 minutes of high-impact aerobic bouncing four times per day.' *LittleMissLottie*

With this kind of baby, if nothing else works, you may just have to wait until she gets older:

'Honestly, they're damned lucky we're not so big on natural selection these days.' *IAteRosemaryConleyForBreakfast*

Many children graduate from two naps to one some time between the end of the first year and the middle of the second. There are likely to be awkward transitions.

'Be warned: it can take a while for your baby to adjust. For a very messy few days after dropping his morning nap, my son kept falling asleep – nose-first – into his lunch.' Porpoise

Some happily drop the single remaining nap not long thereafter; others will have at least an occasional afternoon snooze until they get to school age.

To Train or Not to Train?

There are probably no more vitriolic threads on the Mumsnet talkboards than those about sleep-training methods, and 'controlled crying' in particular. For every parent who thinks controlled crying is barbaric, there is another who feels it saved her life and a third for whom it simply didn't work. The fact that most of the experts claim to have science on their side doesn't help the sleep-starved parent who is trying to make decisions about what to do. The truth seems to be that there is still much we do not know about sleep and infant development, so that all you can do is read around a bit, take much of that reading with a pinch of salt and make a reasonably educated choice which seems to fit your own particular circumstances. And don't beat yourself up too much a couple of years down the line when some new research suggests that the method you chose is 100 per cent likely to turn your beloved firstborn into an axe murderer. Because another couple of years on, chances are there'll be some more research vindicating your choice.

What follows is a whistlestop tour of the dominant sleep philosophies and Mumsnetters' experiences with them for you to read and consider.

Gently, gently, sleepee monkee

At one end of the spectrum of views is American paediatrician Dr William Sears, whose method is perhaps better described as an anti-sleep-training approach. Deborah Jackson and Jean Liedloff, among others, also propound a similar parenting style.

Sears advocates what he calls 'attachment parenting' which involves co-sleeping, cue-feeding and baby-wearing (keeping her in a sling for much of the day). Parents are encouraged to provide calm and peaceful daytimes, consistent naps and consistent bedtimes, and then to use a variety of gentle techniques geared to a baby's temperament to gradually extend her night sleeping and achieve night weaning. Sears rejects the notion that young babies should be taught self-comforting/self-settling techniques. He is opposed to controlled-crying methods and tells a spooky anecdote in his *Baby Book* about a couple who try controlled crying with their baby then rapidly progress (so detached have they become from their tragic infant) to 'getaway weekends' and 'getaway weeks'. On the whole, Mumsnetters don't take kindly to that sort of 'you-bad-mother' style yarn, but many Mumsnetters do like Sears' gentle holistic approach.

Some Mumsnetters also like Dr Jay Gordon, who provides an attachment-parenting approach to issues such as night weaning for babies over a year (www.drjaygordon.com).

'Attachment parenting is about following your own instincts, thinking about how the baby/child feels and doing what feels right. Why do so many people battle with their consciences about letting a baby cry, or letting them sleep alone, just because that's what modern society tells them to do?' footprint

'One of the things about attachment parenting for me is that it is contrary to the current "trend" to insist on babies/children becoming "independent" as early as possible. They "have to" learn to sleep by themselves, to fall asleep without any props and, in particular, without their parents being there; they have to be weaned from the breast, etc. For me, AP is about keeping your baby very, very close, and thereby giving your child the emotional strength to become independent when they are ready.' emkana

'Babies that didn't mind being left in a dark cave to sleep alone probably tended to become extinct. Babies that demanded constant care and frequent feeding probably got better care and more milk. So babies probably feel those things as genuine needs. It's not rocket science. We are all free to adapt our parenting to modern life, but that's not the world a baby is adapted to be born into and it's useful to think about that.' Acinonyx

Some plain-speaking Mumsnetters view this parenting style as 'hippy shite' or, more affectionately, as 'lentil weaving':

'I'd rather slit my wrists with a blunt fork than do attachment parenting.' presidentocustardo

'I think Dr Sears is totally whacked, and some of my worst moments of mothering came after trying to follow his recommendations. My son slept in a co-sleeper for six months, then moved into a crib. His room is separate but very close to ours. By contrast, I have a friend who is still co-sleeping with her two-year-old, although rarely actually gets any sleep; she did wean him recently, as he was still breastfeeding almost continuously through the night, but now feels she has to submit to 15 minutes of painful nipple tweaking before he will settle down. Sorry, not for me.' jabberwocky

Sleep routines: Gina, Tracy, et al.

If they work for you and your baby, the great advantages of the *Contented Little Baby* and *Baby Whisperer* routines is that they regularise not only feeding times, but also sleep patterns. (See Chapter Two for Mumsnetters' musings on the main routine gurus.)

A massive upside of the routine approach is that if you do have a 'contented little baby', you won't find yourself sobbing over the controlled-crying books described below, because baby should sleep through the night from a relatively early stage. Ford's routines, in particular, are extremely detailed, and you will probably need to go with her whole programme to make them work.

Tougher love

Pioneered by Dr Richard Ferber, an expert in paediatric sleep disorders, 'controlled crying' (sometimes called 'cry it out' or 'ferberisation') was – and is – recommended in different forms by a variety of parenting experts. In its classic form, controlled crying begins once a baby is over six months old, and involves leaving him in his cot to cry for a set number of minutes (usually five in the first instance), then returning to comfort him, leaving him again for a longer period, returning to comfort him and so forth. On subsequent nights, the periods may be extended. There are many variations on this method which are somewhat easier on the maternal heart. Some 'allow' you to remain in the room or to pick up your baby at the end of the set time. The idea with all of these methods is that after a period of nights, your baby will learn to settle himself to sleep without crying and this will be for his benefit as well as yours.

'It's not like you just abandon the child to scream its lungs out – you return regularly to reassure the baby that you care and that you are close.' *Rantmum*

The great advantage of controlled crying in cases where it works is that it can produce rapid results for wretchedly exhausted parents and children:

'Sometimes you see photos of children who have fallen asleep while eating and have their face buried in their dinner. I always look at that and think, "How awful that that child was allowed to get so tired that they couldn't hold their head up, even though they are hungry." Or, in contrast, my son would get exhausted and overtired (hardly surprising given the sleep pattern he had) and would just be fractious and impossible to soothe all day. He was just irritable and miserable the whole time. As a loving mother, I don't think it's in his interests to wait passively for the months or years necessary for him to sleep better. Assuming that it would resolve itself. And indeed, the instant that we implemented controlled crying, he transformed into a child who was *much* more content, much less irritable, more able to cope with just being in the world.' bloss

Ferber's rationale behind his method is that the child needs to learn to fall asleep on their own, i.e. without being fed/rocked/patted to sleep. He likens it to an adult falling asleep with a comfy warm pillow and waking up in the night to find the pillow gone. As an adult, he reasons, you would look for that pillow everywhere and wake up big-time to try to find it and get it back; this, he says, is what takes place with a child who falls asleep with a breast/bottle.

So much for the theory, which does make sense – but controlled crying is undoubtedly hard on the parental heart and Mumsnetters who have tried it recommend 'looking after yourself' while it lasts. 'Get in a stock of magazines, chocs, a timer and some tissues, because chances are you will cry as much as the child does for the first couple of nights,' warns one sleep-training veteran.

None the less, parents for whom it has worked often regard it as a small miracle.

'I'm not trying to be mean. I'm not trying to abandon her. I'm not seeing her as an inconvenience. I'm not trying to get some "me time". I'm trying to make sure that I have a happy, well-rested child. How can that be a bad thing?' PinkJenny

On a practical note, controlled crying and other sleep-training techniques may need to be repeated:

'Controlled crying worked, but we had to do it again after the slightest upset in routine, or illness or whatever.' mawbroon

Mumsnetters who don't like controlled crying have a range of criticisms. Here are some which are printable:

'Babies cry at night in order to reunite themselves with a parent as quickly as possible. That is the main reason for them crying. If they are left to find their own sleep pattern, most seem to sleep longer and longer chunks until they sleep for most of the night. For some this might be at a few weeks; I suspect that for most it is at a few months and for some a few years old. Why do they sleep through? Surely *that* is because they have found themselves at a stage where they are emotionally and physically ready to go for several hours without parental contact. Why do they cry? I would suggest this is because they are NOT ready to go without parental contact and the crying is the mechanism which unites them with a parent as soon as possible. Most people argue for controlled crying to improve the parent's mental health, at the risk of the child's.' morningpaper

'To say that your six-month-old baby has "never really slept well" is a bit like saying your six-month-old baby has never really talked well. It's to be expected and you will be happier if you can accept this and wait for her to get the hang of sleeping a bit longer in her own time. Meanwhile, share the burden of the night wakings as much as you can and get to bed as early as possible.' FrannyandZooey

Fractionally less controversial are another cluster of sleep-training techniques called things like 'pick-up/put-down', 'shhh/pat', 'settle-and-leave' and 'gradual withdrawal'. These tend to be a variation on the following:

'Basically, you put your baby in the crib saying, "Sleepy time, time to go to sleep now," etc. When they start crying (which they will), pick them up without fussing or sounding like you feel sorry for them. Talk to them calmly until they stop screaming and put them down immediately. It might take 100 goes the first time, but this rapidly decreases.' Salbow

Some Mumsnetters have found these methods a 'mahoosive faff', others a blessed compromise between controlled crying and their own uncontrolled sobbing after another hopelessly broken night. Again these approaches will not suit all babies:

'About pick-up/put-down – it did not work for my son. It made him very, very upset. Every time I picked him up, he was delighted, then when I put him down he was devastated – and showed it. He settled a lot better, quicker and more happily when I just went in, covered him up, made no eye contact, shushed and walked back out again. It broke my bloody heart, but I only did it for three nights. It's probably controlled crying, but whatever it was, it worked very well.'

colditz

> If you choose a tough-love method and then feel crap about it because it doesn't work, or it does work, but you torment yourself over the damage you may have done to your precious firstborn through bad parenting choices, take some comfort from this. So far as we can all tell (at least until the next bit of paranoia-inducing research hits the headlines):

'There is no evidence that controlled crying does any harm. Only that abandoning crying children for years at a time does harm. Don't let anyone tell you otherwise – check out their claims. And then do it if you want. If you can put up with the lack of sleep in your family and your life, you needn't bother.' bloss

The third way? – Elizabeth Pantley and *The No-Cry Sleep Solution*

Elizabeth Pantley's book, *The No-Cry Sleep Solution* is well liked by many Mumsnetters. Pantley's methods lack the shock-and-awe speed of some of the controlled-crying techniques, but they are gentle, subtle and designed to be tailored to your baby's needs. You do have to put quite a lot of work in with Pantley – work which may be beyond you if you are so destroyed by lack of sleep that raising a cup of tea accurately to your lips is an achievement. You will have to keep sleep logs and work out which strategies are likely to work for your baby's particular issues. Pantley suggests different solutions for different problems and you need to pick and mix to create your own sleep plan. The general idea is to set up new sleep associations for your baby and find ways of helping her self-settle.

> '**Basically, she helps you to cue your baby to sleep without her needing a nork in her mouth.**'
> MrsBadger

There is no quick fix. 'I was too tired for the "gentle" solutions,' says a mum who couldn't make it work the no-cry way. Pantley is, however, particularly good on some intractable conundrums – like the older baby who wakes frequently to breastfeed.

The sleep picture is indeed very complicated, and there simply isn't enough evidence for us to know whether many of the choices we make for our children are a) good; b) bad; c) indifferent; or d) whether it depends on a load of other factors not covered by any given study.

'I find it interesting that while experts offer terrifying predictions about rises in infant cortisol (the stress hormone released during crying), they do not bother to study the effects of chronic tiredness, anxiety and depression on parents struggling to bring up a child on insufficient sleep, usually without help from extended families or communities (such as the Pleistocene or mythical "tribal" mother would presumably have been able to call upon automatically?). An overtired parent will be flooded with cortisol most of the day him/herself because of the struggle of trying to cope and, according to various studies, high parental stress will automatically affect the child's levels (this has been proven with regard to parents with depression, for instance). The "scientific" attachment-parenting argument seems to be a massive red herring.' whywhywhy

No more tears – some (long-winded) *No-Cry Sleep Solution* success stories

'I used some of the *No-Cry Sleep Solution* – mostly to try and persuade my son to start dropping off without the nipple in his mouth. It did work, but it's taken months. However, we did see enough of an improvement to make a big impact on my quality of life pretty quickly, so have faith! I slowly worked on unlatching my son as he reached the end of a feed so that he could be moved away from me. We put our pillows either side of the bed so there was a big enough gap between them for him to lie, and once he'd finished his feed I'd scoot him up there and settle him on his back. It sometimes took a few goes when we were starting the Pantley stuff, but he slowly got better at managing the last bit before deep sleep by himself. Patting helped. As he got better at sleeping away from me, i.e. not with a boob in his mouth, it got easier and easier to feed him and then plonk him between the pillows, which meant I could get good spells of sleep in a position of my choice. It was tedious and slow progress initially, but absolutely worth it to get better-quality sleep.' *IAteRosemaryConleyForBreakfast*

'First of all, I started doing the thing where you break his latch when he's finished feeding, and then put him in the cot when he's nearly asleep; then gradually moved on to putting him down more awake. When he went into the cot I read a story, then said goodnight. At first, if he was still awake at that point, I was sitting by the cot holding his hand, and then gradually moved away night by night. If he cried or stood up, I cuddled him and laid him down, saying goodnight. Once I was outside the room, I then slowly closed the door. I did have to spend 20 minutes or so a night doing it at first, but I really feel that it's been worth it as he only has positive associations with sleeping. Now he goes in the cot, has his story, then lies down and sleeps. It's a nice portable routine in that we can do it anywhere.' *cmotdibbler*

Long Day's Journey Into (Sleeping Through the) Night

So here's the Mumsnetters' guide to juggling methods, philosophies, experts and your own personal snoozemonkey:

- Do not pick a method you and your baby cannot live with:

'You need to pick a sleep solution that suits you and your child. Everyone has to make their own decision. I used controlled crying with both of mine at around eight to nine months and it worked with both of them. It took a week with my daughter and two weeks with my son. To make it work you have to be prepared to stick to it, otherwise you get all the stress and no benefit in the end, if you see what I mean. It's worked for everyone that I know of who stuck with it, but it doesn't suit everyone.' *martianbishop*

- Do not start any controlled-crying-style method before six months because before that age it's quite likely your baby may well just be hungry and need feeding. And then make sure the time feels right for you. Some Mumsnetters who consider controlled crying too harsh for under-ones are grudgingly in favour of the method when applied to nocturnally snacking toddlers.
- Make sure your baby is well and not crying at night because of physical discomfort.
- If you find an approach which appeals, consider whether there is some adaptation to the methods which would suit you and your baby and which feels OK to you:

'Controlled crying does work and I used it with my own child (when he was ten months). BUT it has to be in a form you can cope with. I couldn't possibly leave my baby the suggested ten minutes – five minutes was too much, and in the end I settled for sitting in the room with him and settling him every two to three minutes. I also lifted him if I thought he was getting hysterical as my instincts told me to. It probably took longer than the traditional controlled crying but within three weeks he was sleeping through the night.' *aragon*

- If you do change your method, however, do so with care. Don't just use a load of different techniques at the same time which confuse your junior insomniac:

'I think you need to pick one technique to use and then stick to it. Your daughter may be confused by crying for two hours, then being given milk, then allowed into your bed. So: shhh/pat, pick-up/put-down, rapid return, withdrawal, whatever: start it and stick to it.' *BoysAreLikeDogs*

- Having said that, if you try a method or a change to sleeping arrangements which isn't working after a reasonable period (what is reasonable will vary from person to person), and which is stressing you and your baby, STOP. Try something else or let things be for a few weeks or months.
- If you are really at the end of your tether, consider a sleep counsellor. Some will do telephone or face-to-face consultations, provide you with a sleep plan and remain available for follow-up advice:

'I know sleep counselling isn't for everyone. It's not cheap for a start. But honestly, I think it saved me from completely losing my mind. Also, my husband and I found that having someone else tell us what to do stopped us arguing about whose way of solving the problem was right! (For the record, I was more right than he was.)' *taliclac*

The truth is that most Mumsnetters seem to mix and match and figure out what works for them. You might love co-sleeping, but be unable to carry your baby in a sling because of a bad back. You might be a cue-feeder who eventually does controlled crying. If you read parenting manuals, try to take from them only the bits that feel right for you. If they are making you feel insecure and confused, put them in the bin.

And remember: you are not the Devil just because you make a different choice from someone else whose lifestyle/ability to cope with sleep deprivation/family circumstances/BABY is completely different from your own.

'You don't have to be one thing or another (earth mother/routine obsessed). I think it is sad that we label ourselves in this way – most of us are just trying to do the best we can.' McNoodle

The Closest Thing to Crazy: You and Sleep Deprivation

The blessed thing in all of this is that because the brain cells which would otherwise store memories will not be functioning properly, you will not remember this period clearly.

Sleep deprivation land is a strange place. Time may seem to slow down and then speed up in funny ways. Sometimes, it can be like being underwater and watching your own life ooze by; other times it feels like your emotions have been laid out on a plate and pecked by crows (an experience that may leave you plagued by a tendency to histrionic metaphor). It can be hard to adjust your expectations – you are supposed to be so damned happy and you feel so damned weird.

Bad trip: Mumsnetters' experiences of sleep deprivation

'I find that when I am extremely tired I experience light-headedness or mild dizzy spells, as well as feeling physically sick.' *Pigwig*

'My best description was that it was like having morning sickness all the time (with no baby to look forward to). Do watch your iron levels, anaemia can make me feel similar, as can snacking on sugary food instead of proper stuff, but who has time for nutrition when they've had a couple of hours' sleep and have a baby to look after?' *bluebear*

'I hallucinate if I don't get enough sleep.' *VanillaMilkshake*

'I saw things moving out of the corner of my eye or thought I saw insects. Very strange experience! I also had the sensation of my body moving or the sofa/bed vibrating.' *usandbump*

'I can see sort of shapes out of the corner of my eye, like someone has just walked out of a room, or a folded umbrella leaning against a door. It's very weird; nothing like a hippy acid trip (not that I'd know).' *fizzbuzz*

Getting By (Hopefully With a Little Help from Your Friends)

Here are some Mumsnetters' tips for groping through the long tunnel of sleep deprivation and out into the bright sunshine and fresh air of, er, a good night's sleep – dammit, you know what we mean.

- Eat well and get some exercise: coffee and chocolate biscuits may provide a sleep-defying buzz, but will leave you feeling worse when the sugar/caffeine hit wears off. Don't feel you have to live on a diet of mung beans either; just don't exist entirely on cake.

'I am going to do lots of taking care of *me* for a bit. Am going to make big effort with eating decent food and going to the gym (which I enjoy) and am also going to try to cut caffeine and sugar gradually, all of which I think will help, but am also going to be most sensible.' *FillyjonkthePumpkinEater*

As far as exercise goes, this can be as simple as a bracing walk with the buggy.

- Drink a lot of water: being dehydrated will cause further attrition to your exhaustion-eroded cognitive abilities (try saying that sentence aloud on two hours' sleep).
- It's time for the Night of the Living Dad:

'You will need to equip your partner, if you have one, with a bottle of expressed breast milk or formula, but otherwise leave him to it. You can do this alternate nights or even just at weekends, but you really must have a break or you will be depressed. Someone sharing the night shifts really helps.' *aloha*

- Phone a friend (or your mum): if you can get someone to hang around during the day, you might be able to grab a nap, or even just a reviving bath.
- If you can afford it, get occasional night-time help. If you don't have a willing friend/relative/partner you can even hire some in. It's not cheap but some folks reckon it's worth it:

'I'd struggled through with my first two on very little sleep/help, but when my third came along, someone suggested a night nanny. I was sceptical, but – oh my goodness – am evangelical now! She came at 10 p.m. as I was doing a feed, then took the baby and settled her in the spare bedroom with her while I slept. I left expressed milk and she did a night-time feed. If I woke up with sore breasts, I just expressed for 15 minutes and fell asleep again. It's the settling that takes so much time, not the feeding. She would bring the baby in again at 7 a.m. We had her Fridays and Sundays for about two months and it was the best money we ever spent.' *Biza*

- Set very modest goals, or none at all. Don't make awful lists of things to do which you will fail to complete. Alternatively, if you are a list-obsessive, make a list of very very simple tasks: 'Feed baby, drink water, breathe ...'
- Evolve into a different sort of being:

  'Don't worry, you get used to the sleep deprivation after a while – honestly; you do go through a slightly schizoid phase, but then once you are through it, you just suddenly become a milky automaton.' *whomovedmychocolate*

- Hang out on Mumsnet's 'sleep' talkboard. The chances are that someone else has had your same issue. And you can type as slowly as you like.

Mumsnetiquette: Long dark night of the soul – the things we wish we'd never shouted at babies in the middle of the night

No one's proud of it (most of these posts appeared littered with shame emoticons), but almost everyone cracks sometimes. As they used to say on those old *Alien* posters: in space, no one can hear you scream. It's better if you can go into your night garden and howl at the moon, but if you slip up, at least it is some consolation to remember that your baby won't understand what you are shouting, or remember it:

Night time is not logic time:

'I have shouted, "Stop shouting!"' *martianbishop*

'When my son was a couple of weeks old I shouted, "I've changed your nappy, I've fed you, you're warm, I've cuddled you, now please go to f*cking sleep!" At this point, my partner woke up and said something inane, so I got dressed and said, "Fine, I've had it. I'm going." I left the house (it was 3 a.m.), walked to the end of the road and came back, having nowhere to go. Came back to a bewildered-looking partner, a woken-up two-year-old crying and a newborn baby screaming.' *ledodgyDave*

'Have recently grumbled at an inexplicably crying son, "Oh for God's sake, you're just being a big baby!" Which is ridiculous because he is six months old. And big.' *SpawnChorus*

Some lose their rag, but not their cultural standards …

'I've done my share of cussing out my babies in the small hours, but my most poncetastic moment was with my son. He could not sleep, he would not stop shouting. So I put *Così Fan Tutte* on the stereo, hissed in his face, "Shut the f*ck up you little fiend, this is '*Soave sia il vento*'," and went into the bedroom to have a good cry. He was still going when I went back ten minutes later. Babies need Mozart, my arse!' *Marina*

… or their ability to coin a phrase:

'During a 3 a.m. nappy change when my son was five weeks old: "And now you've soaked my only remaining pair of pyjamas, you piddling little twat."' *VioletBaudelaire*

But after all:

'After 15 or 20 years YOU FORGET IT ALL!' *JanH*

Chapter Five

Food, Glorious Food

In this chapter ...

OK, here's the real reason why people urge you to go to mother-and-baby groups. It's because no one in your former life is going to be even slightly interested in your infant's weaning activities. Even old friends who get a ghoulish frisson out of your sleep-deprivation insanity stories and take a squeamish interest in your bleeding nipples will discover an urgent need to get off the phone when you start rabbiting on about what vegetable you are puréeing today or exactly how large the pieces of carrot in baby's nappy were. And even parents who themselves have been through weaning tend to find that the bit of their brain which was temporarily devoted to it simply disappears after weaning is complete (Annabel Karmel being a glorious apparent exception to this general principle).

Truly, the only people with an avid interest in weaning are those intimately involved in the process. So here is what Mumsnetters have to say about this exacting science. And if you don't find precisely what you need here, the 'weaning' talkboard is full of other gripping discussions under titles, such as: 'Structural integrity of roasted sweet potato compromised' (apparently the aforementioned tuber may be used as a finger food if you can maintain a sufficiently 'crusty' exterior, oh yes).

When to Wean

'If I'd trusted my mother, my daughter would have been on formula milk, having a rusk crumbled into her bottle at six weeks and on solids by two months. If I'd trusted my sister, my daughter would have been formula-fed and eating sausage and chips by three months. If I'd trusted my mother-in-law, my baby would have been on formula milk, with honey and whisky in, from three weeks to help her sleep.' WigWamBam

The World Health Organisation is quite clear that you should wait until six months in most cases before introducing your baby to solid foods. The problem for some of us can be that the WHO doesn't necessarily cut much ice with our chocolate button-brandishing grannies, or with the odd time-warp health visitor, who bangs on at you about 'windows of opportunity' for introducing solids:

'There's a window? That you can miss? How long is this window? What if it happens during the night when we're all asleep? My daughter will have to subsist on nothing but milk FOR EVER!!!'
talktothebees

You can't really blame Granny for trying. She probably did feed you roast beef, gravy and queen of puddings when you were two weeks old, with the blessings of the medical profession. And your health visitor may have spent decades telling mums to wean at four months. Even your friend with an older child may have weaned well before six months. (The Department of Health only started recommending delaying weaning until six months in 2003.) And everyone has anecdotal evidence that early-weaned babies are just fine ... just as everyone knows a nonagenarian who smokes 100 unfiltered fags every day and subsists on a diet of beef dripping ...

Try throwing a little science at the early-weaning enthusiasts in your life, if that helps. But bear in mind that there are various studies, suggesting various things, and that there are no definitive answers about the effects of weaning before six months. Weaning before sixteen weeks, on the other hand, is definitely inadvisable because there is firmer research suggesting links to eczema, asthma and to digestive problems. Mumsnetters can – and do – debate exactly what the scientific evidence means (at considerable length), but many just say, 'Why take the risk with early weaning?'

'The early-weaning consequences can be allergies, eczema and stomach complaints, and some of those effects won't be seen for years and years and years.' simperingbint

'The reason it isn't advised to wean until around six months is due to the fact that there are holes in the digestive tract that don't close until then. At around six months, the baby starts to produce more of their own immunity, so the holes close up and it becomes safe to give them solids.' Wisknit

'The pancreas isn't ready yet, and many different enzymes are missing to aid proper digestion. Also, things like egg (foreign proteins) can fool the body into thinking that they are intruders which need to be fought off, causing life-long allergies. Plus, if you spoonfeed a baby before they can physically refuse food (i.e. bat away the spoon and move their head away), they are at a higher risk of being overweight, as it is easy to overfeed. On top of that, before six months they don't know how to properly regulate food intake. With milk this isn't really a problem, but once they start on solids it can be a huge issue, causing obesity in later life.'
VictorianSqualorSquelchandSquirm

So there is general agreement on weaning at around the six-month mark, give or take a few weeks, and you also want to be sure that your baby is showing signs of readiness:

'... such as sitting unaided, good head control, loss of tongue-thrust reflex (when baby shoves anything that comes into his mouth right out again), pincer grip and being co-ordinated

enough to pick up food and get it to their mouth.' lulumama

A baby who is not yet able to sit well (and some do not sit firmly until well after the six-month mark) should be propped upright in a straight-backed high chair or on your knee when being offered solid foods.

Don't panic if your baby is still tongue thrusting and not really interested in his tucker at six months, seven months or even older. Some babies only really get the point of food around 12 months. Just keep on offering food in a relaxed manner and don't fuss about how much is actually being ingested (they will still be getting most of their nutrition from milk). They all develop at their own pace and they all eat eventually.

Three mahoosive weaning myths, masticated and regurgitated

1 *The baby who grabs your Mars Bar and shoves it in his mouth is ready to eat*

'Reaching for food is not a sign of needing solids. It's a sign of being old enough to see something and grab it. Babies do this with anything, and they may well put it to their mouths.' *tiktok*

Having said that, there are those who think that babies who are physically able to snatch, chew and swallow items of food somewhat before the six-month mark are probably ready for them:

'It seems to me if you leave the baby to decide when to eat, you're probably playing things safe, although my daughter wasn't offered anything until six months. If I have more children, I don't *think* I'll offer before six months (never say never), but if food is swiped then I reckon I'll consider that fair game.' *AitchTwoOh*

2 *Night waking after sleeping through is not a sign of readiness for solids, and solids will not necessarily make your baby sleep through*

This one is also controversial. There are Mumsnetters whose babies have indeed slept through after starting solids and others whose sleeping patterns have altered not a jot. Most agree that sleep patterns often wobble considerably anyway between four and six months (which is a big time in baby's life in developmental terms).

3 *Some babies are too large to wait; they need the calories and other nutrients in solid food*

This is often said to mums of breastfed babies, who are frequently slightly leaner than their formula-fed mates. It is poppycock. Feeding babies under one year old 'is supposed to introduce them to textures and flavours, so that by one year old(ish) they are having a wide enough variety of foods to get their needed vitamins and minerals,' explains a Mumsnetter. Up to the age of six months, they generally get what they need nutritionally from milk. Being more hungry than usual, asking for more feeds and waking to feed are often cited as cues to wean. All of these things happen when a growth spurt is going on – more milk is what they need.

Eat It and Wear It: How to Wean

There are two ways to go on this one:

Weaning style one: you start with very finely squashed up purées, and progress to lumpier ones. You introduce some finger foods somewhere along the way.

Weaning style two (or 'baby-led weaning'/BLW): many Mumsnetters who wean this way, none the less, hate the name:

'The term is a bit wanky, and comes across as a bit cult-like.' TheCrackFox

'It's a three-letter abbreviation for something that most people do anyway.' Alderney

Baby-led weaning is basically making a variety of appropriately sized/shaped/prepared finger foods available for your baby and letting her get on with it. But don't be too purist about letting her choose:

'If I was to truly, truly, truly allow my daughter to wean herself without any intervention from me, she would exist on a diet of Lakeland Limited catalogues and dustballs. (I keep a very clean house, me).' Aitch

You can choose to go either way, and it's fine. As one mum says, 'Purée isn't evil, it's food; so is a broccoli spear.' Some babies choose their own way; a lot of parents do a bit of both:

'I thought you shovel in the wholesome purée and then hand over progressively larger-sized lumps and hard bits until baby stops breathing, then you turn him upside down and bang him until it comes out. That's what I do, anyway.' morningpaper

Foods to avoid

Not everyone's guidelines are the same and the advice does change (see the current NHS advice at www.nhs.uk/chq/), but there are some broad areas of consensus:

Not before six months
If you do start weaning early (or your baby starts helping himself), here are the things to keep out of reach (in addition to all the

foods in the other categories below, which are unsuitable until your baby is even older):

- Gluten: you need to avoid wheat in all its manifestations (bread, pasta, cake, biscuits); also rye- and barley-based foods
- Cow's milk and dairy products: yoghurt, cheese, dairy puddings
- Eggs in any form: raw or lightly cooked eggs should also be avoided beyond the six-month mark
- Fish and shellfish: fish can cause an allergic reaction, and shellfish is a food-poisoning risk
- Meat: not usually given until six months
- Strawberries, raspberries and kiwi fruit: all of these may cause allergic reactions

Not before one year
- Honey: there is a small risk of infant botulism
- Citrus fruits: although some think these are OK from six months

Beyond one year
- Shark, swordfish or marlin: these may have high mercury levels
- Peanut-related products: if you have a history of allergies in the family and/or asthma or eczema, current government advice is to avoid peanuts in all forms until age three or older; remember this can change with new research though, so do look on the internet for the most recent guidance
- Sesame: some say this should also be avoided for a similar period, which rules out houmous, sesame prawn toast (and anything else which lists sesame seeds or oil as an ingredient)
- Whole nuts: some experts say none of these at all for the under-fives, but if you have no family history of nut allergies, you can offer chopped nuts and nut butters

Weaning with Purées

Here is the potted version:

'You go to the shop, buy a vegetable, cook it for a bit, mash it up, serve it to a baby, freeze the rest in an ice-cube tray. If you are daring, you mix a couple of veggies. Advanced method is to mix a fruit and a veg.' threebob

And here is a fuller account of the staged approach to weaning with purées:

'Stage 1 – puréed veg and fruit; stage 2 – puréed meals with protein, i.e. chicken/cheese/fish (no earlier than six months); stage 3 – (approximately seven months) blended meat, but mashed veg, fruit; finger foods such as rice cakes/toast/ cooked carrots; stage 4 – (middle/end of seven months) mashed everything and finely shredded meat. Don't overmash – leave a few lumps of veg, etc. and also start adding baby pasta to some meals. Gradually stop mashing and just mix with a fork, building up to lumpy/coarse food by eight/nine months. It does depend on the meals you do. For instance, for Bolognese, I would blend to just break up the mince and the same with chicken, but then fish I just mash up.' kbaby

If you need the full syllabus, there is any number of decent books on weaning, most of them by Annabel Karmel (see p. 217), and Gina Ford's *Contented Little Baby Book of Weaning* has fans, even among those who don't like her baby routines.

Purée and simple: introducing purées the Mumsnet way

- Start at a time of day when baby is awake and jolly. Morning is better because there is more time to see if he has a negative reaction to a particular food. Mix a little of his usual tipple (by which we mean MILK) in with his first purée to make it more attractive to him.
- Introducing one new food at a time is good way of determining what baby likes and weeding out foods that disagree with him or cause allergic reactions. You can then mix flavours with more and more gay abandon as time goes on:

And now for a little ee cummingsesque poem about good purée combinations:

'avocado and banana is divine
peach and apricot
dried apricots stewed in pan and blitzed
apple and pear
potato and pea
carrot and potato.' *collision*

- He is likely to eat very small amounts indeed initially, but may suddenly get a big appetite. Or get fed up with it all and regress for a while. It's all good.
- Do relax and take it slowly. The early stages of weaning are about him trying out tastes and getting the hang of the eating thing, not filling his belly.
- If he spits it all back at you or resolutely closes his lips, you may want to wait a few days before having another go. Don't force food on him.
- Chill about the mess. The vast majority of the food will end up festooning your kitchen. Not so bad if you have chosen a vibrant carrot colour scheme.
- Some of the slower weaning methods were developed when weaning commonly started at four months. If you wait until six months, you can probably gallop a little more quickly towards consumption of meat, lumps and finger foods.
- One meal a day is likely to be plenty for the first week or two. Gradually increase to two, then three meals (see the weaning guide overleaf).

- Baby rice is dismissed by some parents as wallpaper paste; others like it as a thickener or in puddings, or find it useful mixed with baby's usual milk as an unchallenging introduction to texture:

'I gave my daughter rice and millet porridge at six months – mixed it with veg, a little homemade stock and olive oil. I also did a pudding version with expressed breast milk and fruit. I found it a really handy thing to have; it has the consistency of Ready Brek and you can whip it up in seconds. Nothing wrong with rice, just remember to add flavour.' *Brangelina*

- If you freeze purée in batches in ice-cube trays, as many of the books suggest, watch out for a fluffy exterior on your ice cubes – this is freezer burn, which will render your purées unpalatable.

How much, oh Lord? – an at-a-glance guide to what, when and how much to stuff in (otherwise known as a weaning timetable)

Note: initial amounts are likely to be a teaspoon or two, with much of that ending up on your baby's clothing rather than in her belly.

When	What	How often	Texture**	Breast milk/ formula***
Weeks 1 and 2	Veg/fruit/ yoghurt*	Once/twice a day	Purée/mash well	Yes (no change)
Weeks 3 and 4	Veg/fruit/ meat*/fish*/ cereals*/ cheese*	Twice/three times a day	Lumpy purée/ finger foods	Yes (no change)
From 7 months	Wide variety	Three times a day	Mashed with fork/finger foods	Yes (can reduce amount)
From 9 months	Family food	Three times a day	Chopped or pulsed/finger foods	Yes (can reduce amount)

*Not before six months
**Not applicable for baby-led weaning (obviously)
*** Up to the age of one year, babies should still be having at least 400ml (14fl oz) of their usual milk per day.

Making a first purée

Carrot, parsnip, swede or potato: chop the vegetable into small pieces and then steam or simmer in boiling water for about 15 minutes, until soft. Most root vegetables can be puréed, with a little of their cooking liquid, in a sieve, mouli, food processor or blender, but potatoes are fussier and should be moulied or sieved.

Apple or pear: cut the fruit into small, similarly sized pieces and place in a heavy saucepan with a few tablespoons of water. Cover and cook on a low heat until soft. Purée with some of the cooking liquid.

In either case, serve a little of the lukewarm purée to your baby and freeze the remainder in sterilised ice-cube trays.

That ready-made vs homemade thing

This is not a life-threatening or even life-altering choice, so do what suits you; many, many parents mix and match. Plus, your baby may have his own ideas, whatever your views are:

'I made loads of homemade stuff and froze it … then neither of my two would eat it. So they had jars and packets.' MamaG

Here are some Mumsnetters' views on why you might want to make your own baby food:

- It's cheaper.
- There are short-cuts if you are busy or, ahem, lazy. Mash an avocado or a banana. Microwave a sweet potato and squash it.
- The texture of food in jars tends to be different from 'real' food, so it can be hard for baby to make the transition to lumpier food if he is on ready-made food only.
- 'Loads of them are full of water/juice/fillers which do not fill children up very much,' says one mum (but look at the labels – there are significant variations).
- 'The ready-made food tastes revolting. I did a blind taste test of ten baby jars at my baby shower (don't ask) and they all tasted a) the same and b) faintly of sick. Except for the chocolate pudding, which was yum.' *harpsichordandcarrots*

- 'I love watching them eat home-cooked food, knowing exactly what was put in it, full of goodness, not an additive in sight. It gives me a lovely, warm glow ...' *ThomBat*
- It's a hobby – steaming, grinding and freezing can be a guilty home-makerly pleasure for some parents. Filling your freezer with nutritious coloured cubes makes you feel like you have *achieved* something.
- Much of the nutritional value in jarred food is cooked out. (The frozen varieties are likely to be better in this respect.)

And in defence of bought baby foods:

- There are many new organic and frozen ranges which are better quality than some of the old-style baby foods.
- All baby foods have to comply with standards laid down in European directives relating to salt, sugar, other additives and pesticide levels.
- Convenience:

'They are very handy for when you are out and about.' *TitianRed*

'Jars are convenient in the same way that tinned soups are convenient – you know you can make it better yourself (mostly), but sometimes they're just a handy convenience.' *ginmummy*

- Using prepared foods gives you more time to play with baby, or do something else you find more interesting instead, particularly if you are not a speedy or accomplished cook:

'I really don't see the problem with jars. I had no idea how to cook and purée anything, was totally stressed about it all and it does take extra time when you're getting little sleep and have possibly just returned to work.' *accessorizequeen*

- Prepared foods can be less dispiriting with baby refuseniks:

'It's soul destroying when you have spent your only "free time" preparing it all, only to be scraping it in the bin.' *babybensmum*

- You can still feed lots of 'real food' at the same time (toast and other finger food, pasta, slices of banana, etc.). Some mums chuck some jarred vegetables on pasta for a quick 'sauce'.

- Baby will be getting most of his nutrition from milk in the early days, anyway.
- It is easy to introduce new stuff without cooking up a batch of whatever the flavour of the day is.
- OK, some people say they taste yucky. But do a taste test with some of your homemade purées and you may find them no more delicious than a lot of the stuff in jars. What is new and exciting to a baby is of little interest to the educated/jaded adult palate.
- Give yourself a break.

'Jars are not bad. They are just another option. Read the ingredients, taste them yourself and you'll know if they are OK or not.' *Bugsy2*

And finally, a useful idea:

- 'Top tip for those who are worried about sneering looks when feeding in public from a jar – pop it in a plastic container, either at home before you go out, or when it has been warmed up – hide the jar, and no one is any the wiser.' *TCsMum*

That Annabel vs no Annabel thing

Annabal Karmel is the undoubted princess of puréeing, the tsarina of steaming and the Nigella of toddler cooking in general. Some Mumsnetters love her baby cookbooks, which lead you gently and thoroughly through the wonderful world of weaning and onwards, to pizzas with cat faces, jelly boats and cannelloni which look like dear little people tucked up in bed.

'I like her. Hadn't done the weaning business for eight years, was totally bereft of inspiration, and she came up with more interesting food combinations than just mashing individual veg and freezing. I only do about six recipes from the book, and we're sorted. Easy-peasy fish pie goes down well, as did the lentil thing. I do other stuff as well, mostly our leftovers, but her book just gave me ideas when I couldn't be bothered to think.' Tinker

'I used the book when I weaned my daughter. I knew nothing about weaning kids, had no family support, was generally witless, so I used it and found it quite easy. Made loads in bulk and froze them.' martianbishop

Other Mumsnetters find Karmelisation is a bit labour-intensive:

'She's on that planet where people who have live-in hired help live.' expatinscotland

'It's a good idea in principle, but because I had no other experience, I knocked myself out on her recipes. My husband's eyes used to pop out at all the stuff that used to come through the door for one small recipe, for one small baby, that may/may not end up in the bin.' tinygang

'I hate the thought of making smiley faces out of carrot and cucumber for children. I think it teaches them to play with their food and expect it to be novelty-ised, instead of just getting on with eating it. Bit of a bugbear of mine.' Caligula

As with most baby-related literature, Karmel's cookbooks probably work best if you are selective about what you use:

'This is one of those books that can be enormously useful, if you're confident about picking and choosing and not getting guilt-tripped by the unrealistic expectations. There are some really great, easy recipes in there and some good basic info on how to make purées, but the menu planners are just daft. I would not think it a very good idea to *always* feed your child food in the shape of a smiley face, but nothing wrong with having some ideas for how to do it, if you want to occasionally.' Kathy1972

Mumsnetiquette: Making funny faeces – some weaning foods we have regretted

'Beans at dinner time, in any shape or form. It means I am woken by loud and noxious farts, right in my face, around 2 a.m. Often accompanied with kicks to my head.' *IAteMakkaPakka*

'Cauliflower cheese – she loved it. But she then woke every hour through the night, screamed for a bit till she squeezed out a stinking fart, then went back to sleep. Till the next one ...' *Poledra*

'Kiwi fruit ... it takes for ever to clean all the little seeds off their backsides the next day.' *LeakyDAISYCal*

'Not a mistake as such, but at one time, the only thing on the menu when eating out that my son could eat (allergies) was haggis and tatties. He did a poop in his nappy overnight, and by the morning the spices had burned his bum red raw.' *mawbroon*

And on the subject of strange poo, be warned that consumption of banana can cause nappies to fill with funny black fibres. (Coming soon: *The Mumsnet Guide to Strange Poo*.)

Fishy Fingers: Starting Baby-led Weaning (BLW)

To those of you who have not yet mentally adjusted to the post-baby lifestyle, 'finger food' may conjure up images of prawns in filo pastry or dinky paper cones of fish and chips. Banish those canapé thoughts now! Just offer baby some of your food – but do have some regard to suitability: don't just plonk a bucket of KFC on the high-chair tray and leave him to it.

'Start with "chips and trees". Chips are vegetables that can be cut into a "chip" shape and lightly boiled (root veg are good for this). You can also add in things like toast soldiers if you are happy with bread. "Trees" are broccoli and cauliflower florets – perfect baby-led weaning foods because they come with a "handle". As your little one learns to open their hands, you can add in other things that are fist-shaped, and when they have pincer grip, the gloves are off!' TinkerBellesMum

There is no rush with baby-led weaning; that's the idea, baby is leading. Just keep offering things; it can take a while for babies to get the hang of the whole eating game. Look at the finger food box opposite for more thoughts or check out Mumsnet's weaning board (see Resources, p. 439).

There are some practical issues to consider with BLW:

- Leave out the salt and sugar when making meals to be shared by adults and baby. This also means avoiding ready meals and fast food.
- When you are eating out, pick suitable bits off your own plate. Ask for vegetables and chips to be prepared without salt, and dressing to be served separately from salads.
- It is OK to use cutlery in circumstances where an adult would use cutlery. There is no mad ban on spoons.

'I do use a spoon! We both use spoons for yoghurt, porridge, Weetabix, avocado, etc. My philosophy is not to mush up anything that is not already mushed.' *wherethewildthingsare*

- Teeth are not necessary, except for chewing the tougher meats and fruit and vegetable skins.

'Gums are very hard and can deal with most food.' *minorityrules*

Harder fruits and vegetables should be cooked (carrots, apples, etc.).
- Toast is an easier early finger food than bread, which can be gluey and chokey.
- You don't need to always be making something special.

'Table scraps and sandwiches will do fine.' *MrsBadger*

Although that possibly makes it sound like you are feeding a pig.

Mumsnetters' finger favourites

Here are some of your easiest options:
- Toast fingers
- Pitta fingers
- Slices of banana
- Cheese sticks or chunks
- Pitta bread with houmous (but not where there is any possibility of sesame allergy)
- Dried mango (fruit only, no additives)
- Dried apricots
- Nectarine
- Cucumber slices
- Sliced sweet potato wedges (cut thickly enough to retain their all-important structural integrity)
- Steamed carrot and courgette fingers
- Peach and nectarine slices
- Big florets of steamed cauliflower or broccoli
- Slices of pepper
- Pieces of cold pasta (some parents find cold is better as it goes sticky and doesn't slip); experiment with pasta shapes – many Mumsnetters recommend spirals:

(continued)

When Good Food Goes Wrong: Gagging, Choking, Vomiting

Whether you wean with finger foods only, or with purées too, you will have to face the gagging thing. Remember that choking and gagging are *not* the same thing. Gagging is something babies do when they are learning how to handle solid food in their mouths; they are stopping themselves choking:

'Babies choking is quite unusual; they do gag spectacularly when they first try big lumps, but that's how they learn to control moving the food around in their mouths.' PortAndLemon

'True choking is a total blockage of the throat, when no sound or air can come in or out.' Chirpygirl

Gagging is scary for parents, but try not to let on that you're scared:

'Take deep breaths yourself, to calm down, and watch her breathing. Watch her resolutely not turning blue. She can sort out the food at the back of her throat, all on her own.' NotQuiteCockney

Sometimes gagging leads to vomiting. Babies themselves are likely to take gagging and indeed vomiting in their stride, so long as you do:

'Sometimes he gagged so much he threw up, but even then it didn't seem to faze him. Quite often he would just start eating his vom again unless we cleaned it up smartish. All with the biggest grin on his face.' terramum

Dealing with gagging and avoiding choking

- Sit baby upright while eating; don't let him run/crawl/bumshuffle about with food.
- Remain in the room with him, concentrating at least a reasonable amount of your attention on what he and his food are up to.
- Some mums find that babies gag less when they are controlling the food themselves. An unexpected lump in a purée may be more likely to cause a gagging incident than controlled gumming of a steamed vegetable stick. So let him have some control of the spoon, particularly as the food gets more challenging.
- Texture is important.

'You do need to be careful about giving finger food. I used to give my son "squashy" things, not "pingy" things: so sticks of steamed carrot, but not raw apple – the carrot would "squadge" when he put it into his mouth, whereas the apple might've pinged to the back of his mouth when he bit a lump off.' *Hunkermunker*

- On a closely related point, avoid choking hazard foods in the early days, such as raw apple, uncut grapes, large meat chunks, popcorn and, heaven forefend, hard sweets.
- Do a first aid or infant resuscitation class before you start weaning, if at all possible. It will make you feel a lot more confident when baby starts making those spluttering noises.

Surely shome mishtake: first foods that shouldn't have been

So there you are, progressing carefully through the lovingly blended fruit purées, the vegetable purées and the hand-carved finger foods, when you find junior excitedly munching on the

(continued)

remains of a sausage roll/sugar packet/tea bag. You are so not alone. The infant palate is a many-splendoured, but unpredictable thing. Many Mumsnetters have babies with an inexplicable taste for baby wipes. In the interests of scientific advance, one mum bravely conducted this experiment:

'OK, girls, I'm about to try one ... (moves tongue around in mouth for a while) mmm ... hmmm ... mmm. They're not bad actually. Taste like really mild perfume ... sort of flowery. Doesn't make me want to retch, at least ...' *fastasleep*

But that's not all.

Bad:

'My son at eight months got the coffee essence out, somehow opened it with his teeth and had a good few glugs. I was speechless. Just stood staring at him while he smiled at me, tarlike liquid dribbling down his tiny face ...' *nigeltuffnell*

'Does it help if I point out that BabyDragon's first solids were an inflight magazine (yes, it went all the way through) and a handful of salty beach sand?' *ADragonIs4LifeNotJustHalloween*

Worse:

'My seven-month-old seems to have developed a real taste for cat biscuits. The problem is there are few places I can put them where he can't get them but the cats can. Every time I put him down he makes a beeline for them (even if they're out of sight) and immediately starts chomping them. I don't mind him tasting one or two, but something is telling me I shouldn't be letting him eat huge handfuls.' *Naetha*

'I used to eat them when I was a child, no problems here! <pads off to groom tail and play with toy mouse>' *ellideb*

Worst:

'Could be worse – my colleague's wife was in their kitchen, and wondered what their baby was eating. It turned out to be part of a mouse their cat had brought in. They never established how much he'd actually consumed ...' *jellibob*

Weaning Equipment

You could easily go out and buy a lot of weaning equipment. And who are we to rain on your parade? But if you want just the bare essentials:

'You need a baby, some food and a PVC home.' mrspnut

But if you want to get just that little bit more sophisticated:

For weaning with purées

- High chair – beanbags and bouncy chairs don't give enough support unless your bouncy chair has a fully upright setting. Some parents prefer the kind of high chair you scoot up to the table so baby can feel fully integrated into the family meal. Others like baby to have his own segregated tray for cleaning purposes. Scrutinise all high-chair candidates closely for ease of cleaning (unless you are Mrs StigoftheDump, nothing you own will get dirtier than a high chair). If it has lots of plastic crannies in which banana purée will gradually petrify, possibly preserving intact the fossils of peas for future generations to wonder at, begone with it.
- Ice-cube trays are the classic means for freezing homemade purées. Silicone ones are probably the easiest to extricate the cubes from. You pop the cubes out and into freezer bags. Which you label. Unless you want to feed him random yellowish food of uncertain date (we've all been there).
- Bibs, preferably wipe-clean. Pelican bibs with a lip at the bottom are good for catching at least some of the fallout.
- A good supply of small, sturdy plastic spoons. The soft rubbery ones are less likely to offend.
- Some kind of mashing equipment. This could be simply a fork or a potato masher. Many parents like to use a hand blender to get a really professional finish on the carrot purée and to break up fibrous foods that don't mash well, such as chicken.

'Don't bother with any of the fancy bowls with suction pads – they're useless until the child develops the desire to feed themselves rather than the curiosity to rip the bowl off the suction cup and fling it over their head.' *PrettyCandles*

Many parents have found that the suction bowls are particularly effective at dispersing a meal over the surrounding area because the force required for the baby to detach the bowl from the table ensures extreme acceleration when the bowl does finally come unstuck.

- Some kind of containers to transport food. These could be specially designed weaning pots or just smallish Tupperware.

For baby-led weaning

'High chair, sharp knife, pelican bib.' Aitch

Note: the sharp knife is for you to do chopping with.

Either way, and with an eye to what hits the floor, you might want some bits of PVC tablecloth, a cheap shower curtain, or some other type of splash mat for under the high chair (and a compost bin for that which gets away). A small cool bag is also useful to carry meals in when you are on the move.

Using a Spoon

Give baby her own spoon right from the start, but don't be surprised when she uses it to teethe on, poke herself in the eye or, if she is very advanced, catapult food from the bowl on to the paintwork. Many babies can stick a pre-loaded spoon into their own mouths quite young (and some won't brook any parental assistance in the matter), but the whole getting-the-food-on-the-spoon-in-the-first-place thing takes some time.

Let her keep practising, but don't necessarily expect very accomplished spoonwork until she is well into her second year.

'We went for the two-spoon approach (one for them, one for me) for as long as they put up with it. When they figure out how to shout 'No', 'Mine' and 'Self', then consider yourself redundant.' gigglewitch

Many parents introduce forks some time after the first birthday. Knives we leave to your own judgement. Some of us will probably let them sort that out for themselves when they leave home. If we think they are sufficiently responsible by then.

Salt: How Much Is OK?

The amount of salt that a baby should consume is very small indeed. The Food Standards Agency recommends that babies under 12 months should have less than 1g (0.03oz) of salt per day. From one to three years the limit is 2g (0.07oz). So bearing in mind that small amounts of salt occur naturally in some foods, don't add salt to anything you are cooking for a baby or to any family meal he might be partaking of (until you've siphoned his portion off).

Salt is a sneaky devil. It hides in bread, many tinned foods (including some tinned tomatoes), many breakfast cereals, smoked meats and fish. Ready meals can be especially villainous, as can shop-bought pasta sauces or pizzas. Ready-made stock cubes are often crammed with salt – you can either make your own stock, or there are some commercial low-salt varieties. Many parents think babies don't give a stuff about stock, but if you are making a family meal which baby is going to share, the rest of you might. Don't go mad, but do your shopping with an eye to the salt content. And unless you make your own bread (What? You don't make your own bread!?), keep bread consumption down to two slices a day, tops (that is a stupendous amount of bread in infant terms, anyhow).

But don't go all salt-paranoid:

'I always feel that what carries the salt is relevant, if you see what I mean. Crisps: no goodness in them therefore unacceptable. Houmous: chickpeas provide good vegetable protein and roughage, therefore acceptable. Cheese: also goodness in it, therefore acceptable. If you never add salt/soy sauce/stock cubes to homemade food, and you use homemade food as much as possible, I think baby probably gets the right amount of salt. But also remember that the occasional crust of pizza may also mean the occasional relaxed mummy: therefore good!'

PrettyCandles

And as long as you are mostly careful, the odd excursion to the Dark Side is probably fine:

'Quavers are a bit salty, but not the Devil's toenail clippings.' PortAndLemon

'My daughter discovered at a very young age that she loves Doritos, when she pinched some of ours! And she is still alive!' FanjofortheMammaries

Encouraging Baby to Eat More Vegetables

Some babies get a bit stuck on the apple and pear purées and set their lips firmly against the lovely grass-green courgette entrée you have prepared, the broccoli and potato numnums, the carrot and pea aeroplane (open wide and let it fly in; Mummy doesn't want to keep begging you ...). But it's not terribly surprising he likes the sweet stuff; breast milk is very sweet.

There are a variety of ways of encouraging babies towards a more varied and savoury diet. With a younger baby, mixing a sweet with a savoury purée, then gradually upping the savoury component until there's nothing sweet left can be a good gradualist approach. Sometimes, just getting out the more interesting stuff – spag Bol, fish pie, mild curry, smushed to an appropriate texture – is the answer. Vegetable purées can also be made more interesting by adding a little homemade (or commercial low-salt) stock or other flavourings:

'I've pushed on with the veg though and moved to "tastier" or stronger combinations, which seems to be working, albeit slowly. Things like roasted veg, also mixed veg that has been softened in a little butter or olive oil with garlic, often featuring onions and leeks. For me, these are much tastier than carrots on their own, as I like veg, but am not keen on plain, boiled, steamed puréed veg with no butter or anything tasty!' Babamumma

Finger foods can be your ally here – foods which are spurned in liquid form may be welcomed enthusiastically when they can be gummed to death. Items snatched from an adult's plate may be much more appealing than the dubious muck you have chosen to give him in his own bowl. However, you are unlikely to fool him by sitting down to your own large bowl of turnip purée – he wasn't born (quite) yesterday.

Refined Sugar

When – if at all – do you introduce them to the demon substance, the drug of choice for the under-twos? What do you do if Granny is trying to buy baby's affection with chocolate fingers and fruit shoots, while you are rustling up quinoa and hemp smoothies in the kitchen? Is it too late when you look down at him in the coffee shop to find him drooling at you beatifically, while extruding bits of a sugar packet? And if he gets a taste for it, is he doomed to a diet of marshmallows and Krispy Kremes and a lifetime of obesity?

Your attitude may well depend on your own food experiences. Some of us were cheerfully raised on cherry pop, novelty cereals and Angel Delight at the height of the Western world's enthusiasm for synthetic foods and feel we have emerged relatively unscathed. Others may blame their own crummy eating habits and lardiness of thigh on early exposure to fruit salad chews and marshmallow shrimps, rather than fruit salad and real shrimp.

Many Mumsnetters agree that it is both wise and practicable to keep baby off the hard stuff until he is at least 12 months old.

'Under-ones, who don't know what they are missing out on should have an extremely healthy diet, as we should all make the most of them not being old enough for pester power,' advises one pragmatic Mumsnetter. After that, particularly once you are on to a second or third child and/or he starts attending children's parties, you may struggle, unless you build yourself a no-sugar bunker and repel all intruders:

'It is very, very difficult to stop older babies wanting to share what their older siblings are having. Mine don't tend to have much chocolate and very rarely have sweets, but when they've been to parties and come back with stuff (which they share – they don't get to keep it to themselves!) it is extremely difficult to exclude the baby.' DaisyMOO

Not keeping sweets, cakes and suchlike in the house (or at least hiding your mummystash in the shed) can be a good way of keeping exposure down, as well as avoiding shops where sweeties are arrayed at pram level (this can be tricky though).

The inter-generational sugar battle

So far as this is concerned, many parents choose to concede ground occupied by grandparents:

'My son knows that chocolate biscuits exist at Grandma's house, but are not available at home.' MadamePlatypus

This approach will be harder though if you have a grandparent providing regular childcare, and you may have to have a proper discussion about what foods you are not happy with (or sack Granny when you find her filling baby's bottle with Value Cola). Some parents are firmly of the view that they alone should have control over what their children ingest, at least during infancy:

'My partner has her at his parents' house today – I'm supposed to be sleeping, as I'm on night shift. When I rang him to see how she was, she was eating a biscuit. I could hear mother-in-law in the background saying, but it's a Cow and Gate organic biscuit; yes, but it's still full of sugar and, more importantly, SHE DOESN'T NEED A BISCUIT! My aunt wanted her to try caramel shortbread on Friday and my dad has already asked when she can have ice cream. I don't want her to eat stuff like that until she is old enough to ask for it, and then I will take an "everything-in-moderation" approach, but not when she is only nine months!' LaDiDaDi

But why does Granny push sugar and other crap, anyway? And can you do anything about it? There are various theories as to why the older generation hang about on street corners wearing trench coats, which they open to reveal sherbet fountains and Wagon Wheels, dangling like knock-off Rolexes.
    Some are simple:

- 'Food = love to the older generations, I think.' luckylady74
- 'I think it's because they're stupid, tbh. I've tried to think of other options but, in the end, I always plump for that simplistic explanation. Or they think the child will love them more if they give her as much sugar as she can tolerate without vomiting.' Caligula

Other parents try to appreciate the complex historical factors that have led to their three-month-old gnawing a Walnut Whip. Changing advice may be a big factor:

- 'My mum was told by a health visitor to put drinking chocolate in my milk as I wouldn't drink it; I ended up having quite bad baby teeth as a result.' *pinkmalibu*
- 'Ha, that's nothing to what my mother-in-law tells me about my husband when he was *two weeks old* ... apparently she bought this type of rusky stuff from the chemist that you mushed up in their milk. (Grins while watching many and varied Mumsnetters clutching at their chests and asking for their pills emoticon.)' *sparklemagic*

- Things were, of course, different in all sorts of other ways too, in the olden times:

- 'My brother got dropped on his head when my mum carried him in the car, so they decided it was safer to leave him on the parcel shelf instead.' *gigglinggoblin*
Some parents find they can relax a bit about the whole thing if they remember back to their own childhoods:

- 'But I have really fond memories of the "rules" being broken at my grandparents' houses as a child, i.e. an endless supply of biscuits, cakes and treats. (Lovely days ... can't remember *ever* being told off by my grandparents.) I think this is why I've had to "let it go" somewhat with my daughters. I do have to bite my tongue a lot because the sugar-on-tap is truly *astonishing*. I did put my foot down at mother-in-law's once when my daughter demanded a bowl of ice cream at 10 a.m. and mother-in-law was dithering by the freezer.' *notnowbernard*
- 'When me and my sisters stayed at my grandparents' house, they used to let us have cream cakes for breakfast. We *loved* it. My two stayed with my parents last weekend and I was shocked that my mum had fed them Weetabix with sugar on. <mental note to self: get a bloody grip!!>' *liath*

Sometimes the love is more important than the food:

- My much-missed father-in-law used to cook turkey dinosaurs and chips for my daughter when she visited (about every six weeks) because she never got them at home. It was a lovely thing, and she still remembers it, and how happy she was when he did it for her. We went there for Christmas lunch when she was three, and she burst into tears when he put a lovely roast meal in front of her because: "That's not what you cook me, Grandad!" I was mortified, but guess what he rushed off to the kitchen and did?!' *seeker*

And sometimes you can find tactful ways to edit the food:

- 'I've just said to my mum, "Look, my daughter loves you; she can't love you any more than she already does, not for all the cake in the world. But I will like you much less if you keep feeding her sweet things when she's just as happy with a bit of carrot."' *AitchTwoOh*

And, when all else fails, you can always mutter the unsayable to yourself, or share your pain anonymously on the internet:

- 'What I would love to say to my mother-in-law on the "it-didn't-do-mine-any-harm" theme is. "Didn't it? Your sons are obese, one almost had a heart attack at 41 and the thinnest one lives with me!"' *chipmonkey*

Getting your own (gingerbread) house in order

Parents with their own cake habit may struggle to find the right answer when they encounter tiny fingers in the chocolate icing:

'What about if you are eating some chocolate or cake or a biscuit and your baby comes and asks for some? Do you say, 'No'? I by no means sit there scoffing cakes, etc. all day, but do have them as part of a generally healthy diet and let my daughter do the same. I don't give her her own slice of cake, nor do I offer her mine, but if she sees it and wants some, I'll let her have a mouthful or two. My thinking is that she will want it more if I don't let her try it, but I don't encourage her to eat lots of sweets either.' claireybee

Some babies have a very fit and proper sense of what food is Mummy's food:

'Actually, today he removed a chocolate finger from my hand, inspected it, sniffed it, then shoved it into *my* mouth. That's my boy!'

ViscountessPetitLapin

Note: not all sweet things are created equal. The worst foods from a dental perspective are things which stick to the teeth or hang about exuding sugar in the mouth for a long time – lollipops, hard and jelly sweets, even flapjacks. A child who takes a couple of squares of good-quality chocolate with his parents postprandially is more likely to grow up with better teeth than a lolly-sucker.

Read the labels

It is easy to be beguiled in the supermarket by products marketed for babies which may contain more sugar than you are happy with. Check labels carefully, even on products called HealthyNaturalHappyOrganicBaby fromage frais. You can always sweeten plain yoghurt with a little fruit purée or finely chopped fruit, if needed.

Whatever you do, don't be tempted by 'no-sugar' or 'low-sugar' products that contain artificial sweeteners.

Mumsnetiquette: Sweet surrender

On the sugar question, Mumsnetters tend to converge around a kind of pragmatic Golden Mean:

'Stuff with refined sugar in is far sweeter than the natural sweetness of fruit. If you eat a slice of choccy cake and then a plum, the plum will taste quite tart. So I do worry that giving babies sweet stuff will reset their taste buds to the sweeter end of the spectrum. I've definitely noticed with my two that they went off fruit for a bit after encountering biscuits.' *welliemum*

'I didn't give my son (14 months) sugar until he turned one. He only rarely has it in stuff (if I buy rice pudding rather than making it, for example) but I did say that he could join in at a recent birthday party and have a tiny bit of cake and a couple of chocolate mice. Would never buy them for him, but a teeny bit once in a blue moon is OK – I don't want him thinking certain foods are taboo! There was an interesting experiment that shows if you restrict foods, children want them more (this also applies to healthy foods too, so you can use it to your advantage!).' *bohemianbint*

'Yes, it is marginally healthier for small babies not to have sweets, I'm sure. And fruit is healthier than Sherbet Dip Dabs. But it's not true that in neolithic times babies would taste nothing sweeter than fruit. Breast milk is very sweet indeed! I think we are "wired" to go for sweet stuff (and fatty stuff and food in large quantities, in general) by nature, not nurture. Nature hasn't quite caught up with the fact that nowadays, we live in a world full of food and lovely gadgets and so we get fatter and fatter!' *Aloha*

'The more good food you give them and the more enthusiastic you are about it, and the more they join in with buying/growing/ preparing/cooking it, the better they will eat. It gives them a fantastic start and builds great habits. They may also want shite when they are older, but less than if they had been given it all

(continued)

the time. My son does enjoy horrid sweets when he comes across them, but he also eats mountains of fruit habitually and gets excited about cabbage and leeks.' *TooTicky*

'My uncle was a dentist
kids not allowed sweets (we looked at them in horror)
kids HUGE
clichéd but true.' *LadyCodofCodford*

'My daughter (precious firstborn) had her first taste of chocolate at two and a half. I will never forget the "Mummy–there-is-stuff-this-delicious-in-the-world-and-YOU-KEPT-IT-FROM-ME" expression on her face. My son (neglected second-born) was crawling round the floor at a party at nine months and emerged with a huge grin and a handful of discarded (probably pre-chewed) Maltesers. They are now seven and 12 with a good diet, a good relationship with food, good teeth and there is no discernible difference in their taste for sweet stuff. I think it depends on the child, not the diet.' *seeker*

'Don't be hard on yourself. When my brother and I were growing up, we had a Weetabix with jam on as a special treat! Didn't do us any harm. <gibber>' *AlistairSim*

Food Fight: Fussy Eaters and Food Fads

So one day, you are congratulating yourself on the fact that your baby eats 49 varieties of root vegetable and smacks his lips after each one, and the next day he decides he will henceforth only consume bacon-flavoured crisps and the waxy exterior of Babybels. Despair not. Tattoo the following on your wrist:

- Don't fight about it. If you get all tense and push too much, you are likely to make things worse. If he can get an interesting reaction from not eating, he'll do it again.

- Don't focus too much on what he eats on a particular day. If you look at what he eats in the course of a whole week, you will probably find it's fairly balanced. Or not, so maybe look at a whole month ...
- Keep offering new foods and old foods that have fallen out of favour. Perhaps take a break from something which is really unpopular and bring it back with all the glister of novelty after a week or two.
- Sit down and eat with him. Let him see you enjoying the food. Better yet, find some omnivorous children to dine with him and pique his interest.
- Have a buffet. Serving up little bowls of finger foods often stirs a jaded palate.
- Well, it's controversial, but you could make little faces and scale-models of the Gherkin out of his food. It could be fun for you, even if he doesn't actually eat the damned stuff.
- Some babies do honestly go for that train coming-into-the-tunnel, open-wide malarkey. At least for a period.
- Try hiding nutritious foods he has been rejecting in foods he likes. You can grind up all sorts into pasta sauce or mashed potato or 'gravy', and you can use the cooking water from vegetables to add some vitamins to a sauce.
- Remember that they all go through their own individual phases, and most get fussy or faddy at some stage. Some don't want to eat anything much one day – or week – and are hungry as hippos the next. Babies do not starve themselves.

Vegetarian Babies

You can raise your baby on a vegetarian or vegan diet, but you may have to plan a little more carefully to ensure she is getting enough vitamins B12 and D, protein and iron. Pulses are your friends and tofu is another source of protein, but avoid the very processed tofu which can be high in salt. Some meat substitutes will be unsuitable for similar reasons. Quorn should not be given more than very occasionally to children under two because it is high in fibre, low-fat and highly processed. Try serving foods rich in vitamin C with meals to assist in iron absorption. Some Mumsnetters swear by dried apricots for adding more iron.

'The Vegetarian Society and Vegan Society have factsheets on food for veggie and vegan infants (www.vegansociety.com; www.vegsoc.org). I used quite a lot of fortified cereals. Cereal, plus milk (breast or soya), plus fruit and you've really got most of the essential nutrients for the day.' Fennel

As many Mumsnetters will attest, a baby can be raised healthily on a vegan diet, but if you are planning to avoid all animal products, it's probably worth taking some medical advice, just to make sure you are getting all the right nutrients (and enough of them) into your baby.

What vegetarian infants eat

'Favourites are mild beany chilli with rice or quinoa, chickpea and spinach curry with sweet potato mash, roast vegetables and rice pudding made with coconut milk and cream.' *mmelody*

'My "baby dhal" went down well with my six-month-old – just softened an onion, added red lentils and water. Cooked until mushy, then added a lump of creamed coconut and lots of chopped spinach. He loved it.' *LavenderMist*

'Try low-salt/sugar baked beans, houmous with toast, rice mixed in with puy lentils and/or beans.' *witchandchips*

'You can get almond and cashew nut butters which avoid the peanut issue, and these are great on toast fingers.' *mistlethrush*

'Lentils are invaluable – and popular – especially with garlic.' *TootickyDoves*

'Hiding pulses in pasta sauce is a good move.' *jaype*

There are many vegetarian cookbooks aimed at the junior market but the one most frequently mentioned by Mumsnetters is probably Carol Timperley's *Baby and Child Vegetarian Recipes: Over 150 Healthy and Delicious Dishes for Your Young Family.*

Baby Drinks

A young baby whose main food is still milk is likely to get all the water she needs from milk. As she cuts back on milk and eats more grown-up foods, she may need to drink more water And some babies are a bit water-resistant. Here are some Mumsnetters' tips for hydrating her:

- You can stop using cooled boiled water at six months and just give her tap water. Don't offer her mineral water in the first year.

  'Just keep offering a beaker of water, leaving it on her tray to drink/play with, and she will start taking more eventually.' *Tommy*

  'How about leaving a beaker of water with his toys? This worked with my reluctant-water-drinker – no pressure for her to drink it, so she just played with it and then eventually started to drink it.' *Reginaphilangy*

- Cold water is gripey for some tummies. Try serving it at room temperature.
- 'Try sparkling water with a baby over one. My daughter thinks it is a great treat and calls it "bubble juice". Also, try drinking through a straw as this can seem more fun.' *SazzlesA*
- A Very Special and Personal Cup may encourage a slightly older non-drinker.
- Fennel tea or camomile tea appeal to some infant palates.

And then there is the question of juice. We all know water is better for teeth, but a hardened water refusenik might be lured by juice. Or you might want to introduce some orange juice to a vegetarian baby to aid iron absorption. Dilution is the key – even one part of juice in ten may be attractive to a baby. If you are serving dilute juice, don't put it in a bottle; use an open beaker or one with a free-flowing spout.

Beware of 'baby juice' – it is just diluted juice sold at great expense in small bottles. Watch out for also 'juice dinks' and squashes. These may be loaded with sugar or artificial sweeteners.

Most babies and toddlers will get enough liquid in one way or another, but look out for dry lips, dark or strong-smelling urine, perpetually dry nappies and constipation as possible signs of dehydration.

The Weaning of Life (Wherein We Get a Little Philosophical on the Subject of Nourishment)

Weaning can have its hairy-scary moments and its tiny moments of triumph. It may well bore you senseless and make the contents of your wardrobe look like a pile of casualties from a battle in the Land of Root Vegetables. But remember, the whole process of weaning is one of those formative parenting events, and one which glues the generations together, like weaning utensils coated in dried-out banana purée. And, just maybe, one that brings you to a better understanding of your own parents.

Once you have trained your own child to eat food, you will understand the almost universal look of pride on the face of a parent observing his or her offspring consume vegetable matter (something you can even observe in the natural world if you are so inclined, at least in those species which don't fight their own progeny for food or eat them). And you will know why your father made you sit in front of that heap of really very cold and disgusting broccoli until you ate a bit (which is, incidentally, why you won't touch broccoli as an adult). And why the mothers of lardy thirty-somethings anxiously chivvy them into second helpings of pudding. Or nag them incessantly about their diets. But maybe that is something else again ...

And, perhaps some day in the future – when you no longer have little scabs of carrot on your jumper and your acquaintances have stopped ducking into the newsagent to avoid your tales of courgette-stick success – your eye may alight on a box of tiny pasta shapes in the supermarket and, just maybe, it will stir a sentimental feeling ...

Chapter Six

Baby's Health

In this chapter ...

'Never be afraid to stand up for your baby. It can be hard at times, but a wise consultant once said to me that a good doctor should always listen to a parent's concerns because, sometimes, they can be right and the medical profession can be wrong.' smudgethepuppydog

It is astonishing how many previously carefree and risk-tolerant types – the sort of people who nonchalantly toss scorpions out of their shoes or go to work with raging flu or mild gangrene – develop a sort of Woody-Allenitis by proxy when baby comes along: is he snuffling? Is he hot? Is he breathing? What's that horrific rash?

The thing you don't necessarily anticipate about motherhood is what a fearful condition it is. Of course some of the anxieties are worth getting over, but a sustained attentiveness about the health of a very small and helpless person is actually pretty reasonable.

What follows is in no way intended to be a substitute for medical advice (add the words 'SEEK MEDICAL ADVICE IF YOU ARE CONCERNED' to every section), but is a broad guide to the sort of issues which may arise in relation to baby's health, with some tips from Mumsnetters on how to deal with smaller problems (like cradle cap and nappy rash), some pointers on how you might detect more serious conditions (such as reflux and bronchiolitis) and some thoughts on how you might go about researching issues like when and whether to vaccinate your baby.

Send For the Doctor, Send For the Nurse, Send For the Lady With the Yellow-spotted Purse: When Should You Get Medical Advice?

It's worth having one of those bulky books written by a paediatrician (Sears' *Baby Book*, Spock or similar) so you can look up symptoms in the first instance. But many people take their little tiny babies down to the GP quite a lot. And that's fine. If your instincts say that something is wrong, you may be right and GPs generally expect to see new parents and babies with some frequency. There's no shame whatsoever in just coming home again feeling reassured.

GPs often will make emergency appointments, particularly for babies and will also have an 'out-of-hours' service to discuss issues which arise, well, outside of surgery hours. You can also call NHS direct for 24-hour health advice, but, obviously, if you suspect a baby is seriously ill, you should go straight to the accident and emergency room at your local hospital.

What to Keep in Your Medicine Chest

Mumsnetters' medicine chests come in two varieties: conventional and alternative/lentil-weaver. Many mix and match between the two:

The conventional medicine chest

These range from minimal (some Calpol and plasters) to positively enormous (in the case of a mother from 'a medical and search and rescue background'). This list does hangover cures and nail varnish. So starting with the more widely found items and working onwards to the more obscure, here's what Mumsnetters like:

- Plasters of various shapes and sizes
- Large dressings
- Thermometer (the digital ear variety are pricey, but easy to use on smalls)
- Antihistamine tablets (and liquid for smaller children)
- A paracetamol-based product suitable for babies/children
- An ibuprofen-based product suitable for babies/children
- Vaseline
- Nappy cream

- Teething gel
- TCP
- Dettol
- Savlon
- Antiseptic wipes
- Rehydration sachets for diarrhoea and vomiting
- Tweezers
- Scissors
- Plastic syringe for administering medications and/or plastic measuring spoons
- Cotton wool
- Rubber gloves
- Ice pack
- Torch
- Foil survival blanket

The lentil weavers' medicine chest

Ideally, items might be arranged in a cabinet cunningly constructed from quinoa mosaics and recycled Mooncups:

- Arnica for bruising
- Tea tree oil: disinfectant
- Lavender oil: for burns
- Aloe vera gel: for burns/sunburn
- Manuka honey: for sore throats and burns
- Calendula cream for cuts and grazes
- Homeopathic pills:
  - Aconite 6c homeopathic tissue salts for shock
  - Chamomilla 6c homeopathic tissue salts for teething/toothache
  - Arsen alb for diarrhoea
  - Nat mur for streaming colds
  - Pulsatilla for colds with thick catarrh/discharge
  - Nux vom for nausea/vomiting
- Camomile tea/infusion for sticky eyes/styes
- Echinacea
- Bach Rescue Remedy

Note: remember to keep all medicines safely locked away (see 'Stuff They Swallow', p. 275).

Birthmarks

'Stork marks'are covered in Chapter One. Other marks baby may have include the following:

Strawberry hemangiomas

Basically, an overgrowth of blood vessels under the skin, these are raised red circles which appear in the few weeks after birth, grow during the first year of a baby's life and then shrivel up, usually over the next two years. They generally disappear altogether some time during childhood. They may be very small, but can be as big as a golf ball. If they are on an eyelid or somewhere they interfere with function, they may need treatment. Speak to your GP if you are worried.

Café-au-lait spots

These are light coffee-coloured spots which may look a bit like bruise. As baby grows they will seem smaller relative to her size, and most are cosmetically untroubling: 'We call it her angel kiss,' says a mum. If an older child is bothered by a large spot, laser treatment may be a possibility.

Port wine stains

These are flat marks which may be quite small or many centimetres in size, start off pink and darken to red or purple. They can be of cosmetic concern and sometimes cause other problems. Treatment, particularly by lasers, may be effective in fading these marks. See your GP.

Mongolian blue spots

Harmless bruise-like spots, these are most commonly found on baby's lower back or buttocks. They are most common in people of Afro-Caribbean or Asian descent, but can crop up on any baby. They fade, but never disappear completely.

Do get medical advice (and see Resources, p. 434, for support groups), but try not to stress too much about birthmarks:

'Even if he had never had laser treatment for his café-au-lait spot, our son was and is beautiful, and I regret the time I spent looking at the mark, worrying about it, when I could have been enjoying him as a baby!' pralinegirl

Bronchiolitis

Bronchiolitis is a viral illness usually found in babies under a year. It can last up to about two weeks and is pretty common in the winter months. In some cases it can be very serious indeed:

'Not enough is known about this illness, and I always wonder why we have massive campaigns about meningitis (which we also need, of course), when many more children are admitted to hospital with bronchiolitis each year and a lot of parents have never heard of it. It would be so simple to put a little card in the red book, like you get about SIDS and meningitis, just so more people are aware of it.' Fiveplusbump

Symptoms of bronchiolitis include:

- Cold symptoms with a worsening musical cough
- Rapid, shallow, noisy breathing
- Fever and sleeplessness
- Paleness, lethargy, lack of appetite.

Try propping baby up to sleep, using a humidifier and increasing fluids. Keep him calm and give him small, frequent feeds.

A few babies with bronchiolitis will require hospitalisation for oxygen therapy and/or tube feeding, so seek urgent medical attention if:

- baby is showing any of these signs of respiratory distress: flared nostrils, rapid breathing, drawing in of the chest under the ribcage or between the ribs or of the skin at the bottom of the neck, head bobbing from the strain of breathing, blueness around the lips
- he is very lethargic/hard to rouse
- he has a worsening cough
- he has any symptoms of dehydration
- he is drinking less than 50 per cent of his usual intake
- he has a persistently high fever.

Go to A&E if you are concerned. Bronchiolitis can worsen rapidly.

Spot-U-Like: Chicken Pox

Chicken pox begins with small red spots or a rash which turn into the characteristic fluid-filled blisters. The blisters burst open to leave sores which become itchy and scab over. They can spread anywhere on the body, including – painfully – the genitals, inside the mouth and in ears and the eyes. Baby is likely also to be feverish and may have stomach pain and nausea. The blisters last up to ten days, and baby is infectious from 48 hours before the spots appear until all of the blisters have scabbed over. The incubation period for those exposed is up to 21 days.

Chicken pox is not usually dangerous in children, but can be serious in adults and in tiny babies (up to about a week old), so make sure you aren't visited by any newborns, women about to give birth and adults who have not had chicken pox while your baby is suffering. The Mumsnet consensus is that it is not right to take an infectious child to public places where tiny babies, immune-suppressed adults or pregnant women may be exposed, so you may have a tedious week with a grumpy baby at home.

To while away the hours:

- Lukewarm baths with sodium bicarbonate in the water or oat baths (as described under eczema, p. 263) or Aveeno baths are soothing. Try popping in a couple of camomile teabags as well. Pat baby dry afterwards.

- Calamine lotion painted on the spots works for some – but not all – babies. 'Calamine cream is much better than the lotion,' thinks one Mumsnetter – and the cream is easier to apply to the scalp or for a bigger baby or toddler to apply himself.
- Cut baby's nails so she doesn't scar herself too badly scratching.
- Baby paracetamol or ibuprofen are good for pain and fever.
- For a very very itchy baby, a prescription antihistamine may help. **Note**: if you are using over-the-counter antihistamines and antihistamine creams, check that they are age-appropriate (they are generally for children over one year).
- 'Calpol and keeping as cool as possible helped. My son couldn't wear a nappy, as it was too uncomfortable. Getting warm made him itchy.' *triceratops*
- 'Try the homeopathic remedy Rhus tox (available from Boots).' *Prufrock*

You should generally take baby to the GP to confirm the diagnosis and especially if symptoms are severe (particularly fever, headache, cough, aversion to light or respiratory distress).

Cold Comfort: How to Get Through the Winter Bugs

Some babies seem to have an almost constant cold. Here are some Mumsnetters' favourite ways of alleviating symptoms:

- A humidifier can be great. Or run a hot bath or shower and sit in a steamy bathroom with baby for half an hour. Be careful the steam is not scalding.
- A nasal aspirator may help to evacuate a very stuffed-up nose. And can be, you know, quite good fun to use.
- Give lots of fluids.
- Raise the feet at the head end of the cot with about 7.5cm (3in) worth of books.
- Try saline nasal drops to clear really blocked nostrils.
- For a feverish baby, administer baby paracetamol or baby ibuprofen.

A very high or prolonged fever and breathing difficulties are the main cold-related symptoms of concern to watch out for. And remember there's no shame in taking your baby to the doctor: many Mumsnetters suggest you take any newborn or tiny baby with a cold to the GP, just to be on the safe side. Very small babies can get sicker very rapidly.

Be careful about cough and cold medications. Many, for example Medised (formerly prized by parents for its famous sedative effects), are no longer recommended for the under-sixes.

The Crying Game: Colic

Pre-parenthood, most of us probably had a dim idea that colic was a kind of digestive discomfort suffered by babies, associated with burping and farting. Or possibly something that sheep get when they eat a load of apples then lie on their backs with their stomachs blown out until someone punctures them.

In fact, colic is the Loch Ness Monster, the Bermuda Triangle, the Area 51 of infant health. No one is really sure what it is:

'The definition of colic is unexplained crying for at least three hours a day, at least three times a week. It's not a diagnosis of an illness.' tiktok

Colic tends to start around three weeks. It's generally over by about three months, but can go on longer. It is unexplained crying which occurs in an *otherwise healthy* infant. So don't conclude that your miserable crying baby is 'just' colicky without considering (with your GP) whether there may be a root cause of the crying and discomfort, such as reflux or food allergies.

Some babies suffer only in the late afternoons/evenings. Some babies are colicky all day. The general modern view is that colic is probably not caused by gas, but that colicky babies may appear to be especially windy because they gulp air while crying. None the less, a lot of colic-relieving techniques focus on getting the air out of baby's system.

So here are some things which might help baby to be less unhappy, you to be more sane and both of you to get through what can be a nightmarish period:

- Some parents swear by cranial osteopathy – gentle application of pressure to the baby's head, neck and spine to release tension believed to be caused by the squishing of the skull bones during birth:

  'In case you're wondering, it's terribly gentle what they do – it looks as if they are caressing the baby's head with their fingers.' *mistlethrush*

- Things which help to eliminate the windiness – whether that is causing the crying or being caused by it – can be a blessing. Wind treatments such as Infacol and Colief are popular.
- Some bottles seem to be better than others for windy bottle-fed babies, so experiment with bottles and teats.
- Feeding relatively upright, then keeping baby upright for half an hour after feeding is good.
- Cluster-feeding (small, frequent demand-feeds) in the afternoon/ evening often soothes a colicky baby.
- Sling-plus-dancing-plus-music gets many parents and babies through those difficult late afternoons. The colic dance, as you will discover, is quite fast, but not entirely manic, and probably involves movement up, down, back, forth and side to side. Your partner may be held upright or (with care) in the 'tiger-in-the-tree' position described overleaf. Or he may be suspended in a sling. Music is a matter for your own personal taste and that of your partner – it doesn't *have* to be Classic FM, but loud disco is unlikely to be the right thing for him at this stage of his life.
- Various massage and exercise techniques work with some babies:

  'Try really working her legs. I push them around like she is on a bike, then squash her knees into her chest. I really work them, and it squeezes wind out.' *treedelivery*

- 'Positioning – we always winded our daughter in an upright position, rubbing left-hand side (massaging stomach). Also, in the middle of a colicky attack, we used to drape her over our knees, letting pelvis and legs hang down under their own weight. This is supposed to create loads of room for the digestive tract/bowel, aiding the movement of trapped wind and bubbles.' *west3*

'The other good holding position for colic is called something like "the tiger in the tree". It's really hard to describe, but goes something like this:

Hold your arm at right angles across your body with your palm upwards. The baby's body rests on your forearm, with an arm and a leg on each side of your forearm. The baby's head rests on your arm, tucked into your bent elbow. With your other hand, use the heel of your hand to rub from bottom to top of the baby's back.' *Littlefish*

'We used to find that the "tiger-in-the-tree" hold worked for us. Our son would fall asleep like that. We also used to put him on a playmat on his tummy during the day a lot, and that helped too. Moving his legs around, as if he were cycling, was also great for him, as was gently massaging his tummy in a circle. I also used to find winding him regularly during feeds would help (say every ten minutes). And I used to prop his Moses basket up at night too, and this helped him sleep better.' *intergalacticwalrus*

- 'We found a few coping strategies that worked with us. Put her in her pram and roll back and forth over the edge of a rug or a power cord. Something about the bumpy ride that helps. You or your husband could have a deep bath and take her in with you.' *sdr*
- 'Try swaddling baby (wrapping a blanket/sheet fairly closely round), then holding her against your shoulder and patting her back slowly. Apparently, if you do this once a second, it reminds them of the heartbeat in the womb, and the swaddling makes them feel secure. This calmed her down at times when nothing else worked.' *Joanne*

For many people, living with colic is just a question of coping until it passes. You will be so damned happy when it's over. Truly.

Eyes Wide Shut: Conjunctivitis

The term conjunctivitis tends to be used for a variety of viral, bacterial and allergic eye complaints in babies. Baby is likely to have red, weepy eyes, swollen lids and a pussy discharge. Watching an interested pram-peerer recoil from the sight of your beloved squinting up through a little veil of pus is yet another of those magical moments with which infancy is so liberally strewn.

If you can manage it, breast milk may be the miracle cure for baby's sticky eyes, as it 'contains antibacterial agents and stuff that dissolves the gunge', as one mum puts it. Also, regular cleaning with warm, recently boiled water on a piece of clean cotton wool is a good idea. Wash your hands after you touch baby's eyes and throw away the dirty cotton wool. Make sure you use a fresh piece of cotton wool for each wipe – never use one piece for both eyes. Wash his bedding and anything else which comes near his face, including his hands.

If the symptoms are severe or do not respond to these home remedies, see your GP who may prescribe saline drops or an antibiotic.

Tough Jobs – Someone Has to Do Them: Constipation

Frequency of pooing is not the main issue here. Some babies poo very frequently, especially when tiny, while others, as they get bigger, seem to save their waste products for up to several days at a time, in order to delight you with a really sizeable, right up-the-back-grazing-the-hairline-style poo.

What *is* a problem for baby are dry, difficult-to-pass poos. Constipation is not common in breastfed babies, but some formula-fed babies will be afflicted. Generally, constipation is most common once baby is eating solid food. So if baby is struggling, straining, in pain and is producing sad little pellets or nothing at all, try the following:

- Give water at frequent intervals. If your baby isn't drinking from one kind of bottle or cup, try something else. Some babies struggle with sippy or sucky cups and need an open cup, perhaps a Doidy cup (one of those slanted cups).
- Some babies are constipated by bananas, so try cutting these out for a while if they feature in baby's diet.
- Give her lots of fresh fruit and vegetables (full of soluble fibre), but don't overdo the non-soluble fibre. A baby who is eating, say, two Weetabix in a sitting, may suffer from constipation, much as a baby who is getting too little fibre:

'I find the whole fibre thing confusing. I just thought fibre was fibre, but now I know that soluble fibre in fruit and veg is different to insoluble fibre, in bran, for example.

As I didn't know this, I think I made the mistake of stuffing my daughter with insoluble fibre, which then sucked water from her bowel and also made her full. She'd have been better with soluble fibre, as it's less filling, so she would have had a varied vitamin-rich diet. All fibre was not created equal, it turns out.' *treedelivery*

- Try diluted prune juice but, again, don't overdo it or you may find yourself with an extreme poo situation of the opposite kind.

'For my son, when it got bad, I used to purée prunes and mix with stewed apple or some natural yoghurt.' *thisisyesterday*

Dried apricots chopped or puréed and mixed in food may also help.
- Try changing formula. Some babies seem to be particularly bunged up by 'follow-on' milk.
- And:

'I KNOW you're not doing this, but just in case ... Are you sure you're not making formula too "strong"? My son had a few bottles of formula, and I put the powder in the bottle then topped it up to the proper level with water instead of measuring the water first, then adding the powder. He was incredibly constipated almost immediately. Worth checking, even though I'm sure you've got more sense than I did!' *seeker*

If baby struggles frequently with constipation, is really distressed when pooing or has bleeding from his anus, see a doctor. He may need treatment with a laxative or may be suffering from a food intolerance.

Cradle Cap (or 'Cradle Crap', As It Is Sometimes Known)

The main issue with bad cradle cap may be overcoming your own shame, as well-wishers peer into the pram and their faces curdle as they are confronted by your infant wearing what appears to be a tight-fitting hat made of old earwax. Ach, it's not usually that bad; *your* baby may well just have a few scaly yellow patches, well hidden by hair.

Cradle cap is a generally harmless condition, but it can be unsightly. It is a form of seborrhoeic dermatitis (which, in another incarnation, causes those baby pimples discussed on p. 47) and it usually improves with age.

Many Mumsnetters confess, a little shamefacedly, to prising cradle cap off baby's head while baby is feeding. It is an enjoyable pastime from the same stable of disgusting hobbies as nit-combing and using that snot-sucking device to clean babies' noses. But it is not *really* recommended because it can leave sore patches.

For mild cradle cap, try rubbing a little olive oil into baby's scalp. (Do not use arachis oil – peanut oil – which was, at one time, recommended for cradle cap, as it can trigger peanut allergy; nor should you use 'baby oil', which often has additives, such as perfume.) Leave the oil for a few hours or overnight, then wash out using mild baby shampoo. Repeat if necessary. Brush baby's hair with a soft brush regularly to stimulate the scalp. Scaly patches behind the ears and lurking in neck folds should be gently washed with warm water.

For more severe cases, try a medicated shampoo such as Dentinox and comb *very carefully* with a nit comb to remove the loosened flakes (assuming your baby has hair). A soft toothbrush may also be effective. Brush or comb against the grain of the scales. Don't shampoo more than once a week or you will dry baby's scalp and make the problem worse.

If none of the above works, consider slathering your baby's head with petroleum jelly morning and night and doing some gentle massage.

Or just leave it – 'it's only skin', and the hair will eventually cover it.

If baby has red patches on her scalp and/or other parts of her body, you may be looking at seborrhoeic eczema and should see your GP.

Croup

Croup is an infection of the larynx and trachea and is characterised by a barking cough and often wheezing or laboured breathing. Baby may also have more common coldy symptoms like a runny nose and fever.

Mild croup will get better on its own. You can help baby feel better by keeping him upright and propping his cot at one end when he is sleeping. Open a window, so he gets fresh air, and make sure he is not exposed to smoke. Do not give any sedative medication.

'The best treatment we found was to take them into the bathroom and get it really steamy (put a couple of drops of Olbas oil in the bath too) and keep them there for 20 minutes. A bit of a pain at 2 a.m., but they normally get a good night's sleep afterwards.' mersmam

'Humidifier, steaming baths, showers do all help with milder attacks.' Kewcumber

'Invest in a good humidifier – mine has been a godsend. I have a program plug, so it monitors how dry the room is and switches itself on and off accordingly. Helps during the worst coughing period – between 12 and 2 a.m., which is common for croup sufferers.' twinsnikki

Note: do be careful that you do not expose baby to hot water or to steam which is scalding.

Fresh cold air is generally helpful – which is why some babies make remarkable improvements on the way to A&E.

'The thing I find is to take them out on a cold night and walk around. The cold air shrinks the swelling, improving their breathing.' twinsnikki

'Iced drinks and ice lollies were our lifesaver – they help reduce the swelling in all the little tubes and soothe the throat.' seeker

Go to A&E/call an ambulance if baby has the following:

- signs of respiratory distress: flared nostrils, rapid breathing, drawing in of the chest under the ribcage or between the ribs or of the skin at the bottom of the neck, head bobbing from the strain of breathing, blueness around the lips
- blue or grey skin
- noisy breathing in his upper respiratory tract ('watch out for a "whooping" sound when she breathes in – this is called stridor; if that develops you need to take her to hospital')
- unusual sleepiness.

In the odd case, croup can be very serious but treatable:

'Our first son had croup at eight months, blue light in ambulance, team waiting for us outside on our arrival – bloody scary, went downhill rapidly, but after steroids was out in 24 hours. Had an inhaler for a while, as he had a couple of chest infections as baby/toddler. Now a strapping eight-year-old who suffers with bad hay fever during the season.' CaptainUnderpants

Ordure in the House: Diarrhoea

How can I tell if he's got diarrhoea, you may well ask, given the generally soupy contents of baby's nappy. Actual diarrhoea in infants usually means much greater frequency of runny poos and runnier runny poos. A gastrointestinal infection may involve very watery, smelly, explosive, sometimes mucusy and, occasionally, bloody poos. However, mild diarrhoea may accompany a cold, teething or the introduction of new foodstuffs. Generally speaking, once solid foods are on the scene, stools will firm up.

When your baby has diarrhoea, make sure you wash your hands thoroughly after nappy changes unless you want to spread the misery.

The time to worry and seek medical help is if you notice some of the following:

- Severe diarrhoea
- Diarrhoea accompanied by vomiting which continues for more than six hours
- Diarrhoea accompanied by fever
- Signs of dehydration: weight loss, quiet behaviour, dry mouth, infrequent urination in mild to moderate dehydration; lethargic or very irritable behaviour, sunken eyes, sunken fontanelle, dry mouth, no tears when crying, very dark urine and very infrequent urination, dry, pale, wrinkled skin in severe dehydration

'Pinch some skin on her arm and see how long it takes to get back to normal; if hydrated will return straight away, but if dehydrated it will take longer.' *kreamkrackers*

'Tears and wet inside of mouth are good indicators that she's hydrated.' *bundle*

In addition to the above, it's always relevant to see how baby appears to be in himself – is he happy and playing or is he miserable and lethargic?

It is very important to rehydrate your poor, runny infant:

- Oral electrolyte solution is the best thing for baby to have if he will take it.
- A breastfeeding baby should generally be allowed to feed as much as he wants.
- Try ice cubes/ice lollies, with a bigger baby.

A baby who is eating solid foods and is able to continue doing so can try the BRAT diet (assuming he's not allergic to or intolerant of any of the constituent parts):

'BRAT = Bananas, Rice, Apple, Toast.' palermo

Or another alternative:

'I have the most fantastic GP. I took my son and my daughter to see him, both with unbelievable exploding bottoms. He said to make carrot soup (or purée some cooked carrots or just go and buy a jar of Hipp Organic puréed carrot – doesn't matter which), then give to your children and I PROMISE poo will solidify (nice) in 12 to 24 hours. By the way, the poo might be orange for a bit, but don't worry. If they won't eat just carrots on their own, you could mix with a little boiled rice. But try just carrots first.' lostinfrance

For teething diarrhoea:

'Overcooked, mushy white rice with plain yoghurt is easy to eat during teething, and it's binding, so may help ease the diarrhoea. Avoid acidic foods/fruits for a while.' clucks

Princess of Wails: Ear Infections

Another fiendish device for destroying baby's equanimity and your will to live is the ear infection. Here are some of the signs:

- Tugging at ear when the baby has cold symptoms or fever
- Crying and screaming

- Drainage from ear
- Refusal to lie flat

Generally speaking, if you suspect an ear infection, you should see your GP. For a more serious ear infection, they may prescribe antibiotics. If the first lot don't seem to be working, you may need to take baby back to the GP to try another kind or rethink the treatment. If you suspect your child might have an ear infection and you can't get to the GP (because it's the middle of the night or they're shut), treat it as you would a bad cold or fever, i.e. with baby analgesics and lots of fluids. Feed baby in an upright position and keep his nasal passages clear (sit in a steamy bathroom or try a humidifier). Help baby get to sleep in an upright or propped position with the sore ear facing out.

'Try a warm hot-water bottle on the ear for comfort.' Ottavia

It is worth asking for a referral to an ENT (ear, nose and throat) specialist if baby has repeated and persistent ear problems. He could be suffering from a dairy intolerance or from glue ear (thick, gluey fluid in the middle ear). Glue ear can cause hearing loss, and surgical insertion of grommits may be necessary (tiny tubes in the eardrum which allow fluid to drain out).

Eczema

Eczema is a group of skin conditions characterised by dry skin and dry patches of white or red, bumpy skin, caused by a combination of genetic and environmental factors. Very mild eczema may require no treatment at all. Different treatments will work for different conditions and different children. Generally speaking, you are looking to keep the skin hydrated and reduce exposure to allergens and irritants which trigger eczema. These will vary from child to child.

'Kids with eczema seem to respond to different creams, etc. differently, so obviously, what works

for one will not necessarily work for another. We actually went through about four different emollient creams before we found the best ones for our son (as well as the bath stuff, we use Cetraben to moisturise generally), so you may have to experiment a bit.' naturopath

Here are some Mumsnetters' tips on how to make your eczematous child more comfortable:

- 'Use a liberal coating of aqueous cream on afflicted areas; I'm all for steroid cream on really bad patches.' *KerryMum*
- 'Put oats in a muslin bag (or I use a pillow case and tie it with string) and put it in the bath water. It turns the water cloudy, but oats are so soothing, and help stop the itch. It also softens the skin.' *twoisplenty*.

Oilatum bath oil has a similar effect.

- Use mitts or socks over baby's hands at night if he is scratching himself raw.
- The advice on bathing is not entirely consistent, and some people still advocate very limited bathing:

'The current advice for eczema sufferers is to bathe *at least* once a day (in severe cases specialists recommend twice a day), BUT the key thing is to use a specialist bath oil such as Oilatum or Aveeno (never soap, bubble bath or even plain water) as these are key in replacing the oils in the skin. Not bathing can also increase the chance of infection.' *MegBusset*

Baths should, however, not be too hot or too long.

- Use cotton rather than synthetic bedding.
- Use clothes washing products designed for sensitive skins.
- Consider investigating Chinese herbal medicine – some parents swear by it.

Severe cases of eczema need to be tackled with medical help. Some will require treatment with steroids, and an antihistamine is sometimes prescribed to treat the itching. If eczema is associated with allergies, seeing an allergist may hold the key to reducing baby's outbreaks.

Very eczematous children may need careful handling in extreme weather and temperature conditions:

'We don't holiday in hot countries in August, and tend to limit our time outside in the garden to first thing and last thing. Plenty of water to drink and keeping cool are key to managing things, so paddling pools are great, if in the shade. We tend to cover her up in loose clothing rather than use suncream (a big, floppy hat helps). Yes, we are restricting things, but the penalty for not doing so in our experience is a hot, scratchy child.' Utka

(See Resources, p. 434, for useful contacts.)

Fever

Average body temperature for a baby is 37°C (98.6°F), but it can vary a bit between babies, and in relation to the same baby (depending on what he's wearing, what he's up to, time of day and the prevailing weather conditions). Anything over 37.4°C (99.3°F) is considered a fever.

For reducing a fever, try:

'Cooler rooms, fewer clothes (vest and nappy and socks), cool drinks, fans.' emma1977

But don't go overboard on cooling, as the body will overcompensate if it gets too cold. Underdressing a baby will cause shivering, which can worsen the fever, as will the old trick (no longer recommended) of sponging with cool water, then putting the fan on.

Child formulations of ibuprofen and paracetamol are the usual medications for treating fever. Current NICE guidance is that they should not be given at the same time, but they can be given alternately, when necessary, to keep fever down.

Note: Make sure products and doses are age-appropriate.

Fevers can come with a range of other symptoms, depending on what is causing them, so the following are only broad guidelines on when to seek medical help:

- Any fever in a baby under three months. Urgent help should be sought if baby has other symptoms such as lethargy, lack of appetite or persistent vomiting.
- Any fever which is not responding to fever-lowering methods.

'Try paracetamol, tepid bath, hardly any clothing on, turn the heating off, etc. and give it an hour. If it goes back up, take him to A&E. I did with my son when he was very small. They gave him a pessary – sorry, yuck, but it did the trick and brought his temperature down quickly and they let him go home after a couple of hours.' *littlemissbossy*

- Any fever accompanied by worsening symptoms.

'I'd only take him to casualty if you can't get the temp down or if you're worried about him (rash, listless, high-pitched cry, etc.).' *Hunkermunker*

Febrile convulsions

Apart from making baby comfortable, the other main reason to bring down a fever is to avoid a febrile convulsion, which is a fit caused by a rapidly rising fever.

Here is a Mumsnetter's description of a full-blown convulsion:

'Bright purple, soaked, whimpering and then the convulsions started. Rigid body, fitting, then short periods of unconsciousness. The most terrifying thing I have ever seen.' OlaMamas

A febrile convulsion may just happen as a one-off but some children are susceptible to further bouts:

'We could always tell when he was about to get one as his eyes would just vague out and he would be gone.' 100yearsofsolitude

'Don't panic thinking these will occur every time your child is ill. Even with my son, who seems to be a fitter, he doesn't always fit if he's ill. It's been ear infections and tonsillitis which have done it! Also what I've been told and which seems to have turned out to be true is that the convulsions seem to signify the beginning of the end of the illness.' Weegle

For a baby who is prone to febrile convulsions:

- Use fever prevention medications at first sign of fever
- Cool child down by dressing lightly
- Sponge with tepid flannels. Cold water will probably make baby scream which can raise temperature
- Seek medical help.

'My advice would be to carefully stagger the meds and I was also advised to give them for a low-grade fever rather than waiting to see if it went up.' MissAnthrope

Alarming as they are, febrile convulsions rarely cause harm.

Infant Scissorhands: Fingernails

Babies can do themselves a surprising load of damage with their little papery nails, but you can end up feeling like the worst parent in the world when you chop off a little sliver of skin with those fiddly baby nail clippers.

Clippers and scissors can just be too scary to handle next to tiny fingers. Mentally it is very easy to picture the entire end of a digit disappearing into the maw of the clipper and being guillotined off. Shudder. A lot of mothers say, just bite the nails off yourself, while baby is asleep or feeding: 'It is so easy and you can feel exactly what you are biting,' reassures one mum. Try nibbling after a bath when the nails are softer, and just nibble across rather than trying to tear off a strip of nail.

If the biting idea scares or disgusts you, try using a smooth emery board to gently file the nails down while baby is asleep. Or use either a baby-size nail clipper or safety scissors with blunt ends. Push the finger pad away from the nail, so you can see what you are cutting.

A Spoonful of Sugar: Administering Medicine to Your Baby

So here is the big health warning: always read the guidance on medications carefully and only administer over-the-counter medicines which are age-appropriate and in age-appropriate quantities. Be very careful if you are using more than one product that you are not overdosing on any constituent ingredient.

Then, once you are satisfied you have the right tools for the job, consider these techniques:

- Pin down: hold tightly, use a plastic syringe and 'squirt it into their cheek, a bit at a time, so they can't spit it out', as one mum tactfully puts it.
- Make medicine time fun time, oh yes:

  'If you make a game of it – kind of peepo, where every time they open their mouths, you squirt a bit in – that might work.' *scootergirl*

- Concealment: for a child who is eating solids, some medicines can be mixed into an attractive foodstuff.
- Positive reinforcement: an older baby with some notion of cause and effect could be, er, positively reinforced:

'I always find a couple of Smarties "in view" while medicine is being administered, then given once medicine is swallowed, works well; it's not bribery – it's a reward for good behaviour.' *Seeline*

- And, you know, there's always suppositories ...

Meningitis

Meningitis – the possible symptoms

Viral meningitis can cause flu-like symptoms with a high temperature, muscle aches and headaches. Bacterial meningitis is very serious and can be fatal, especially in young children. Recognising the early signs is very important, as the bacteria can multiply rapidly once in the bloodstream. Symptoms in babies and young children can include the following:

- High temperature (possibly with cold hands and feet)
- Vomiting and refusing feeds
- High-pitched moaning or whimpering cry
- Blank, staring expression
- Pale, itchy complexion
- Floppiness
- Being fretful and not wanting to be handled
- Neck retraction with arching of the back
- Convulsions
- Lethargy and difficulty waking
- Tensing or bulging fontanelle (the soft top of the head)
- A rash of red or purple spots or bruises (or darker than normal in dark skins) that do not fade when you press a glass against them (this might be septicaemia or blood poisoning)

(Source: www.nhs.uk)

If you suspect meningitis, always take your child to A&E. An important point which emerges from Mumsnetters' experiences of this frightening illness is that you should act quickly – there isn't always a rash and they don't always have all the symptoms:

'Meningitis is a terrible disease. My son had pneumococcal meningitis at six months, but did not develop a rash until he started intravenous antibiotics in hospital. He had all the other signs though – high temperature, not feeding, high-pitched cry/moaning when moved. His bulging fontanelle was the tell-tale sign, and the diagnosis was confirmed by lumbar puncture. Although the rash of meningococcal septicaemia/meningitis is classic, there are other forms of meningitis that do not present themselves in the same way. If concerned at all, always seek a medical opinion, rash or not.' mears

(To find out where to go for more information on meningitis, see Resources, p. 434.)

Fire Down Below: Nappy Rash

There are actually several different types of rash which afflict the nappy area, and different rashes respond to different over-the-counter creams, so you may have to try juggling to find the one that works (but give each cream a chance to work before trying a different one or you'll just confuse the poor thing's bottom). Here are some general nappy-rash prevention tips:

- It may be stating the obvious, but do clean baby's bottom carefully at each nappy change, and don't let her sit for too long in a urine-filled nappy. Some babies will get nappy rash however assiduous you are, and the Mumsnetter who set her alarm clock to wake in the night for nappy changes was probably taking attentiveness too far.

- Use a barrier cream containing zinc oxide at each nappy change if baby is prone to rashes.
- Air baby's bottom for as long as humanly possible. Let a naked baby lie about on some towels.
- Consider changing products if baby suffers from frequent nappy rash – it is possible that something in your brand of disposable nappy, detergent or baby wipe is irritating your baby's skin.
- Some rashes, particularly around the anus, are caused by new foods such as citrus fruits or wheat. Try discontinuing the suspect foodstuff for a period and reintroducing it later. Teething can also cause stool changes which trigger a painful bottom.
- 'Ditch the wipes. I've found that using cotton wool and warm water helps sore bums clear up loads faster.' *MrsMattie*

In terms of treatment, Metanium, a disturbingly yellow paste-like cream in a tube, is much recommended by Mumsnetters for fast healing of some of the more acute nappy rashes, but it won't work for thrush or a serious bacterial infection. Some also recommend calendula cream.

'I found the Kamillosan I used for sore nipples equally good on nappy rash.' bundle

A raised rash with some spots around it which may appear as pustules could be thrush: get an over-the-counter or prescription anti-fungal for this. A very persistent or infected rash should be taken to your GP. There may be a bacterial infection which requires antibiotic treatment. Or baby may have a seborrhoeic dermatitis which requires a prescription cream.

Spongebob Squarehead? – Positional Plagiocephaly

Positional or deformational plagiocephaly is a condition in which baby gets a flat area on the back of his head due to sleeping in one position (i.e. with his head to one side or the other). It occurs because the baby's skull is still relatively soft, and can be pressed out of shape. Many people say the incidence of the condition has increased since the introduction of the 'back to sleep' campaign to reduce cot death, but also that lying on hard surfaces (car seats, baby gyms on hard floors) contributes. It is, in the majority of cases, a purely aesthetic problem, which can be resolved with some simple measures:

'Turn him! Turn him! Turn him!' DBXMum

'Lay your baby to sleep on its back. Then, in a three-day cycle, place the head to the left for one night, straight up (looking at the ceiling) for one night, then to the right for one night. Then start at the left again. This way, the heaviness of the head is not always putting too much force or pressure on one point.' NoNickname

Changing ends of the cot regularly can also be an effective way of getting baby to sleep with his head angled in the opposite direction from the one he usually likes.

Lots of supervised tummy time is a good way of ensuring baby does not have his head pressed against a flat surface for excessive periods. Sleeping in a sling or baby hammock is also good, as is time being held upright or sitting in a Bumbo, provided your baby is not one of those who fall out of Bumbos.

Avoid too much sleeping in car seats, swings or bouncy chairs which can not only flatten heads, but also scrunch up spines and digestive systems.

In some cases, there is an underlying condition causing the plagiocephaly:

'One of the main causes of plagio is neck stiffness or torticollis in one side of the neck, meaning the baby finds it hard to turn the head one way. If you suspect your baby has this, ask your GP for a referral to a paediatric physio (paid for on the NHS) who will show you some stretching exercises you can do at home to resolve the torticollis or stiffness. Doing as much repositioning as possible, putting towels under the mattress to lean it one direction, toys on one side, cot/change table, etc. moved round, so he has to look to the other side, are also helpful.' kekouan

Many parents say that minor asymmetries of the skull which remain are often covered by hair and become unnoticeable. Severe asymmetries, however, can lead to interference with sight and hearing and jaw misalignment, so do seek medical advice if you are concerned about the level of flatness or asymmetry, and persist if you think you are being fobbed off. Sometimes, in severe cases of plagiocephaly, a pressure helmet is used to remould the skull.

Reflux

Posseting babies have what doctors sometimes quaintly call 'happy reflux'. But some babies suffer from gastroesophageal reflux disease (GERD), in which not just milk comes up the oesophagus, but also stomach acid. This condition may be associated with vomiting, but in some babies the stomach acid does not come all the way up (a condition known as silent reflux). GERD is very painful for baby and needs medical attention:

'Reflux is not a question of squawking and puking a bit. It is *horrendous* to deal with. It is utterly demoralising to have an otherwise happy baby who is constantly getting attacks of heartburn as stomach acid enters his throat. Most refuse to sleep lying down, which is exhausting for the mother, and the baby's unpredictability – not to mention the mess – means that it is hard to find anyone willing to look after him and give the parents a break.' lalalonglegs

'Mine would projectile vomit – literally about six feet – across the room after *every* feed. It was awesome to witness – if I had ever managed to video it, it would be a very popular YouTube hit.' padboz

'If you are meeting mums, you will generally know the ones whose babies have reflux – they are the ones with a haunted, glassy expression, who often break down in tears before you, and are so tired they can no longer remember their own names ...' elffriend

The following signs may indicate GERD:

- Spitting up or vomiting (sometimes projectile)
- Excessive, inconsolable crying
- Excessive drooling
- Wet burps, gagging and hiccuping
- Irritability, arching of the back, stiffening, often after eating, writhing as if in pain
- Night waking, accompanied by crying, etc.
- Improved mood when carried upright or sleeping propped up
- Weight loss, failure to thrive
- Respiratory problems (coughing, wheezing, stridor, gagging, choking at end of feed).

Many babies with reflux will need medication (possibly just over-the-counter antacids, possibly prescription drugs) and you should seek medical help if you suspect GERD. Here are some other ways to help your baby:

- 'I have had three babies with confirmed reflux, and also one who we now think did have it, but as she was gaining weight well wasn't tested for it. I found the best way to feed mine was to prop them in an almost upright position, with many towels and pillows around to help. I needed to be mega-organised for each feed, and so had everything to hand, so as not to disturb baby while she/he was feeding, as that seemed to aggravate the sickiness more. With my third daughter, who was our worst, we went through many, many towels, bibs and outfits each day (both her and me!). I also found she fed much better when my older two girls were well occupied, so I could feed in silence, or at least, with no disturbances. The white noise suggestion is a good one ... Warm baths helped lots, as did baby massage.' *psychomum5*
- Elevate the end of the cot, Moses basket or wherever the baby is sleeping or let him sleep upright:

  'I would second the sling suggestion, keeping him upright as much as possible, feeding little and often.' *ib*

- As you would for colic (see p. 252), keep baby upright for 30 minutes after each feed.
- Dress him in loose clothing, so nothing is binding his tummy area.
- 'I have been taking him to a cranial osteopath for a few weeks (not just for the reflux though). I do think he is improving – whether it is the osteopathy or the Gaviscon or just the fact he is getting older, I'm not sure.' *mhorne*
- Use a dummy: relaxed suckling of a dummy produces soothing saliva.
- Some reckon that the foods a breastfeeding mother eats have an effect and that you should try avoiding possibly offending foods. You might try cutting out all the possibles at once, or experimentally removing a few at a time, depending on how desperate you and baby are: caffeine (in coffee/chocolate/tea/cola mainly) is often a culprit, and in one mum's experience, 'milk/dairy, fruit in large quantities (strawberries set my daughter

off). Some vegetables ... mainly the green, leafy types (cabbage/ sprouts, etc.), spicy foods (curry and chilli in our house were the main culprits).'

Other foods that have had the finger pointed at them are citrus fruits, egg whites, corn, nuts, soy products, tomatoes and wheat. You may wonder what that leaves ...

- For chokey refluxers, who choke, gag, cough or even inhale vomit, one mum recommends propping them up for sleeping. A baby swing can be good too, or, again, try a sling for more upright time, both sleeping and waking.

The good news is that most babies with reflux will grow out of it within the first year. But it may be a pretty miserable time for both you and baby. Try to get some breaks for yourself – looking after a frequently unhappy baby can be soul-destroying.

You've Got to Eat a Peck of Dirt in This Life (and a Few Buttons, Coins, Shells and Bits of Reading Matter): Stuff They Swallow

Some days, half the threads on Mumsnet's children's health forum (www.mumsnet.com/Talk/childrens-health) are about things children have ingested or sucked: multivitamins, silica gel packets, loo brush, dog vomit, washing powder tablet, to name but a few.

If baby mouths or consumes something dubious, ringing NHS Direct is a good idea; they will tell you if you need to go to A&E. Or ring the poisons unit of your local hospital.

Note: act quickly – it may well be harmless, but if it's not, baby may need fairly urgent attention.

Prevention is always better than cure. So put medicines, household cleaners and such like in places where even a mobile and ingenious baby can't get to them. Take a good, stern look at your beloved pot-plant collection and check on the Royal Horticultural Society website (see Resources, p. 434) to see if any is toxic and should be evicted. (But you should also train your baby/toddler not to stick any old green thing into his mouth too.)

The power of the internet: mums giving each other detailed specialist medical advice about accidental ingestion of inappropriate materials

'My son has swallowed a CBeebies magazine sticker, what should I do? My inclination is to watch and wait, but am slightly paranoid, along the lines of: "What if it moves down his airways in the night and he chokes?" or "What if the sticky side is facing out and it obstructs his bowel?"' *whenwillisleepagain*

'It will be dissolved by his stomach acid. My daughter has eaten quite a few Iggle Piggles in her time and is kicking around. The Upsy Daisies taste better, apparently.' *whomovedmychocolate*

'If it's one of those plastic-coated stickers, it will probably roll itself up – like a short piece of drinking straw – and pass through his system. I know this because I once found a piece of plastic in my son's nappy which unravelled to reveal Peppa Pig.' *LiberalIdleOlogy*

The Inconvenient Tooth: Teething

There is some controversy over what symptoms teething actually causes. Everyone seems to agree on sore gums, red cheeks, drooling and grizzling. But modern medical opinion tends to discount, in particular, the digestive symptoms that a million parents will tell you accompanied their babies' teething process. Although everybody has their own list:

Mumsnetters on teething

'Dribbling, red cheeks, temp, sore bum, whingey.' *MrMalloryTowers*

'Does the poo smell a bit vomitous? That's teething.'
FlamingTomatoes

'My son started teething at about 12 weeks – dribbling, red cheeks, chewing on everything he could get in his mouth, and he gave himself a sore on his hand where he kept chewing his fist, but a tooth did not actually appear until six months. He is now nearly 15 months and has seven teeth. Just before each tooth appears, all these symptoms intensify and he also has wakeful nights with lots of screaming, a temperature and very disgusting loose, green nappies. For his first back tooth, he was also physically sick the night before it cut the gum.' *Ten10*

And as for the suggestion that diarrhoea and accompanying nappy rash and teething are unrelated:

'Yep, it's bollocks – along the lines of "PMT is in the head". So many doctors insist it's coincidence, but it can't be. I don't know what's wrong with admitting it.' *PhoenixSongbird*

'Teething = increased saliva = swallowed saliva = more acid in the system = upset stomach = bad nappies = nappy rash. I think that's how it goes, anyway.' *NineUnlikelyTales*

'My take is that teething by itself doesn't cause any other symptoms apart from sore mouth and dribbling. BUT it a) makes them more run down and b) makes them put loads of things in their mouths, and a) + b) means they are more vulnerable to low-grade infection.' *witchandchips*

Whatever the truth about what goes on (or not) at the nether end when babies are teething, here are some things you can do about the sore gums and general miserableness:

- 'I used to cut up some carrot into chip-sized sticks and put them in the freezer. *littleboyblue*

Try refrigerated apple and pear and frozen banana too.

- Celery from the fridge apparently has a natural anaesthetic effect.

(**Note**: common-sense reminder – don't use any foodstuffs which are not age-appropriate and supervise their use carefully!)
- Try teething granules, teething gel or baby analgesics:

'My biggest find was homeopathic teething powders, either by Nelsons or Boots own brand. I was worried about over-medicating, but these powders cut down meds by about 80 per cent. Chemist in Boots told me that he and his wife called them "miracle powders"! They contain homeopathic Chamomilla which soothes baby, as well as helps with the pain. Now when my son sees me open a packet, he opens his mouth ready!' *JellyBelly2007*

- 'Give a dummy! Really, it's not the end of the world and it will help ... especially if you rinse them in water and freeze them first. Bliss! You could also freeze a muslin dipped in water, but to be honest, a dummy is a lifesaving device! It's easy to get rid of too, if you don't leave it too late, in my experience.' *lilQuidditchKel*
- 'I bought some gum massagers from Boots: you put them on the end of your finger, then put some teething gel on the comb bit and let her chew away. It was the only thing that really worked when she was tiny.' *twoshakes*

Note: be aware that adult mouth ulcer formulations should never be used on babies and children.

Vomiting

Some babies posset a lot – this is when a small amount of milk comes up after a feed because the valve at the top of the stomach isn't very strong yet, and baby has gulped air with his milk or just drunk too much milk. These babies seem always to have a slimy trail of whitish drool emerging from their mouths. (Sometimes you see those baby pictures where possety babies look like they have a full set of eerie white teeth, because they are smiling through a mouthful of vomit.) Babies eventually grow out of posseting, and apart from the wear and tear on your washing machine and your nerves, there is usually nothing much to worry about.

(However, see also Reflux, p. 272 ...)

Vaccination Vexation

OK, well. Let's start with the easy bits.

That immunisation schedule in full

The current UK system for the under-twos is:

Two months

- Diphtheria, tetanus, pertussis (whooping cough), polio and *Haemophilus influenzae* type b (Hib)
- Pneumococcal infection

Three months

- Diphtheria, tetanus, pertussis, polio and *Haemophilus influenzae* type b (Hib)
- Meningitis C

Four months

- Diphtheria, tetanus, pertussis, polio and *Haemophilus influenzae* type b (Hib)
- Meningitis C
- Pneumococcal infection

Around twelve months

- *Haemophilus influenza* type b (Hib)
- Meningitis C

Around thirteen months

- Measles, mumps and rubella (MMR)
- Pneumococcal infection

The schedule will be in baby's red book and it can also be found on the NHS website. Do always let your GP know if baby is poorly when due for a jab.

Possible side effects

Some normal side effects of vaccines include swelling or redness or a lump at the injection point, mild fever, crankiness or sleepiness. Treat the fever in the usual way (see p. 264). More rarely, a child might have a severe reaction (fever, prolonged crying, lethargy or convulsions). You should consult your GP and consideration may need to be given to the wisdom of administering further vaccinations.

Vaccination aggravation: the MMR controversy

The issue of whether to give your child the combined mumps, measles, rubella vaccine (MMR) or pay up for separate vaccinations for each of these conditions ('single jabs') excites feelings on Mumsnet Talk at least as strong as those aroused by breast vs bottle spats, the running sore that is the controlled-crying controversy and the question of whether it is reasonable to wear shiny, pink metallic stretch leggings outside the home once you have sentient offspring.

The debate has waxed and waned since Andrew Wakefield's 1998 paper in the *Lancet*, poisiting a link between the MMR vaccine and some serious conditions, including autism. The NHS says there is no evidence for a link between autism, inflammatory bowel disease and MMR, and good evidence against such a link. Many parents will feel that this is all they need to know. Some commentators, medically qualified and otherwise, will tell you that a lot of the research is in its infancy, that there is some evidence that a small minority of children are at risk from the MMR and they will point to a case in the US where a vaccine court concluded that a child's autism was connected with the vaccines she received. It is all very complicated, and many Mumsnetters agree you need to read up yourself, consider the pros and cons and make the (educated) decision that feels right for you and your child (usually MMR on the NHS or single jabs administered privately).

The main disadvantages of single jabs are cost (they can be quite pricey) and the fact that they are administered at intervals, so your child will be unimmunised against some diseases for longer than if she had had the MMR.

'If you go for singles, avoid the big companies and go for somewhere where an actual doctor will be overseeing what you're given and making the choices. Some give you a consultation first. The one I use gives his NHS patients single jabs on the NHS if they request it, so is motivated by what he believes is best for the child rather than money, if you see what I mean.' jimjamshaslefttheyurt

Mumsnetters on the MMR

There is some very well-informed and surprisingly civil debate on the talkboards on these issues. There are parents of autistic children who feel there is a connection with MMR. And there are also other parents who have seen the devastating effects of some of the illnesses immunised against:

'I am too old to have been immunised for MMR. My mother caught Rubella when pregnant. Result: a brother with hearing defects. I caught mumps from an unimmunised child. Result: in and out of hospital for two weeks, potentially fatal complications. (It was touch and go there, for a while.) My husband, when it comes to viruses, knows of what he speaks. It's his profession. The only circumstances under which he would not immunise his child is if there was a history of autoimmune disease in the family or a previous child with a bad reaction. Your decision affects not only your children, but anyone who might come into contact with them. Consider that the next time you take your kids to see an elderly or frail relative.' *slug*

'My son was fine and absolutely neurologically typical until he had his MMR at 18 months and is now very severely autistic, so I, personally, couldn't vote with the "There-is-no-real-concern-about-it" point of view.' *pagwatch*

(continued)

'The Cochrane Report did conclude that safety trials on the MMR were inadequate (there weren't many!), but as it's been given to millions without mass numbers being struck down by something it's probably safe for the majority. I don't think anyone disagrees with that. Of course, as a parent, you're not interested in whether it's safe for the majority; you want to know if it's safe for your child. You can tie yourself up in knots, really. The only negative with the single jabs is that your child would be unprotected for longer. Although you might feel that is countered by being more likely to have a successful mumps jab (not that mumps is really a problem for young children). You won't be able to suss out an absolute risk factor for your child before having the MMR (as you can't for any jab). You just need to make the decision you feel happiest with.' *jimjamshaslefttheyurt*

'I had all of my jabs as a child, as has my daughter. There was never any question for me, she was getting done. Again, like one poster said, the risk of my daughter getting sick after having the jabs was far less than if I didn't get her jabs done. If I hadn't vaccinated her and she'd caught a serious disease she could have been immunised against, I'd never have forgiven myself, knowing that I could have prevented it and opted out. I know of some cases in my family and among friends, whose children have caught measles and meningitis and the outcomes of that, well, not nice and completely heartbreaking. However, it's a personal choice and, as parents, we do what we feel is best for our children.' *CatchaStaR*

'I only found out the other day (after making a comment that mumps is only important for boys) that apparently mumps can affect girls ... it can make you infertile by affecting the ovaries, in the same way that it can affect the testes of boys. Do what you think is best for your baby, but please be aware that many of the internet anti-vaccine pages are heavily biased towards scaremongering against vaccines. Try and read some literature/ web stuff that also gives you the opposite side of the coin before making your decision, at least.' *thehairybabysmum*

'The hypothesis should NOT be that MMR has caused the rise in autism, but that MMR has triggered autism in a small number of children. The children Wakefield looked at also had severe, debilitating bowel disease (ulcerated guts). This group is estimated to form about 7 per cent of cases of autism. The vast majority of children will not be adversely affected by the MMR. Doesn't mean that we should just pretend that those that are don't exist. No one has answered the question of why some children regressed dramatically and developed severe physical symptoms in a very short time period following MMR. Severe diarrhoea is actually quite difficult to "not notice". Only people who have never observed a regression say that it's not noticeable. Believe me, a child stopping speaking is really quite easy to spot. "Ooh, we've got 50 words; oh no, make that none. Eight years later? Nah still none – must just have imagined those 50 early on." Luckily, some of us have video to remind us of the sound of our children speaking. Faced with a child who developed encephalitis in the days following MMR, and at eight years old is still non-verbal and in nappies, you will find that paediatricians will tell you that they think MMR was involved. They won't say it on record though. Don't blame them.' *gess*

Chapter Seven

Parenting – or What to Do With Babies All Day

In this chapter ...

'The perfect mother is a mythical creature who lives in stories and some films. My failure to realise this has probably contributed to my increasing propensity for panic attacks.' trefusis

'I feel, frankly, as if parts of me have been swallowed whole by the python of parenthood. I thought this only yesterday. I don't want a bloody romantic evening in, I want a bloody good evening out at the theatre seeing something devoid of puppets; more to the point, I want the energy and will to arrange said evening. My life used to involve that sort of thing. The python has eaten it.' motherinferior

You feed them. You change them. You get them to sleep. You try to get some sleep yourself. And about the time you are mastering all of this, they start changing. And it occurs to you that perhaps there are other things you ought to be doing with them. Stimulating their brains, monitoring their development, recording their milestones, propping them in front of DVDs which will help them turn into baby Einsteins. Or not?

What *do* you do with babies all day? How do you know if your baby is 'normal'? Does it matter? Do you need some kind of parenting master plan? Are you supposed to be enjoying all of this?

For some parents, day-to-day life with a baby in its first year is, to be honest, a monotonous purgatory. It can feel relentless, tending to this wordless, mysterious, demanding beast all day. One day he likes you singing that humorous song about his bottom, while you stand on one leg, twirling a carrot. The next day he screams and throws blocks at you. Then he refuses to get into the pram to walk the two miles which will take you to the soft play centre, where you can have a cappuccino and a chat with an adult person; he won't let you put him down, so you can deal with the flood in the bathroom and the cat's diarrhoea; and he cries bitterly all afternoon. And you wish you could just walk out of your house, leaving your baby and all his plastic tat behind you and go to the gym. Or read a book by yourself. Or have sex in a taxi. Or whatever it was you used to like doing before your broodiness got the better of you.

Other people actually just love this time – the freedom from the world of work and deadlines, the drifty, long afternoons with baby in the park, the constant small achievements – and feel that underneath the welter of repetitive tasks and nagging anxieties, they really are embarking on a great adventure. Or maybe they just love carving root vegetables into characters from *In the Night Garden*. A lot depends on the baby you get, frankly. Some are just much easier than others.

For many of us, it's all a complicated patchwork of the two states, stitched together by a fine thread of anxiety. And sometimes you do wish it was possible to step off the roundabout and have a break for a week (or a year) and then come back to it again when you've visited a few more countries and experimented with a few more cocktails.

'How many women do you think look back at their life and say: "What I really regret, the GREAT mistake of my life, was – having children." I don't think it's that many; not really. Though I reckon about 94 per cent of women with children under four DO think it at the time.'

favourthebrave

'My biggest worry is that their childhood will pass before I've learnt to be a good mother. Every day I promise myself, "Tomorrow I'll get the hang of this," but I don't. I'm going to run out of tomorrows soon, and meet the two miserable men that I messed up. No, that's not my biggest

worry, thinking about it: my biggest worry is that my trendy new neighbours will see my massive, saggy maternity pants on my washing line.'
BEAUTIFUL

This chapter is about riding it out, and what you do between or around the eating and the sleeping. Because, as one Mumsnetter asked rhetorically, 'What else interesting is going to happen between now and death?'

Motherhood: molluscum contagiosum and all

'I like being a mother. On balance it is quite an interesting and rewarding part of my life, all usual caveats applied. I found work infinitely easier actually – people would largely leave me alone and do what I told them to do.' *sfxmum*

'I have never been as unhappy as I have been since becoming a mum. I drink and smoke to get through the day. Even my mum says she understands why I do this when she has had my son for a couple of days. My son has flashes of brilliance – when I think, "Oh my word, this is what life is all about". They are few and far between though.' *SilkCutMama*

'I love motherhood. Bits of it are rubbish, obviously, like the sleep deprivation and constantly smelling faintly of farts, but it is *much* more rewarding than my supposedly fascinating career that I worked and fought so hard for. Little did I know that I should have got myself up the duff asap.' *TheProvincialLady*

'For me, being a mother has enabled me to be happy in a way that I now realise I was never capable of before.' *LittleBella*

'I really enjoy arranging food into faces (or trains or flowers). But I did this before I had children/had heard of Annabel Karmel.' *Othersideofthechannel*

(continued)

'I think maybe there are two schools of thought on motherhood: there are those who love being mothers, *despite* the domestic/ dull/tiring stuff, and who need to let off steam about the aspects they dislike; and there are those who love being mothers, and who don't find the domestic/dull/tiring stuff particularly problematic. And, as ever, whichever camp you fall into, you'll hear the expression of the opposing point of view as a criticism.' *policywonk*

'I will never stop worrying, feeling guilty, inadequate and dreading the next stage; and if I'd known it would have been this emotionally demanding, I'd have got the coil fitted at 18.

I could hyperventilate at having to entertain this little person for the next 17 years.

Sometimes, I want to put my shoes on, just walk out of the house and leave him to climb, destroy, chew and rip as much as he wants.' *JamesandTheGiantBanana*

'At the same time as being bored and irritated, I live in fear of anything happening to them, and can be brought to tears at the thought of time and their childhood passing. I want to grasp them to my bosom and squeeze them with love, and then read my book in peace for a couple of hours. (This, I imagine, is why celebrities find motherhood so fulfilling, it's probably what it's like.)' *Communion*

'I don't think anyone ever said looking after small children was incredibly fulfilling, not anyone I know, anyway. But in the long term, with the long vision, I think you might see that having children was a good journey, and an interesting one, and you learnt lots during it, and it broke your heart a few times, but then it made you proud, and made you smile a whole lot too. That's not so bad you know, for a life. In the meantime, everyone should have something else that they do at the same time to keep sane. Preferably a job of some sort.' *favourthebrave*

Childcare Experts: They Are Not the Boss of You

As we've said before, when talking about feeding routines, keep your sceptical head on when approaching childcare books. Some of them are too bossy (or feel bossy) and are likely, if you are not feeling robust, to make you feel inadequate.

'I personally think reading those books did me a lot of harm, but I also know that that is probably because of who I am. For others they might prove useful. I needed a lot of reassurance that most people muddle through, and that a lot of people find it very hard to cope with their first baby. I also needed to know that it didn't have to be perfect at all; in fact even "good enough" is pretty difficult to achieve. For me the books were a two-edged sword. Each promised that if I followed their technique, I'd have a wonderfully happy baby. The more routine-based ones would promise me more control, the attachment-parenting ones would promise me a happy baby/child with no psychological issues.' lazycow

On the other hand, it's all very well for people to tell you to just get on with it and trust your own instincts:

'I had no bloody instincts whatsoever. Was totally flummoxed and bothered by my first baby.' motherinferior

These days, most of us in Western society don't live in an extended family of mothers, aunties and sisters, helping us out and teaching us what to do with our newborns. (Hoorah, many of you cry.) And even if we consult our own mothers, via Facebook or text message, we may find they are firmly espousing the parenting fads of the '60s/'70s/'80s or the old wives' tales of our grannies. ('No, Mum, I'm not going to give him a bit of gin for his colic.')

So the books are not necessarily your enemies. Try to take what you need from what's out there. Not all of the 'science' is necessarily convincing, and just because someone is a 'Dr', doesn't mean they aren't (arguably) talking crap. You may, for instance, find that not every theory derived from what cavemen did is suitable for you:

'It's one of my pet peeves, actually. The use of evolutionary anthropology to justify various bits of nonsense in current society – typically women's roles.' margoandjerry

'One of *my* pet peeves is the way we cite "traditional societies" where, ahem, women tend to do things like die in childbirth and spend their lives subjugated to blokes.' motherinferior

Many parents find that some books, or bits of books, suit their babies and/or fit in with the demands of their lives (work, other responsibilities, their own health and wellbeing):

'Parenting isn't a "one-size-fits-all" technique.'
Olihan

'I would be a basket case by now had we co-slept. I think it is a terrible thing to do.' shrinkingsagpuss

Defenestrate any book that really demoralises and offends you. Most of us eventually think our way through a proportion of the advice, maybe debate it with other parents, analyse the more outré theories and reach some kind of coherent or, frankly, muddled synthesis which works for us. Or just get by, somehow.

But try to avoid those moments of despair along the way, when you become convinced you have inflicted irreparable psychological damage because you have not followed some piece of advice which only became available last week. When Dr Jekyll published his new study, showing that the IQ of children who are not provided with dummies is ten points lower than their dummy-sucking peers'.

If you can find the time, try reading Christina Hardyment's book *Dream Babies: Childcare Advice from John Locke to Gina Ford*, which is useful for putting it all into perspective. And then, when some new childcare expert appears on TV, swaddling babies and hanging them on pegs, you will be able to point out to your partner in an erudite fashion that this practice was popular in the 1800s.

'I'm pretty grateful for the occasional parenting book. It has enabled me to retrospectively justify the accidental, chaotic and random acts of mothering I've found myself executing over the last nine months, and call them by a name. I can even pretend it was all deliberate and a Good Idea.' verylittlecarrot

Baby Personalities

In your teens, when you were gloomily blaming your mother for your neurotic/depressive/gluttonous tendencies and she cheerfully told you that you were like that from earliest infancy, you may not have believed her. And then you get your own baby and, contrary to your dearest-held 'nurture-versus-nature' beliefs, he really does seem to come equipped with at least some aspects of his personality already hardwired in:

'My oldest son as a foetus seemed to spend most of his time dancing on my bladder; from day one, he was a lively little tyke. I could distinctly feel my youngest son's roving fingers a few weeks before he was born; days after his birth, he showed an early fascination with his hands. He is a pretty dexterous two-year-old. My oldest son smiled broadly at anyone who took notice of him from five days old, and loved meeting strangers. Yes, I know experts would put the smiling down to wind, and yet I can't help wondering – my son was, and still is, very outgoing and people-orientated. Call me mad – I don't care what developmental experts say, I just know my son was being his inimitable self even before we left the maternity ward.' tigermoth

'I read an interesting book recently by a behavioural psychologist. His argument was that all the research shows that personality is innate. Twins raised apart are more like each other than they are like any adoptive siblings raised in the same household, for instance. Adoptive siblings are no more like each other than any pair of random strangers, apparently.' edam

The sins of the mothers: did I make my baby like this?

In that introspective postnatal interregnum, when you may be sitting around with no adult company to jolly you out of your darker and dafter thoughts, you may also start drawing a connection between your demonic infant and your strung-out pregnant self. Scientific studies (well, OK, threads on Mumsnet) have indicated no correlation between how miserable you yourself are in pregnancy and how easy or ghastly your baby is.

That scientific study – the highlights

'I was a joyous ray of sunshine during my pregnancies with my daughter and son, and they were both easy, happy babies. I am now five-to-six weeks pregnant and am the most miserable, grumpy harridan to have ever stomped the Earth. Poor husband is developing a haunted expression. Am I going to produce a ratbag child? <<fervently hopes hypothesis is a bag o' shite>>' *MadamAnt*

'Pregnant me – demonic. Daughter – demonic. Case closed.' *CharCharGabor*

'My second son is an angel baby. Almost never cries except when very hungry or teething. Air of calm and benign wisdom, like a little Buddha! I was actually suicidal during the pregnancy with him, I'm ashamed to say. One day, I had the most powerful urge to throw myself, bump and all, out of my attic window. The midwives were desperate for me to go back on antidepressants, telling me how badly my depression would be affecting my baby (which didn't help!), I spent most mornings crying, I was finishing a PhD and felt I didn't have a brain cell left in my head, I thought I was stupid, monstrous and unemployable!

I really think they have their own innate personalities. You can make no predictions.' *DomesticGodlessyoumerrygentlemen*

'I am always a miserable evil hag when pregnant. Lots of stress and shouting at my partner. I had one incredibly easy-going baby. And one Devil incarnate.' *thisisyesterday*

[Twenty similar posts later:]

'<<Permanently retires lab coat and safety goggles>> Phew! I can officially declare my worrying hypothesis as a Bag O' Shite.' *MadamAnt*

The, ahem, difficult baby: maybe you shouldn't have named him Damien ...

Different books describe different baby temperaments in different ways, but the sort of baby people post most frequently and desperately about on Mumsnet Talk is the type variously described as 'high-need' (a Dr Sears term which many Mumsnetters have adopted), 'fussy', 'demanding'. These babies tend to be intense, active and sensitive. Some of them want to be carried all of the time. Others seem to reject cuddling, as one mum knows: 'Holding him is like holding a ferret sometimes.'

Here's an example of a Mumsnetter's 'high-need' baby:

'My son really hates his high chair – screams as soon as he feels he is being lowered into it! Hates spoons, hates being put down, just hates everything, other than milk and being carried by Mummy all day long. Just putting him down can upset him. My family keep saying that it's just because he's clever and wanting to be on the move, but it does worry me that he won't even be cuddled unless on the move. Sometimes I pace around with him for so long that my legs are throbbing and my back is aching as he now weighs almost 10kg (22lb), so it's like carrying a toddler around all day!' Meandmyjoe

So what do you do with your high-need baby? Here are some ideas:

- You should always get a miserable baby checked out by a doctor, just to make sure he is not suffering from a physical condition such as reflux. Don't conclude you have a 'high-need' baby until you have made sure he is not crying because he is in pain.
- Check out pp. 252–4, for some ideas for coping with colicky babies.
- Some parents find they just have to weather the early months. If he is clingy, they carry him everywhere (some find this less

stressful than screaming); if he needs to be out and about a lot, they keep bloody moving; if he hates his high chair/spoon, they feed him on the floor/let him eat with his fingers:

'Just do whatever it takes to get you through the day. Sometimes, it's more stressful trying to make them do what you (and others) think they should be doing than to just let them do their own thing and you fit in with them.' *Biza*

- Some parents find that at least some of the problems are sleep-related, and if they can sort out the naps and work towards a consolidated period of sleep at night, there is some (and sometimes radical) improvement.
- Some babies cry because of over-stimulation. The big, wide world is just a bit too much for them:

'My son got very easily overwrought and upset, within a few minutes of waking sometimes, and hated strange people and places. He found lights and noise really hard to deal with for his first few months. The sling gave him a haven away from the outside world, and I was careful not to expose him to too much passing round and prodding from family members.' *IAteMakkaPakka*

- You may be able to counter fits of boredom in very restless active babies:

'I say get lots of toys out, especially musical and touch ones, books that are textured, etc. If unsettled, try walking around the house telling him random information about where you got things from, what they are, about people in photos, what you are doing when you make a meal/cuppa, etc. This might help.' *Tori32*

- Wait. There are many happy stories of difficult, unhappy babies gradually turning into contented toddlers around the one-year mark. It is as if some babies are deeply dissatisfied with the condition of babyhood. Being able to move about themselves works wonders for some. Other high-maintenance babies, however, become high-maintenance children.

'Let's face it, she's going to be a gregarious, strong-willed, stubborn, excitable toddler, and I for one, would prefer that (although some days more than others!). We've all met boring people, haven't we? I bet they started off as boring babies.

This is the way I choose to make myself feel better, anyway.'
PinkJenny

- Love the one you're with:

'Her demonstrations of joy and affection can be just as forceful, so it's fair to say that while her rages have been, and still are, truly awful to cope with, her happier times are exuberant, hugely fun-filled and a great laugh for all concerned.' *Pennies*

'Your Velcro baby will be the cuddliest, most loving child you could ever wish for. At school, I am the only mother who gets bear hugs for watching her ballet performance, whose daughter screams with joy and runs to me with arms outstretched when I collect her from school, and, at random, will just pull my face to hers and plant a big kiss. I am not sure how I deserve all this, but just to let you know, there is a payback for all your hard work.' *blueshoes*

The concept of 'goodness of fit', as found in some books (good old Dr Spock), is a useful one to bear in mind if you have a baby whose temperament you find challenging. Successful parenting is not, ultimately, about whether you get an easy baby or a difficult one, but about how well you fit the way you deal with your baby to his temperament. And remember, if you are managing a difficult baby through the early months, you are a bloody champion.

What Babies Do: Some Ages and Stages

Big disclaimer: these things are averages; all babies are different and, on the whole, it is best not to read all that much into these differences. There are very detailed developmental calendars on websites and in books like Dr Sears' *Baby Book*, and they are interesting and informative, provided you read them in their contexts. Although babies follow a general arc of progression, they go through different stages at different speeds, and some skip some stages altogether. It is not unusual for a baby to have an area of late development – walking and talking are common ones. And premature babies and multiples are also likely to develop more slowly in the early stages. Some very clever children we know seemed to lie around snoozing their babyhood away and then emerge suddenly with their talents fully formed, like butterflies from cocoons.

Having said all of that, here is *roughly* what you might expect.

Six weeks

To the untrained eye, he may appear to be doing nothing at all beyond eating and excreting. But to anyone who has been intimately involved with him, he is a changed beast.

He is probably:

- making small, grunty noises and cries, and watching you when you talk; he may well be mouthing at you when you speak to him (it's a conversation of sorts)
- smiling – the random 'Hello trees, hello gas man' smiles you may have already been seeing for a while if your baby is an early smiler are probably beginning to focus on you and other beloved objects and people; a few weeks more and he will be laughing and turning his neck around to hear you
- focusing on you and seeing your face; staring intently at objects, like he wants to consume them
- lifting his head off the ground when lying flat (but if yours is the only baby at baby-massage class who lies there drooling, his cheek squashed to the floor, don't fret; try giving him some more time on his stomach); he is likely also to be able to hold his head up for a few moments, if gently brought to a sitting position.

Three months

He is probably:

- keeping his head raised a bit longer when lying on his front, and making some crawling movements with his arms and legs; he may have already learnt to roll or he may be storing that up for another month or so
- doing a bit of haphazard grabbing at objects and managing to clutch some of them for a while; if he drops them, he won't look for them because what he cannot see does not yet exist for him

- responding to you more; smiling when he hears your voice or sees you approach
- beginning to babble and coo and make different sounds when pleased or displeased.

Six months

Some parents find this age a blessed relief. He is starting to turn into a real person with some mastery over his body and his own thoughts about how things ought to be done.

He is probably:

- babbling in more detail, with some consonants entering the vowel soup and variation in pitch; he will also respond to and understand the emotional overtones of language
- gaining eye–hand co-ordination at a rate of knots, patting his own reflection in a mirror, concentrating on an object while reaching for it and then grasping it and probably popping it in his mouth for further investigation
- becoming highly responsive to you, putting his arms out to be picked up or cuddled, laughing inordinately at your jokes, patting you, etc.; he may also begin to socialise in a minimalist sort of way with other babies (pat/poke), and he may also be learning how to express fear and anger
- gaining a sense of cause and effect, in terms of his interactions with objects
- beginning to distinguish tunes and respond to his name.

He may be rolling quite busily now from back to stomach and vice versa. And he is possibly raising himself to a crawling position and looking like he might take off. Some babies hopefully rock their bottoms back and forth, while in crawling stance, as if this will somehow lead to forward motion of their entire person. He might even start crawling properly or begin to stand supported by furniture for a few moments. He may also be sitting a bit but should be surrounded by cushions as he will be prone to topple.

Nine months

Some babies this age are crawling about busily. Some are bumshuffling amusingly. Some are cruising about on their legs by grappling the furniture. A very few are even walking. And some are doing none of these things and are sitting about on their bottoms plotting future world domination. Any old way, it is probably time to think about getting some stair-gates installed.

If you train him, he may be able to clap, possibly to wave, although probably not at the appropriately adorable time. It is also possible he will be able to lay one block precariously on another.

He is probably:

- sitting reasonably well for up to about ten minutes unpropped (but he may not be); he may well also be able to reach for objects from a sitting position without crashing on to his nose
- transferring objects well between his hands and using a thumb-and-fingers grip to pick up small bits of food/dirt to eat
- looking for objects he has dropped out of sight; he now knows they are still there, somewhere
- understanding the word 'No'; but he may well like to tease you a bit by repeating banned activities to see what happens:

'He treats it as more of an observation than anything else. In fact, it's quite handy because he says "No" *as he's about to do* the thing he isn't meant to. So at least I know when to pounce.' *frazzledgirl*

- getting clingy about you, if he is not used to other caregivers
- beginning to understand references to favourite people or objects; he is probably chattering away in quite a convincing simulacrum of language too.

12 months

He may have a meaningful word or two – a noun, like 'duck' or 'car' – but otherwise will be mostly babbling sociably. He might be able to draw a line with a crayon. He may be crawling well and possibly walking. He may like to practise those walking skills with a well-balanced trolley.

He is probably:

- using objects in a more grown-up way (brushing your teeth for you, excruciatingly) and remembering where objects he is interested in live around the house, so he can go and retrieve them
- understanding simple instructions (although not necessarily following them)

- enjoying social situations (but not necessarily strangers)
- using a fine pincer grip with thumb and forefinger; perfect for tiny, chokey objects, so make sure none is to hand
- able to throw toys at you – quite hard
- able to feed himself with his hands, and possibly, in an approximate sort of way, with a spoon.

Getting Over Yourself: Coping with Milestones (or Lack of Them)

So here are some thread titles, out of gazillions on Mumsnet's development talkboards: 'Nine-month-old daughter still not sitting', '18-month-old son still not walking', '12-month-old only pointing with middle finger', 'Seven-month-old can turn full circle, but no interest in crawling'. Arggghhh.

'STOP THIS NONSENSE RIGHT NOW. STOP IT AT ONCE.' Quattrocento

And this is the problem with milestones. They tend to make first-time parents anxious. Especially if you have the baby who is the last to do everything in your antenatal group, or the baby who decides to move about in mysterious ways – the strange one-leg-out-to-the-side crawl, the commando-style swim across the floor or the multiple roll, for example. Alas, everywhere, highly educated parents are peering and poking at lumpen infants, fretting that their lack of gross or fine motor skills will bear negatively on their prospects of getting into the higher educational establishment of their choice:

'You are certainly not the first person to feel this way. I sobbed after a meeting with my antenatal group, when my son was the only one at six months who wasn't sitting up without a cushion.

Yet at 24 months he sits up *astonishingly* well.'
TheProvincialLady

'None of this, do you hear, none of this, has any bearing on her future intelligence or how she will turn out in life.' Niecie

Hell, you will be lucky to remember any of this a few years hence, unless you have assiduously kept one of those baby journals/ development charts some books encourage you to produce. In the meantime, if you are suffering, keep away from other mothers of first babies. Try socialising with mothers of ten who will turn their eyes blankly to the horizon when you ask when No. 3 crawled and No. 7 achieved a pincer grip. Or hang out with other people altogether:

'It's BORING. Find some different mates that talk about shoes or plants or the economy or Corrie. ANYTHING.' MalloryTowers

It is utterly anecdotal and unscientific, but a lot of Mumsnetters report that children who do things late seem to pick them up quickly: the late walker who just gets up and perambulates the room, the late talker who suddenly produces a haiku. Some late walkers, in particular, just cannot see the point of making the effort. Until, one day, they do.

Of course, there are sometimes developmental delays that should be checked out. The fact that there is progression happening is more important than precisely when a particular skill is mastered. If you have a specific concern, because everything is late or something seems especially late, take it to your GP. The chances are that investigations will show it's nothing to worry about, but it's better to get it checked out than to worry. See p. 310 for further thoughts on babies with special needs.

'It depends which milestones are being missed and how many. If a child is late with all milestones, it should definitely be looked at.

But things like crawling vary wildly (and don't always happen). Different milestones have different degrees of importance. Rolling is less important than things like sitting up.' Jimjams

'To those who are worried, I would say do follow it up, but don't get over-the-top paranoid. It's about the whole child. Whatever you do, don't go down the line of looking up stuff on the internet because you can drive yourself insane ...' smallwhitecat

Remember that your baby is shaped by your genetic material, however dodgy that material may be, and is likely to have some of your idiosyncrasies:

'We have noticed that our son's body always sees to be a little behind what he wants to be able to do. So he realised that crawling was out there, but didn't have a clue and came up with a bizarre lunge-and-pull method of getting himself about. It was totally inefficient and painfully slow. He was very funny about clapping. Can't remember the age, but everyone else's baby could already clap. He watched very closely while I clapped. Then he rubbed his hands together, while smacking his lips to make the sound. We figure that with both parents being people who cannot run/jump/throw a ball or do anything that requires physical co-ordination, that is just the way he is.' fisil

And comfort yourself with the thought that early walkers and crawlers can be a logistical nightmare. Their physical skills may be so far in advance of their ability to appreciate danger, that you find yourself wishing you had one of those Buddha-type babies instead.

'He could walk at ten months, climb at 11 months, had a huge head which invariably hit the ground and never stopped running. We often fantasised about having a padded cell we could put him in for a few minutes, so we could have a cup of tea without worrying ...' duchesse

Getting Over Yourself Part II: Precious Firstborn Moments

After you have driven your 'precious firstborn' (PFB) home from the hospital at a steady 2mph (safely cradled in the most up-to-date infant car-seat technology), sterilised your entire house and put up notices banning the consumption of hot drinks on the premises, it is just possible you will find yourself doing some of the following that parents of PFBs have done before:

- dressing her exclusively in white (cashmere)
- carrying a changing bag with 100 nappies, half a dozen changes of clothes, suncream, sunhat, rainhat, mittens, hospital-grade antibacterial handwash, resuscitation equipment ...
- compulsively kitting her out in (ironed) vests, whatever the weather
- panicking when other people touch or hold her, spraying said persons with said hospital-grade antibacterial handwash
- imagining that random strangers are going to steal her
- minutely recording her consumption of solids, in grams
- taking 20,000 photos of her sleeping, at different angles
- dusting your guests for peanut crumbs and breathalysing them at the door

- ringing the midwife to discuss the colour of her poo (the baby's, not the midwife's) and/or keeping a poo diary
- attaching her bibs to her outfits

And do you know, it is OK to do most of these things. Because, in some weird way, you are ensuring the survival of the species.

'It's absolutely right that new, inexperienced parents should have safety margins the size of Australia until they've sorted out what is truly risky and what isn't. In fact, I'd go further and say that that's the ONLY sensible way to parent if you're new to the game.' welliemum

'Second time round, you realise they're not quite as fragile as you thought they were. If they *were* that fragile, the human race would probably have died out by now and the world would be run by squirrels.' SoupDragon

OK, so some of it you should strive to get over: anger at the *enormous, bullying* 18-month-old who snatches baby's toy at toddler group, hysteria about your mother-in-law handling baby while wearing that cardigan with the *dangerous buttons*, apoplexy at the postman because the *loud flapping* of the letterbox has disturbed baby's nap ... But you may well not succeed. The truth, for many of us, is that early parenthood is a delusional state, and all of the above (and below) will seem rational at the time.

The posts of shame: Mumsnetters' PFB moments

These fall into a number of categories, illustrating the various type and degree of neurosis and besottedness:

Medical

'I once took my daughter to A&E because she had a bruise.' *Slur*

'I made A&E x-ray my daughter's head after a bump and *would not leave* until they had done so.' *Plonker*

'I held my finger over my daughter's two-week-old nose at 3 a.m. and was convinced there was no breath, so snatched her from her bedside Moses basket and shook her awake in panic, then was sleepless with fear for five nights over possible shaken-baby syndrome.' *snigger*

'I phoned NHS Direct the first time my son slept more than two hours ...' *PHDlifeneedsanewlife*

'My husband asked our midwife, "If his dummy drops out in his cot, do we need to sterilise it before we put it back in his mouth?" She fixed him with a steely glare and said, "Well, I don't know ... *you're* the microbiologist [and yes, he really is] ... you tell me."' *SorenLorensen*

Psychological development

'I used to "spend quality time" with my son under his baby gym, gently patting at the dangling shapes. I was convinced if I took the time to enjoy a cup of coffee/read a magazine instead then I was a terrible mother and not making the most of my baby. I don't think he noticed I was actually there with him, and he certainly doesn't remember it now.' *Notalone*

'My mum said she had seen a baby on the telly who was the same age as my son (three months) who seemed more alert than my son. I cried into a muslin.' *Anchovy*

Security/crime prevention

'I used to take him to the bathroom with me in a tiny one-bedroom flat, where, if I left the doors open, I could actually see the living room from the toilet! When I finally plucked up the

(continued)

courage to leave him in the (totally unoccupied and secure) living room, I drew the curtains, to ensure nobody coveted his beauty through the window.' *colditz*

'At two weeks, I went to get petrol and left my son locked in the car while paying. About halfway down the queue I panicked that he might have used up all the air in the car (WTF? he was tiny!) and went back to open the window a crack. Then, again about halfway down the queue, I panicked that someone might jemmy the window down further by means of the crack and steal my darling. So I had to run back *again*. Eventually, I queued up with him. I think the cashier thought I was barmy. Which to be fair I think I was, slightly.' *MissGolightly*

Health and safety
'I screamed at my partner and kicked him because he tried to cross the road with our baby in a pram without asking me if it was safe to do so. I then stayed awake all night sobbing about the dreadful trauma of my son sensing, in his sleep, that his parents had rowed.

   I also rubbed neat Johnson's shampoo into my eyes to see if it really is tear-free (it's not quite as painful as you would think).' *SmugColditz*

'We had ONE small step in the hall. And a STAIR-GATE! Hahahaha.' *wickedwaterwitch*

The Second Coming
'It took us at least an hour to bathe my daughter for the first time when we got home from the hospital. We videotaped it too! Think I would die laughing if we watched it now. It took two of us to first carefully swaddle her in a pristine fluffy white towel, to wash her holy head in water, which was, of course, at the perfect temperature. Then we did her body, which must have taken at least another half hour.' *milkysallgone*

'My friend and her husband would get up together to change their daughter's nappy several times in the night, not only cleaning her with boiled water and cotton wool but then gently blow-drying her bum with the hairdryer. She was chatting to her neighbour and asked if they were ever disturbed by the baby's crying. The neighbour assured her they were not, but that they had been woken once or twice by what sounded like a hairdryer.' *mehgalegs*

'The first time my mother looked after my baby son for the night (he was maybe six months old), I typed out eight pages of detailed notes on what to do and when (down to when to change a nappy and what time to wake him from his nap). The fact that my mother had had four babies of her own seemed to escape me; I was a complete twonk about it all.' *Ghosty*

'I took careful note of every gift she received. I then spent hours carefully dressing her in each outfit/posed her next to the stuffed toy or whatever and took a photo, then had the photos printed and made them into thank you cards, with an ink footprint on the inside. My great-aunt called to say thank you, it was very lovely, but she hoped I was getting enough rest.' *TheDevilWearsPrimark*

'When my PFB was little, I used to do a Pramercise class. That, in itself is mildly embarrassing, but here's the really frightening bit: I used to dress my two-month-old daughter *in sportswear* to do it. Yes, I would be sagging around the park in my ratty old trainers and one of my partner's T-shirts, while my daughter slept through the whole thing in her pale pink tracksuit.' *BroccoliSpears*

'We have over 4,000 photos of our daughter (seven months).' *Penthesileia*

'When my son was about nine months old, we had booked a holiday to the Canaries. Being very informed and clever first-time parents, we also took the precautionary measure of booking a Manchester/London flight for the sole purpose of gauging his "flightability" before we set forth on the mammoth four-hour real flight. Armed with most of the stock of the ELC, we spent the 45-minute flight beaming with pride, as our obviously gifted traveller slept all the way there and back ... Dear God, we needed a slap.' *alienbump*

Special Needs

OK, this is really a book in itself. Or several books and many websites.

Some websites to look at

There are numerous organisations that can offer support and advice in relation to specific conditions – here are just a few (see Resources, p. 437, for more information):
Association for Spina bifida and Hydrocephalus: www.asbah.demon.co.uk
Birth Defects Foundation: www.birthdefects.co.uk
Down's Syndrome Association: www.downs-syndrome.org.uk
Department for Children, Schools and Families: www.dcsf.gov.uk/everychildmatters/healthandwellbeing/ahdc
For help and support and general chat from other parents of children with special needs: www.mumsnet.com/Talk/specialneeds

Coming to terms with your baby's special needs can be very difficult.

'A diagnosis or the realisation of one is a time of bereavement with the blessed difference that we can still hug our child. The steps and a great many of the emotions – grief, anger, fear, guilt – are the same though.' PeachyLaPeche

'A diagnosis can be great for parents and therefore great for the child too. To be able to dump all those "What ifs" and "Maybes" is such a relief, and to let go of all the self-blame too, as it turns out you're not such a rubbish parent after all. You can also forgive your child too for their behaviours and all the times you've resented them for your lives not being like other families'. Your head will be cleared for focusing on the future and fighting for your child.' LoveBuckets

Many mothers, particularly those whose children have an impairment as a result of a birth accident, may experience feelings of guilt:

'If, if, if ... little word, but Oh My God so big. What if they had got my daughter out five minutes earlier? What if I had laid 100 per cent still the whole time? (I knelt.) What if the midwife had been better at her job? What if the doctor hadn't walked out of the room. Oh, we all have lists. BUT IT IS NOT OUR FAULT.' 2shoes

Helping him develop to his full potential may involve hard work and a lot of research. You may need to push for the medical and educational help he needs:

'Nothing wrong with being a pushy mother – if you don't push for your kid, then who else will? As long as it's velvet bulldozer, rather than foul-mouthed and abusive mother, then bring it on.' TotalChaos

Also, while it may not be the first thing you think of, do investigate what benefits you and your child are entitled to (such as Disability Living Allowance or Carer's Allowance). There is a variety of benefits available, particularly for children with significant disabilities:

'Do you have a social worker from the children's disability team? You might be able to get respite help if you are exhausted looking after your child? He will need more care and attention than a child without impairments. Blue badge (for disabled space parking) at two, for non-walkers. From two, you could think about statements of special educational needs as there may be SN playgroups/nurseries he could attend.' Riven

You know you have a child with special needs when ...

'... you use syringes instead of water pistols.' *2shoes*

'... your mobile phone contacts section is FULL of weird acronyms – ENT, PT ...' *ShinyHappyRocketsGoing*

'... your baby's five-year-old brother uses words like "interact", "gluten-free" and "sensory".' *sphil*

A Life in the Day of Babydom: How to Pass the Days

With a very small baby, the answer may be obvious: sleep, feed, pose in tiny outfits for pictures (see earlier in this chapter), sleep, feed, pose for more pics, change nappy, etc. Then they get to be a couple of months old and it can strike you that you should be *stimulating* them in some way every waking minute. That way madness lies. You can turn yourself into a gurning, toy-bobbing book-waggling wreck. Which is pointless if in fact you have a very sunny and contented baby, although it may be brute necessity if you have a very demanding infant.

Remember that the world as it is is intensely novel and stimulating to her – what Sylvia Plath called the 'zoo of the new':

'Teeny ones get stimulation from lots of "boring" things, like lights, moving trees, balloons, faces, voices, etc.' Tutter

> Much of the point of finding other, more structured or elaborate things to do can be to save *you* from profound ennui, at least in the early weeks. Mothers of multiple children often consider they have entertained their small baby if they have flapped a tea towel in his direction. But then again there is nothing more entertaining to a small baby than a bigger baby or toddler, so mothers of, say, three under five, are laughing.

'You have years where they *need* to have activities – take advantage of this time to recharge your batteries after nine months of growing a baby and the early months of tending to his more immediate needs.' fullmoonfiend

> And here is the advice we know you are unlikely to take:

'Ignore him. My friends who are on to their third and fourth children healthily neglect their babies and they seem all the more relaxed for it.' Litchick

> So, for those desperate moments, we present:

Some things to do with a six-week-old

- Chat to her and make funny faces at her. Try sticking out your tongue at her slowly and repeatedly when she is paying attention to you. She may start doing it back. Ditto other facial expressions.
- Lie her under a colourful musical mobile. Give her safe things to touch and hold.
- Prop her upright safely, possibly in a bouncy chair or baby nest, so she can watch what is going on around her.

- Try some walks with her in a sling facing outward, so she can see the world – trees, dogs, children playing in a playground.
- Give her a bath and swim her around a little. Show her a bit of splashing.
- 'Strip them naked and let them kick around with no nappy on. My son was a bit colicky, and this always made him really happy, so from about six weeks he was naked at least once a day! It can be really messy, lots of towels required, but it allowed me to get things done!' Katyjo

'They have to be gazed at a lot – it helps them grow!' *seeker*

- Try some baby massage. Find a class or read a book.
- 'I used to go out for whole day trips with my son in the buggy – as well as doing errands, like food shopping, I would do museums, zoo, clothes shopping, trips to other towns – as long as you're equipped for feeding and changing, you can do what you like, and the baby will often sleep a lot in the buggy. I'd time it so when he was asleep I'd roll up at a Starbucks and read a magazine with a coffee. Use this time to do and see things you've always wanted to.' *snowleopard*

Things to do with a three-to-four-month-old

- Take him for walks in the pram.
- Let him lie on baby gym or mat with toys. Grabbing and shaking toys and things he can kick which make noise are good.
- Let him watch the washing machine or tumble dryer for a while. Or a real fire if you have one.
- Play peek-a-boo or other hiding and silly-faces games.
- Read some board books together.
- Dance about together to some music.
- Look in the mirror together.
- Do a little swimming. Go to a baby swim group or just take her into the pool yourself. 'A lot of babies are somewhat unimpressed at the start of the course; the key is to make it fun and don't stress about it. Keep smiling at them and talking in that funny, cheerful voice they seem to insist on!' *GunpowderDragonsandSoup*
- Go to a mother-and-baby screening at the cinema (that's for you – it doesn't have to be animated/about animals).
- Try 'some baby groups if you can be arsed – for you to socialise', advises a Mumsnetter. Pretty much everyone says you need to find some excuse to be out of the house every day, to save your sanity.

- 'Do stuff around the house which she can watch, and chat to her while you do it. The dreariest and most repulsive chores are new and fascinating to her. Embarrassing external monologue: "Look here's Mummy washing dishes. Look at all the lovely bubbles! Now here's Mummy getting poos out of the cat litter tray. How stinky they are! Now see Mummy pouring herself a lovely large gin ..." When mine were little and I needed to get on with something – or just rest/read/drink tea, etc. – I used to lie him between two chairs with a string tied across. Then I used to hang pretty or interesting things (like Christmas tree ornaments which sparkled, coloured ribbons, leaves, fir cones, beads, etc.), and I would wiggle the line every so often so things spun gently or moved (like a mobile does). Often, it was either interesting enough to keep him looking or he would drift off to sleep.' *fullmoonfiend*

Things to do with a six-month-old

- 'Get out as much as possible. It's hard being a one-woman entertainment complex.' *MrsMattie*
- Some soft-play centres have a babies bit – those ballpools are good for this age group.
- Local libraries may have a story time. Even going out to look at Things Happening can be diverting – the bin men going about their business, tractors, builders, gardeners, ducks.
- For a bored child, having different boxes of toys to investigate in different rooms of the house can keep things interesting when the weather is bad.
- Building blocks may come into their own at this age. Watching Mummy build a tower can be a laugh, even if he's not up to it himself.
- Those bouncers which you hang in a doorway (see p. 13) may provide some diversion.
- 'When all else fails, Watching Mummy Dancing is good for at least five minutes.' *MrsBadger*

Things to do with an eight-month-old

They tend to be getting more mobile now, less plonkable and more of a risk to themselves and others.

- 'Get a hamster and put it in a ball and let her chase around after it. My daughter loves doing this with ours.' *KnickersOnMaHead*
- 'Banging pot lids and other kitchen utensils.' *nailpolish*
- Let her help you 'clear out' the kitchen cupboards and involve her in other things you are doing around the house.
- Treasure baskets or 'heuristic play' (see box below). These provide a rich, sensory experience for babies by giving them pine cones and other interestingly shaped and textured bits and bobs to play with, instead of all the buzzing and singing plastic toys/junk you have already bought them. And actually they do seem to love them. You can go to organised heuristic play groups or put together your own basket of bits. The basket should be large and preferably sturdy enough for baby to lean on.
- Other toys which may come into their own at this age: shape sorters, stacking toys (rings on a stick, cups).

'I also bought a play mobile phone, because I read somewhere that they like to be able to copy you, and she can interact with it. She loves it, and has spent all day waving it around near her ear.' *PinkyRed*

- 'Set up an obstacle course with cushions, sheets, etc. and favourite toys for her to find along the way.' *ILovePudding*
- Blow bubbles.
- Go to playgrounds and more playgrounds.

One Mumsnetter's treasure basket advice

'This is the list of suggestions I give to parents who attend my treasure basket group:

Natural objects: pine cone, large pebble, loofah, large shell, pumice stone, large feather, large cork, natural sponge, citrus fruit

Wooden objects: egg cup, clothes peg, curtain ring, nail brush, small bowl, coaster, wooden spoon, napkin ring, small ornament, small lidded box

Metal objects: spoon, bunch of keys, egg whisk, small sieve, length of chain, jar lid, small bowl, curtain ring, bracelet, bicycle bell, egg cup, bulldog clip, lemon squeezer, garlic press, small mirror in frame, metal keyring, tea strainer

Aromatic objects: citrus fruit, leather purse, lavender bag, rubber doorstop, leather glasses case

Noisy objects: bell, whistle, piece of cellophane, chime ball, harmonica, castanets, small maracas, other shakers made from wood or metal, beanbag, rattle, bunch of keys, tin or box filled with dried beans and glued firmly shut

Fabric pieces: scrap of velvet, fur, silk, corduroy, etc.

Other interesting items: paintbrush, toothbrush, ribbon, small, thick glass jar (e.g. individual-sized jam jar), marble egg, empty salt pot, string of "pearls", raffia mats, small baskets, shaving brush, wicker ball.' *FrannyandZooey*

Parent-and-baby Groups

Well, there are wildly varying views on and experiences of parent and baby groups (touched on already on pp. 40–41).

Some people go in order to: meet new people; make friends who have small children; entertain baby. Other people go to: chill out; drink the tea; get out of the house. And still others would sooner spend the day with Jeremy Kyle and/or their own thoughts.

Not every parent and baby group involves a bunch of forbidding drabs in a draughty church hall, drinking pallid cups of tea and snubbing newcomers. Some probably do, but there are many sorts – council-run Surestart things, baby gyms and soft-play sessions at leisure centres, one o'clock clubs, baby yoga, baby massage, baby singing, heuristic play, library story sessions ...

If you find that sitting around in a municipal environment with manky toys is not for you, you might, none the less, find the more structured stuff is OK – an hour of singing and clapping, for example. Do what you enjoy.

'I would have gone mad without M&T groups, as I moved to a very rural village from London with a nine-month-old and probably never would have spoken to another adult if I hadn't gone to the groups. It's for me as much as my baby

– we then do stuff together in the afternoon, but as I work from home, I really need adult company to stay sane. They can be cliquey places, but there's one group I go to where there are only about ten of us, and no cliques – very welcoming and friendly. If you can find somewhere like this, it's great.' Boco

'Is there anything worse than mum and baby groups? I don't want to feel I have to bond with strangers over stories of cracked nipples. I spent the first year of my son's life dipping horrible biscuits into stewed tea in a string of grotty community halls, screaming inwardly: "Who gives a fuck whether you formula-feed or breastfeed? Or if little Johnny pushed little Annie over in the Wendy corner?" I used to be a contender, y'know! A contender, I tell ya! Doesn't anybody care?????' MrsMattie

If You Don't Have Anything Nice to Say ... Unwanted Parenting Advice

It's just horrid. You struggle on to the bus with your pram. It's probably raining. Your baby is almost certainly crying. The bus is crowded. And one of two things happens:

a) A person, possibly – but not necessarily – from the older generation, suggests you should feed baby immediately/stick a dummy in

OR

b) Two persons start commenting loudly on your rotten parenting skills/selfishness in bringing your pram on the bus in the first place.

It is tempting to cry. Somehow, having children exposes you to the scrutiny of the world and to a wealth of unwanted and, generally, ill-judged and inappropriate advice. Public transport, supermarkets, cafés are all hotspots for not very sotto voce grumbling about your baby and your handling of her. Or bog-obvious advice – that the baby you are rushing to feed is hungry. Or insane advice – that your colicky screaming baby needs a slap. 'Suddenly everyone is a paediatrician,' observes one mum – every shop assistant and every crusty in the park knows when your baby is teething or hot, what to do about her eczema, why her head is flat on one side ...

The other time the stickybeaks get you is when baby is not crying, is clean, is beaming at the world. You think they are about to say something admiring, and your heart opens, and your brain sends smile messages to your mouth, and wallop, they hit you with it – she shouldn't be holding those keys/in that buggy/dressed inappropriately for the weather/wearing that hat with the ties ... you bad and careless mother.

'The first time I got old-biddy nonsense was when my daughter started crying in the pram in the street. It was raining and I was rushing her down the street to get her to a café to feed her. "Give that baby something to eat," shouted some old crone. Because I was just going to stop in the street in the pouring rain and whip out my boob.' chequersandroastedchestnuts

'We had the "miracle cures" for eczema as well. My daughter used to have cracked and bleeding cheeks. Thanks to the "sharing" from random strangers, I now know:

1. Quite a lot of people in southwest London have a friend or relative "much worse than that".
2. It disappeared completely on the single application of a "cream", which was either homeopathic or E45.
3. I really ought to think about changing my washing powder.
4. I shouldn't feel guilty about "giving it to her". But it was clearly caused by me drinking/ eating milk/wine/peanuts/coffee while pregnant/breastfeeding.
5. On no account was I to give steroid cream, whatever the paediatrician said. There were much better-qualified people in the coffee shops of southwest London who knew all about the dangers of it.' Anchovy

Mumsnetiquette: handling unwanted advice with aplomb

Try to remember that stuff about how it takes a village to raise a child. Even if you wouldn't necessarily choose to people your particular village with some random strangers on the Piccadilly Line or the gentleman with the large bottle of Woodpecker from your local park ('Give her a bit of thish. Rassin frassin. Who you fink you looking at ...').

Remember that many people who do not at present have (or never have had) babies or small children just forget (or don't know) that there are moments when you simply DO NOT HAVE CONTROL. And that, statistically, most of these moments occur on public transport or in places where comestibles are offered for sale. Also, that when much of the rest of the world is at work or at school, parents of infants and the elderly are having to co-exist in public spaces. And that each side has its own issues.

Avoid violence:

'I was walking around Sainsbury's with my three-week-old in a sling and I got told by an old woman that I'd "be better off with a pram, as they're much more practical and comfortable".

I resisted the urge to bop her over the head with my French loaf.' *MrsMattie*

Tune it out, relax:

'People see a couple of minutes of you and your children, and if they happen to be crying at that moment, they assume you are an inadequate mother and your children are monsters. God forbid that a child should just cry. I now totally do not care about these types of comments. I used to go into a blind panic if my children were less than angels. It made me a nervous wreck until I understood it was unfair on my children to be so stressed out all the time. Now I deal with crying/tantrums in public more calmly, and the situation is usually resolved much quicker.' *Gorionine*

Avoid the advice altogether by looking scary:

'I highly recommend shaving your head. Seriously, I had a brush cut for nearly all the time my sons were tiny and I had *very* little advice.' *NotQuiteCockney*

You may have to accept that you are an advice attracter:

'I get advice on parenting from EVERYONE. But then I get advice about everything from EVERYONE. Even got advice about sugaring my legs from the doctor, when she was stitching up my third-degree tear. They were hairy, I admit, but it was quite hard to appear grateful when sucking on the gas and air and having a hook put through my bits.' *grumblinggirl*

(continued)

And, if so, you may need some prepared ripostes:

'You need a withering reply. Ask for their phone number and say you'll give them a quick ring for more advice when you're up in the night with your baby.' *TsarChasm*

Smile sweetly and fight fire with disingenuousness:

'I'm not into this fighting rudeness with rudeness. I go for "I'll bear it in mind – have a super day." I like the "super day" bit. I really do hope they have a super day, and don't just go around hurting people's feelings.' *twentypence*

'The trouble is, people like this always catch you on the day the washing machine's broken, your husband is working late, the kids all have colds, you've lost your house keys, etc., etc., and it's dead hard not to punch them, never mind wish them a super day!' *KatieDD*

Express your own real or feigned mental-health issues:

'A good, hard stare works wonders. Just practise looking someone up and down from their Carmen Miranda hat to their footgloves a few times. Don't say anything, just look curious. That really gets them running.' *zazen*

Don't, however, assume that all old people are lip-pursing carpers who think they own the Marks and Spencer's café (ah, let them have it):

'I was once sat down on the window sill in Tesco's, breastfeeding, when this old biddy stormed over, waving her stick at me. "Here goes, anti-breastfeeding spiel!" I thought. She shouted at me: "Jolly well done. That's all I've got to say, jolly well done." And stormed off, no doubt to wave her stick at someone else.' *jeee*

And try to keep an open mind. The reality is that some of us, with our Precious Firstborn goggles on, are itchy-scratchy nightmares, who see the mildest suggestion or comment as a wounding critique of our parenting skills. The odd person with unsolicited parenting advice will actually have something helpful to say, some useful assistance to give, will actually be motivated by kindness rather than mean-spirited interferingness:

'Once, a traffic warden came up to me and my daughter while she was having a monster tantrum in Waitrose. She stood in front of my daughter and said, "Now stop that nonsense now and be a good girl for your mum! She has shopping to do!" My daughter took one look at the uniform, probably thought it was the police, stood up nicely and held my hand quietly. Said traffic warden winked at me and said, "I find the uniform usually has the desired effect."

I could have hugged her!' *VirginBoffinMum*

TV or Not TV? That Is the Question

There is a fear that stalks new parents. The fear that TV will make their child stupid. Or hyperactive. Or something else awful.

It is quite right to say that the American Academy of Paediatrics recommends no TV at all for the under-twos and there are occasional scare stories about TV in the press, but if you look at what there is actually evidence for, it seems to boil down to the following:

- Lots of TV is bad.
- There is no clear evidence that a little TV does not cause harm, hence if you are being super-cautious, the advice is to avoid television altogether. It's the old problem of disproving a negative.

In the real world, while some parents abstain altogether from TV for the under-twos, many think half an hour of TV now and then is unlikely to destroy baby's brain – especially if it is CBeebies rather than *Die Hard*, and especially if you sometimes sit and chat about what Thomas and Diesel are up to. You may find that trying to concentrate on an episode of *Thomas the Tank Engine* sufficiently to follow the plot is an interesting intellectual exercise, akin to reading and assimilating the information in your tax return. And, frankly, once you have more than one child, you may also find that the only way to change your baby's nappy is to let Mr Tumble babysit for a bit.

'Mine has been watching *In the Night Garden* from five months; she's now eight months. It makes her very happy indeed – she claps her hands and laughs loudly at the introductory songs and the bandstand finale. Logically, I can't see how it's worse for her than plastic light-up musical toys or squidgy toys. I'm not really very frightened of her being turned into an angry fool by it. I think there are rather more powerful influences and factors at play in the development of a child's intelligence – genes, the amount we talk to her and read to her, her innate personality (I do believe in those) and whether she's of an academic bent. I think we probably oughtn't to hold television wholly responsible for behaviour; we have quite a lot of influence over that. It just makes her happy, and sometimes it calms her when she's too angry to look at books and play.' macneil

The Tooth, the Whole Tooth and Nothing But the Tooth: How to Clean Them ...

Most parents (in this century, anyway) agree that 'teeth are non-negotiable', and dentists say you should start brushing as soon as teeth start appearing. They talk of little else at dentist lunches and golfing dates. Cleaning may simply mean rubbing round the gums with a finger wrapped in clean gauze during the first few months. Towards the end of the first year, when you might be getting a brush out:

'... let her have a go before you do. Even if she just chews or sucks the brush for a bit, it's good practice. Try novelty toothbrushes – musical is good. Finger brushes (brushes which fit over the parental finger) may work as a next stage from the gauze on finger approach. Brush in front of a mirror, so she can see what's happening. Brush toys' teeth as well. (Or where teeth would be if toys commonly had them.) Sing a song very loudly as you do it (mine is "This is the way we brush our teeth" to the mulberry-bush tune) and he will pick up on it and get distracted by it eventually.' 2point4kids

Let a bigger baby brush your teeth. It hurts less than childbirth. Make up a game – 'Open wide like a tiger', for example.

'My "magic bullet" has been the *Night Garden* episode where the Tombliboos clean their teeth. We now have "Tombliboo teeth cleaning" every day in our house, complete with songs, and my son loves it.' black31cat

Some Mumsnetters sadly admit that that for some children, when all the blandishments have failed, reasonable force may have to be applied:

'If you think about it, there are probably sound evolutionary reasons for not wanting anyone messing around with your mouth. We persevered. At one stage, I was pinning our son down on the floor with my knees either side in order to get to his gob, but it had to be done.' edam

So if none of the games and novelty brushes works, you may have to resort to one parent gently, but firmly, holding baby's arms, while the other brushes, or the one-parent pin-down technique described above.

These Shoes Were Made For Walking

Shoe shops are often quite bossy about selling you baby shoes. There you are, all SJP-ishly aquiver to start investing in a shoe wardrobe for young Tinkerbelle, and the shoe salesperson tells you to come back when Tinkerbelle has been walking unaided for six weeks. Most advice you read suggests that the shoe salesperson is right. It is better for baby to get the hang of walking barefoot before graduating to big-girl shoes.

If you have a baby who is likely to be crawling or cruising in places where there are dangers to feet, there are any number of unstructured soft shoes or 'cruisers' or 'crawlers' on the market which will protect feet from hazards. Once she really is ready for walking shoes, get her properly fitted at a decent shoe shop. And walk her about the shop to see how she gets on. Even if she is walking well, she may find the sole of the shoe too stiff, in which case try something more flexible:

'My daughter (then 14 months) sat down and howled in the first shoes we tried on her. They fitted fine, but as she was walking well, they'd put her in walkers and the soles were too stiff for her. We tried a pair of cruisers which were less structured and more flexible and she was fine.' MrsBadger

Mumsnetters' Idiot's Guide to Dummies

Satan's most fiendish invention or a harmless, blobby rubber thing that can come in handy with a baby who likes to suck? There are many self-confessed dummy snobs who just don't like the look of the things. Other people are squeamish about toddlers who constantly have dummies attached to their face, but OK with a dummy judiciously used to soothe a sucky baby. Whatever you think of them aesthetically, dummies are harmless so far as anyone really knows.

Dummies – the dos and don'ts

- Some babies do like them, some don't:

'If my son had taken a dummy, he'd have had one, but the little sod kept spitting it out. Do what keeps you sane, I say!' *beckybrastraps*

'My son is eight weeks old and I've finally given in and given him a dummy! He was always either sucking my boob or trying to suck his hand and then getting arsey when he couldn't get it in his mouth – so we tried him with a dummy and he settled down almost immediately.' *Mandymoo*

- Don't introduce a dummy too early if you are having any difficulty establishing breastfeeding. Some babies learn poor latch techniques by sucking dummies when they are supposed to be learning to open wide to latch on to a nipple, but if a baby who knows what she is doing is munching your nipples to tatters just to comfort herself, consider answering the siren call of the 'infant soother'.
- Do sterilise dummies when baby is under six months old.
- The dummy/thumb debate in a nutshell:

On the side of thumb: it doesn't fall out in the middle of the night and get lost in the bed, causing deranged screaming from infant, followed swiftly by deranged screaming from parent; baby can control usage; it doesn't get manky and old and require frequent replacement.

On the side of dummy: as one mum puts it, 'I always felt it's easier to remove a dummy than a thumb.'

'A thumb is there for life. I worked with a 25-year-old who still sucked her thumb at her desk when she was stressed, tired or bored.' Tillyboo

Very prolonged and intense thumb-sucking can lead to orthodontic issues. The Foundation for the Study of Infant Deaths advises that use of dummies for settling to sleep can reduce the risk of Sudden Infant Death Syndrome. (Have a look at the FSID website for more detailed advice.)

- Do take the dummy out. If you can keep it for naps and times when baby needs soothing, you are less likely to be the mother taking her child to reception with a dummy. Also, it is a little sad when you get out the baby photos and find yourself wondering what baby's nose and mouth actually looked like.
- Size matters, but shape is a question of personal preference. Go with what your baby likes.
- Kicking the habit. Dummy-disposal ceremonies are popular. You know – making a little coffin for dummy, then burying it in the garden while you recite a mass. Or perhaps not.

'I decided that because my daughter was into fairies, I would tell her it was going to the dummy fairy. We went out for the afternoon and she voluntarily placed the dummy on the doorstep. When she came home, there was no dummy but there was a note saying that it was nice of her to be giving the mummy fairy her dummy for the fairy babies, and there was a penny for her to spend. After two days, she hadn't asked for her dummy back, so the fairies sent her another note to say that she was to get a present for being so nice.' *singyswife*

Others find gradually restricting dummy to fewer and fewer times and venues (and hiding dummy away between-times) is less painful. Some parents find the dummy habit doesn't last more than a few months because they simply remove it from baby after an initial unsettled period. Note use of the word 'simply' in the specialist sense here, meaning 'possibly involving nights of screaming'.

And Then We Were One: First Birthdays

There are a couple of schools of thought on how best to mark this momentous event. On the one side, the austere/miserabilist 'don't bother, they'll just eat some wrapping paper while older children break their toys and grind birthday cake into your carpets' favoured by the parents-of-more-than-one-child faction. As one mother describes the ambitious one-year-old birthday party:

'Eager-to-please parents shuffling their babies around soft play and doing pass the parcel when all the babies want to do is gnaw shoes and admire their own hands.' chevre

On the other hand, many think it can be a bit joyless to do nothing at all, so you might consider the tasteful tea party for grandparents and/or a few close friends. This may be most fun for baby, who gets a bit of cake, a bit of 'interaction' with other babies or doting relatives and is not overwhelmed by stampeding older children, party bags and clowns. A picnic is a good variation for a summer baby. Or an activity, like a trip to a zoo or one of those farm-type places. The great big party for all and sundry can be enjoyable too, if you are party-giving types:

'They say the first birthday party should be a celebration for the parents more than the chid (who will be oblivious), so do whatever you want and congratulate yourselves for having made it through the first year.' wickedwaterwitch

But, then again:

'I find the classic middle-class one-year-old's birthday party dull as f**k. I remember my parties as a child and they were an excuse for all the family and our friends (adults and children) to get together and have a party. None of this, "Let's all sit round in a circle and stare at a bunch of babies" malarkey …' LoveAngel

Mumsnetters' non-advice on the subject of first birthday parties

- Make easy food, unless you really want an excuse to make one of those great phalluses of profiteroles held together by a cage of spun sugar …
- Baby will no doubt be happy with a sponge cake stuck together with jam or something in the shape of Iggle Piggle from the supermarket, but if you want to make the Island of Sodor out of trifle, that is truly your prerogative.
- Have some wine. If you like wine.
- There are many years ahead to wrap pass the parcels and fill party bags. A few balloons will probably seem like pretty hot stuff to your target audience. Remember before you drink too much wine that babies and balloons do need close supervision because popped balloons are a serious choking hazard.
- Don't worry. Be happy.

Memory Books/Scrapbooks/ Photo Albums ... And All That

We all deal with the passage of time in different ways. Some find that gathering up lots of stuff keeps the fears at bay. Much depends on how disciplined/sentimental you are:

'I've got stacks of photos, little video clips on the digital camera, videos of our holidays and the dreaded baby books. I have to confess to making up some things that have gone in these, but no one will ever know! I stick lots of little mementos into the books too – swimming certificates, etc. I also have casts of my sons' hands on my wall and also their first trainers in deep frames.' SoupDragon

'I keep a journal. I started it the day I found out I was pregnant and have kept it going. I record all the little things she does for the first time. I've listed people she's met so far, people who came to her Baptism, stuff like that. In the book, the first 30 pages are one colour and the next 30 another and so on. So on the yellow pages, I've got friends and family to write a message to her when they meet her, the lilac pages are her first year, etc. etc.' Thomcat

'I have a box for each child, containing key objects like reports and photos and letters that they send to me. Paintings and school work. However, I feel that this only portrays one aspect of the child, i.e. what they can do and what they look like. I also keep a diary and have done since they were born. Doesn't include the mundane matters ("Today I went to Tesco!"), but it does record things that they say, their struggles and achievements, their traits and hopes and dreams and their personalities. Also records how well/badly I am coping with motherhood.' crystaltips

Others of us just don't manage:

'The books would be so lovely if only there was the *time* to fill them in. I've got a couple of empty books. Well, I managed to put some foot and handprints in them, but that was it and it was a huge palaver, as I recall. I found it was always on my "to-do" list and eventually dropped off the end. The list never got any shorter and the twins are seven next week.' TsarChasm

'While I LOVE being a mum, I guess I'm just not sentimental about all that kind of stuff. I kept my first son's hospital ID bracelet until he was about one, then looked at it one day and noticed it had a distinct yellowish taint from a disastrous early nappy change, and promptly threw it in the bin. I have got a lock of my first son's hair that got too long when he was two, and it was just so cute that I wanted to keep it; I must admit though that I look at it from time to time and don't feel *that* nostalgic, and wonder why I kept it. I have also kept a tiny newborn hat that both sons wore, but it was hand-knitted by my mum and it took her AGES, and that's more the reason why I kept it.'

rachelp73

Some parents suggest that if you are feeling guilt-ridden about an empty red book, you could 'creatively remember' the information and fill it all in ex post facto:

'You care now, but really in 15 years' time will you or your kids want to know the EXACT date they lost a tooth or crawled? In fact, if you can wave the dates at them when they have children they will hate you – you'll be able to say, "Well, when you were little you were walking/talking/pointing by now," and undermine all their efforts with their own children.' greenandpleasant

Although it is also true that six-year-old narcissists will listen dreamily for hours to accounts of their first word/when and how they first walked/how hairy or bald they were, and will laugh hysterically at anecdotes about their infant selves which would bore the most besotted granny. So there is another argument for ultimately inventing what you are too fatigued to record. And not forgetting what you have invented, six-year-olds being terrible pedants with total recall of every white lie you tell them ...

Chapter Eight

Relationships

In this chapter ...

It's not just that you have a new relationship, with your baby, it's that a mighty wind has blown through all of your other relationships and left them tumbled and tousled and with some of their furnishings and ornaments irretrievably broken or lost. And while adapting to the new and central relationship with the baby, you have to start feeling your way round these other relationships, and work out how they might be rebuilt into something different, but still good – something which can usefully form part of your own altered life.

Look at photos of people with new babies – that after-the-shipwreck look of the unshaven dad uneasily cradling a newborn, the random bits of new baby tat strewn around in the background. Even the grandparents look dazed, the aunties and uncles slightly demented. And at the outer edges of the catastrophe there are the childless friends who perch uneasily on the sofa averting their eyes from the new mother's breasts and trying to maintain a conversation about clubbing or spelunking or what's going on at work or whatever it was they used to talk about with the new parents, aka their old friends.

It can be lonely, feeling the distance that opens up in some of your closest relationships. At least it can be lonely when you finally have a moment to notice. And other relationships with family members who are keen to be involved in your baby's life can suddenly become claustrophobic. Childbearing tends to suck you back into your extended family in a way you may have become unaccustomed to during your 'freedom years' (as we call them in women's magazines and panty-liner adverts). The people formerly known as your partner's mother and father may suddenly mutate into 'in-laws', with a new programme of expectations and demands. And having your own baby may bring you closer to your own mother in particular, for good and/or ill.

So here are some thoughts on some of these changes and how to handle them ... or at least feel philosophical about them.

Husbands/Partners

Often men are slower to adjust to life with baby. Whereas women are essentially *forced* to learn how to be mothers, men do not have the same level of physical connection with the baby and may feel like rather helpless spare parts in the early days. The same may be true of any non-Dad partner. So for Dad in this chapter, read partner, co-parent or significant other.

'Essentially you've brought another person into the relationship, another person who comes first, is very demanding and does not, at this age, seem rewarding to some men.' Cathpot

While Dad is not bleeding from his nethers and his nipples or buffeted by the retreating tide of his pregnancy hormones, nor is he awash with soothing oxytocin either. He has no natural high to carry him through this period. And a new baby who needs to be comforted and fed to sleep may at times seem like an insoluble puzzle to a person without breasts. 'This leaves dads with the crying bit,' observes one mum.

'My baby's cry makes me want to grab a spear and chase predators. I never knew it would make me go this *crazy*.' TheHerdNerd

And if Dad is unable to settle baby so you can have a moment to yourself or a nap, it can be easy in your sleep-deprived state for you to start seeing him as an incompetent enemy. He feels left out, you feel unsupported, you both feel exhausted. Don't divorce him just yet.

How he can be more involved (How you can be more involved, Dad! Listen up!)

- It helps for you both to realise that there is likely to be an order in which the baby bonds. She will bond with her primary carer first and then more slowly with a secondary carer. That's normal and OK. You may just both have to be patient.
- It can also help a bit with the bonding process for the mum to wear one of her partner's shirts before he does, so that to baby it smells of Mum.

- Allow him to be and become competent in his own way:

'Make sure that even though you know you could do everything better/quicker, causing less stress and screaming, that you don't say so/tut/raise eyebrows/shove him out the way, etc., etc. ... Really, really try not to say anything negative, and be as encouraging as you can about what they are doing, possibly not standing over and watching everything that they do. He will be much more likely to want to help with the baby and form a bond if he and you believe that he is just as capable of caring for baby as you are.' *Bky*

- If you are breastfeeding and also able to express, it can be a great relief for you and a bonding experience for Dad to give baby a bottle. Obviously if you are formula-feeding, he can share the feeding:

'We persisted by my wife expressing milk in the morning, so I could bottle-feed our daughter in the evening, with the long, lingering eye contact and positive associations that develop.' *Daddster*

- Taking baby out in a sling can be a snuggly pleasure for Dad and baby. And Dad may find he gets admiring looks from passing laydeez. Which is always good for the morale.
- Giving baby a bath can be an enjoyable bit of physical contact, especially if Dad is unable to help with feeding.
- If Dad is off work for a period, baby massage is a good way of building physical bonds with baby. One of you could go to a baby-massage group and train the other.

There may well come a stage, particularly if Dad has gone back to work after a week or two, when baby resists settling for him, even if he has previously been able to soothe her:

'In the end, I just had to let my husband get on with it. It was really hard for me, sitting downstairs, listening to my son cry – I had to sit on my hands, zip my trap shut and let them find their own way. I'd tell my husband the things I did to help baby settle, so we were both singing from the same hymn sheet, but other than that I let them get on with it. It was so hard at the beginning, but it didn't last long in hindsight, and now there's nothing I can do with my son that my husband can't. They have a great relationship and my husband has him one day a week while I am at work, and they get up to all sorts of things together. Try and give your husband/partner the space to find his own way. Tell him what you do (not in the heat of the moment, but at another time) and encourage him to do the same, but when it comes to it, if you possibly can, just stay out of it.' Jojay

'Leave the house and leave your husband to it, even if it's just to go to the library or sit in the Morrisons café.' rookiemater

Some advice on bonding from a Dadsnetter

'In my experience, it will be up to you as the mother how involved your partner will feel. The more you can let go and completely hand responsibility to him, the more he will feel included. Letting go might be more tricky than it sounds, though! Try and combine "Dad time" with "treat time" for Mummy, i.e. while he entertains baby for an hour, you enjoy a bath/power nap.

If there are Dads out there who are disappointed with the lack of involvement and bonding in the first six months, then maybe some expectation-management is in order:

- Don't expect the first six months to be a bed of roses with lots of fun around – expect it to be bewildering, knackering and, at times, downright boring.

- Expect to play an important but, ultimately, peripheral supporting role.
- View the first six to 12 months as the start-up investment. You are investing your energy, your time, your sleep and a chunk of your sanity. You are investing in new skills and in your new team. Don't expect any returns until after the first year. The returns will come, though, and by God they are pure magic!' *DaddyJ*

Fight Club: you and your partner

Judging by the Mumsnet discussion boards, there seem to be three main areas of potential conflict, misunderstanding and hurt feelings between new parents:

Housework

In any relationship there may be a disparity of, er, standards. If he lived in a hovel filled with takeaway containers and mouldy mugs when you met him, you probably had a reasonable sense of what you were getting. But we all have to grow up. And there is more housework to do with a baby, and ultimately with children. Lots more. HE IS NOT ALLOWED TO GO ON LIVING LIKE A STUDENT FOR EVER.

Care for the baby ...

... and, its flipside – each of you having time to do your own things, e.g. seeing friends, pursuing hobbies, spending time posting on websites ...

Er, couple time

Things that were small issues before can suddenly feel like reasons to chuck your partner in the bin when you are both knackered and stressed and life is just generally weird.

'We have always struggled a bit with chores – doesn't everyone? Although we are very much on the same wavelength in some ways, we are very different in others. Pre-baby, we got round this by giving each other lots of space and independence. Obviously, this is a bit harder now. I think it is about finding ways to negotiate chores/childcare, and making time to do our own thing, BUT hopefully have a bit of family time too. Impossible?' dustbuster

Good housekeeping

Please note: the discussion that follows proceeds on the assumption that the mother is the put-upon party, but of course there are all manner of people in all manner of relationships, so alter roles and genders to suit!

This confession from a slatternly Mumsnetter may help you to enter the mind of the Untidy Partner as a useful prelude to what follows:

'I love my partner very much indeed, yet I know I upset him by not doing as much as I could about the house, and I often do feel terrible because of that. Since I don't live alone, I do accept that this isn't on, and try to keep the place as habitable as I can. The fact remains that I find it extremely difficult. I've never really learnt how to manage a house, I guess, and I'm quite lazy and not very skilled at it.' *ScummyMummy*

Some partners form the erroneous view that because you are on maternity leave, you have lots and lots of time to do housework and IT IS ALL YOUR JOB. They need to be disabused of this notion pronto. Yes, of course, they cannot do housework when they are at work. But with some babies, it can be difficult for you to get any housework done in the day either. And you are not obliged to run about like a maniac every time baby falls asleep.

If there is housework to do in the evening, and you are both home, it's probably down to both of you:

'It's not *your* housework; it does not belong to you. Delegate it, ignore it, but don't own it ...' harpsichordcarrier

But also try to keep housework in perspective:

'I think all couples spend quite a bit of their time bickering competitively over who is most tired/does most in the house, etc., etc. – it's certainly not unique to your house, honest. Work on enjoying your day as much as humanly possible. If you find it impossible to relax unless the house is OK, most of the time, then just do enough to make it OK, most of the time. There are no medals for housework.' aloha

The appropriate division of labour around the house will vary between relationships, depending on individual circumstances:

'There has to be a balance of power within a relationship, and as all relationships are different the dynamic will be different. Somehow, you have to feel you are not being taken advantage of by your partner.' Bugsy2

'I think in the division of house-type chores, it really helps for each of you to have responsibility for specific things and each play to your own strengths/priorities.' alarkaspree

So if he is good at Hoovering and terrible at laundry, you know what to do. But what if he simply does not see or care about dirt and mess?

'It's not that he won't do it. It's that I have to ask, and I hate being cast as a nag.' Cathpot

Housework, let's face it, can be an amorphous nightmare, with no discernible beginning or end. Some people cope much better if everything is spelled out for them:

'This is my usual advice on this: sit down, agree the list of jobs that need to be done each day, and then decide who they belong to. Then you don't have to nag about it. If he doesn't do his agreed jobs, it's clear, and you can just ask when he is going to do them. Men seem to like this approach (it's what my husband came up with when I went back to work), as they don't have the same "floor needs Hoovering" radar, but will look on their list and think, "Ah, Hoovering today," and get on with it.' cmotdibbler

The quality of the housework is a vexed issue. Some men are very good at high-quality housework. Some heterosexual men, even. But others are not. Some women ditto.

Some Mumsnetters take a very dim view of housework incompetence:

'Doing the housework badly is the number-one passive-aggressive tactic of men who don't really want to do the job.' Dittany

Others are more pragmatic:

'My husband usually puts the washing on and we were having a problem with whites and coloureds. I did the whole "sandwich criticism" thing with him, and then showed him the benefit of NOT having grey grundies ... I said: "I really love that you do the laundry, it's so helpful. Do you think you could separate the whites out, because they're going a bit grey, and it's such a shame to send you to work in grey shirts. Thank you so much, I love you, hug, hug."'

ThePregnantHedgeWitch

You need to find a way to help him improve his housework skills without you feeling beaten down:

'I don't think you have to be slavishly grateful that he does something. Really, in an ideal world, it should be normal for a husband to share the housework with his wife, even if he does work out of the house. And if he's going to do it, it's no particular help if he does it badly.' bloss

You may have moments when you feel you would rather bin him than have to *manage* him. You may find yourself grinding your teeth and seriously wondering whether feminism has had any successes at all. But you may also take the view that if you want to maintain a relationship with your decent man who happens to be a slob, then your life will be easier if you are not feeling wound up by the small stuff (the very big heap of small stuff) all the time.

'It's not how much housework/childcare an individual does that matters, it's whether his/ her good points compensate for the bad ones. SO if you're married to someone who hates housework, but is always available to drive you and your friends and relatives everywhere/a constant sympathetic ear/makes you laugh and is fab in bed, then you could probably overlook the slobbiness. However, someone who does f*** all round the house, but whines that *your* standards are not high enough is probably not a keeper.' madamez

How to turn Mr Messy into Mr Clean or, failing that, not kill him

- Train him. Show him how to do tasks he is crapping up.

  'You just have to stand firm, and keep telling yourself that if he is able to work in the real world, then basic shopping, cleaning and food prep are well within his capabilities.' *MorrisZapp*

- Have a 'niggle list' or a whiteboard in the kitchen – somewhere you can write down things that need doing which are your partner's job. So you don't find yourself nagging.
- Some people, male and female, don't really understand the constant small tasks which are performed by people who like a really tidy house. And possibly no amount of training is going to change these people. So try to agree some big jobs that the unnoticing person can do regularly, which will compensate for the constant bits and bobs the other person is doing. Remember: it can be hard to be the less tidy person who is not meeting the tidier person's standards.
- For some people, leaving it all during the week as much as possible is the answer. Then at the weekend, you each have specific tasks to blitz while the other person holds the baby or takes her for a walk. Struggling to do housework with a baby in tow is like wading uphill through custard, as one Mumsnetter memorably describes life with children. Unencumbered, you can each fly about in your pinny with your mops and dusters.

  'My husband and I consider specific time to do chores considerably easier than childcare. Quite relaxing actually.' *blueshoes*

- Consider whether there are things you can do to make housework easier for both of you, like getting a dishwasher. Or a double laundry basket so you can sort whites from coloureds easily. Think about whether you have 'storage issues': if you have no proper places to put baby toys, clothes, other bits, they may sit in heaps until they topple over. This adds to your housework burden.

- If you can afford a cleaner, now may be the time to hire one. But recruit carefully. You don't want to be shivering in the park with the pram for hours because your cleaner doesn't like anyone around when she is ironing/watching *Trisha*.
- Remember that you are probably both under a lot of strain. As one mum says, he may well be just 'a good man being a bit of a pain, rather than a horrible man being true to type'.
- TRAIN YOUR BOYS. You know you owe it to the women of the future. And your daughters need to grow up seeing men taking on a fair share of work around the house. And doing a fair share themselves.
- And, last resort of the desperate – trade sexual favours for housework:

'I, ahem, "surprised" my husband on Saturday night, and he spent most of Sunday doing housework (most unusual for him) in a state of dazed stupefaction. I shall certainly be repeating the exercise.' *rookiemater*

Childcare/time for yourself

You both had that baby. You should both be looking after her. The tips for Dad-bonding (see p. 338) are also a useful template for Dad pulling his weight. But there are some other specific issues which come up:

The night shift

If it is possible for him to feed at night, because baby is taking something from a bottle, it's generally right and proper for Dad to do some night duty, particularly once you are both back at work. But even before that, as one straight-talking mum points out, 'Being knackered at work is part of being a parent'.

The appropriate division of labour depends on your exact circumstances. If one of you is performing brain surgery, it may be sensible for the surgeon to do night duty only at the weekend or on off-days. If one of you sits in an office drinking coffee and looking at price comparison sites on the internet, a different division is likely to be appropriate: 'There are lots of variables actually, and what is fair depends on the sort of people you are, as well as what jobs you have.'

Different people have different sleep patterns and requirements, and some parents may be able to make up a bit of sleep by napping, when others can't. What is true is that it is not right for one parent to shoulder the entire burden of sleep deprivation.

Lie-ins

> 'I have to "book" a lie-in the night before … then he takes forever to get out of bed, so I am well and truly awake. I used to read *Cosmo*, and believe in equality, for God's sake, and now I'd sell my soul for a lie-in.' marthamoo

Lie-ins should be distributed equally, and the non-lying-in partner must make a genuine effort to facilitate the lie-in for the other. The same applies to other bits and bobs of rest and recuperation:

'We try and give each other little breaks during the day (weekend) or early evening. It's lovely to take it in turns to sneak off with the paper and a hot drink.' *onepieceofbrusselssprout*

Nights out

It may well be that the person getting less sleep and suffering more from a leaking, cracked and bleeding body is less up for nights out in the early days. If so, it may not really be equitable for the other person (let's call him Dad) to go out three or four nights of the week, on the basis that the first leaking, etc. person (whom, for convenience, we will call Mum) is welcome to go out the remaining nights. Especially if the Mum person is, in fact, the only person from whom the infant will accept nourishment. It may be reasonable for both persons to curtail their social life during the early period and then work out what is reasonable and sensible as they go along.

Similarly, if one person has a very time-consuming hobby, some discussion should be had as to the extent to which it would be reasonable to curtail or rearrange said hobby, either in the short or longer term. There are sometimes cunning ways you can arrange 'you time', 'him time' and 'family time' in the same outing:

'We started going to a health club. I'd take our daughter swimming or to the play area, while my husband went to the gym (his idea of a good day out). Then we'd have a family lunch (no cooking or washing up), then he'd take her to the play area (or swimming, if I hadn't done that) and I could either work out or just go and sit in the steam room/jacuzzi. That way, we all went home happy.' Bon

'My husband did the hobbies thing when our son was born. He pursued a hobby every weekend, leaving me isolated and alone. It very nearly destroyed our marriage. Eventually, I said that I could not go on in this way any longer, and I was more lonely than I had ever been in my life. He was shocked, and I realised that he really had no clue how isolating the entire experience was. I told him that of course he was entitled to pursue his hobbies, but for every hour he did something, I had to have a corresponding hour. We soon ended up doing more family things, as my husband did not like to be alone too much with our baby.' GooseyLoosey

Admin

There is a certain amount of admin that goes along with having a child (taking him to GP appointments, buying nappies, packing spare clothes and changing bag when you go out, etc.) which steadily grows and grows as the child grows, until it is a veritable mountain in the school years (paying for and arranging childcare, lunch money, sports kit, homework, after-school clubs/lessons ...). And many mothers wake up one day and find they have become the Queen of Remembering Everything. Only they have no retinue of servants to assist them in their royal duties. So try to share the burden early on if you can ...

You and him

This is an area where you may have to do some more 'expectation management'. You may be a bit lost to each other in some ways during the first few weeks or months of your baby's life. A lot of this parenting lark is about bearing in mind that the hard bits end. And then some new hard bit begins. But at least it's a different one.

Lost that loving feeling? How Mumsnetters keep lurve alive

Some of this advice is really for a few months down the line. For God's sake, don't feel you have to do anything at all, except help each other survive for as long as that takes.

- It's not all about sex. You don't have to transmogrify once a week or so into what one Mumsnetter described as 'a wide-eyed deranged woman grinning wildly, while wearing some questionable undercrackers'. (But do see below for thoughts from the dubious underwear school of relationship maintenance.)
- No, love can be maintained more sedately. Have a sort of two-person book club where you read the same book and chat about it, or listen to the same new album and 'review it' together, or sample the same bottle of wine and critique it. Or do all three at once for a really happening evening.

- Get away from him sometimes. See a film with a friend, or do an evening class. It will refresh your head. And make even the most tired old partner look more interesting.
- Perform small kindnesses. Send affectionate text messages. What you sow in this regard, you may well reap.
- During those long evenings at home, try to have the occasional meal where you actually sit together at a table. With no televisions, laptops, mobile phones or other electronic devices for company.
- A staid Mumsnetter makes these suggestions:

'I would have a go at a jigsaw. I am sad and proud, I embrace my inner saddo-ness. Quick crossword? Sudoku. Seriously! We do the odd crossword together.' *Doggiesayswoof*

- Getting a little less sedate, some Mumsnetters suggest engaging in a snogging session. Don't have sex, just snog.
- Upping the stakes a bit:

'We play cards. Sometimes while naked.' *Lauriefairycake*

- There are some Mumsnetters who seem to think that doing things naked generally is the answer, but even these wanton funsters warn: 'Don't cook naked if using hot fat.'
    Others subscribe to the theory that men, in some respects, are a bit like dogs.

'Men are easy creatures to please. Buy some dubious-taste underwear in crowd-pleasing colours and surprise hubby in front of TV/computer game in it. Repeat randomly on a monthly basis (or more frequently if you can be bothered).' *rookiemater*

- If you are feeling underconfident about your body, try a little PR:

'I am a fatty and I never bitch about how I look. Instead, I encourage him by talking about how gorgeous I am, fluttering my eyelids at him sexily. As a result, he does not notice any of the less attractive bits – I find that with most men, if you sashay and have sex with confidence, they are utterly seduced.' *Lauriefairycake*

(continued)

- And for racier activities in 'couple time', some Mumsnetters share the following (look away now if you are squeamish):

'Sometimes what we do is have Pizza-in-Bed nights. Have baths, pour wine, husband puts oven on, have shag, husband puts pizza in oven, more wine, talk, eat pizza, have another shag, if capable. Nowadays, if I buy pizza, my husband says, "Ooh, you naughty girl".' *BalloonSlayer*

'One that works well for me is to text my husband when he is watching telly and I am already in bed, and tell him a shag is urgently needed; never heard him lock up so quickly.' *VinoEsmeralda*

But before you break out the board games and the gimp masks, remember to allow for some ebb and flow:

'In my experience, you will become distant again. And then you'll fall in love again. And then become distant again. It seems to be the pattern for long-term relationships.' *OrmIrian*

Let's talk about sex (post-) babeee, let's talk about you and meee

As far as the question of when to do it is concerned, you don't *have* to wait any particular length of time before you have sex, if you have had a straightforward vaginal delivery. But there are many reasons why you may feel tempted to tell your partner that it's not allowed for, say, a year after birth. Whatever you feel, don't do anything you're not physically up to. You are unlikely to want to go for it if you have a catheter for example. Or zillions of stitches.

Some women don't feel very sexy while breastfeeding because prolactin can be a libido-killer. Or they have so much physical closeness to the baby for so much of the day that even the cat gets short shrift when looking for a lap. Having a husband or partner who is looking 'ratty and petulant' may not be entirely aphrodisiac either. Nor is being desperately tired. So here, on the subject of 'When?', is the very, very, very wide spectrum:

- 'I was really confused when I was gagging for it three days after the birth! To be honest, I felt so incredibly achy, immobile and racked with SPD (symphysis pubis dysfunction) at the end of the pregnancy, that even despite the stitches afterwards, I felt sooo much better and was well up for celebrating getting my body back! Plus, as someone else said, I had a huge rush of love for my partner for giving me such a beautiful baby, so I suppose I wanted to show him.' *JamesandTheGiantBanana*
- 'Weird it's so different for everyone. I'd prepared my husband it might not be for months, then was gagging for it when out of hospital – just after the 3 a.m. feed too. What's wrong with me?!?!!! My husband likes to think it's cos he's so studly ...' *mossycow*
- 'When I was a health visitor, I once visited a woman who had love bites all over her neck and bosoms – at the 11-day check.' *ggglimpopopo*
- 'Three weeks, once the stitches had healed and the piles shrunk away. Felt odd for a bit, then normalised. Sooner the better I say!' *pigletmaker*
- 'Six weeks – I think my husband had a reminder set up in Outlook, so he pounced on me that evening!' *Meeely2*
- 'Oh God. It's making me feel ILL. The thought of it days after – all flappy and bloody and ewwwwwwwwwwwwwwww.' *HUNXXXX*
- 'It was literally more than six months after my first son – and we conceived our second baby the second time we did it, heh heh.' *policywonk*
- 'Didn't know you were *expected* to do it *again*. Is that why I got divorced?' *NoNameToday*

When it comes to how to do it, yes, OK, we know you have a baby, so you have probably mastered the basics. It's just that postnatal sex can be a bit like starting over. You may feel uncertain as to how it will all feel down there, and a little bit shy about doing it after a break.

Take your time. You may both suffer from performance anxiety, if it's been a while. Talk about it. Take it as slowly as you need. Explain to your partner if you are feeling unconfident in your body.

There are different ways to improve your feelings about your body:

'Try pinning him down and smearing Vaseline on his eyeballs; that way you'll appear in flattering soft focus at all times.' suzyJ

'I have vivid memories of refusing to meet up postnatally with ex-boyfriends, because I was so embarrassed about the way I looked. Pathetic or what – and yes, my partner still fancied the pants off me, even though I was obsessed with the rolls of fat hanging over said pants. Maybe some other sort of physical exercise might make you feel slightly differently about your body, and/or burn up calories, release endorphins, etc. The thing that did make a difference for me was swimming and aqua-aerobics.' motherinferior

Getting out without baby in some becoming duds may help you to remember that you are a sexual being. As many a Mumsnetter has lamented, you don't get many admiring glances when you are pushing the Buggy of Invisibility.

Don't feel you have to rush into full penetrative sex with all the foreplay trimmings. Maybe get your own body back for yourself a bit:

'Try going for a massage. It might start making you feel more "in touch with your body" and remind you that your body is yours, and there for your pleasure as well as everyone else's.' Enid

'Do everything you can to take care of yourself, eat well, dress up when you can, read a favourite book, go out, etc., etc. You will then be much happier. And I always find that happy is a good step on the road to sexy.' pagwatch

Or forget all the sensitivity and talking and go for this streamlined approach:

'Two glasses of wine. Lashings of KY Jelly. Bish Bash Bosh.' mrsmerton

Multi-tasking: Mumsnetters talk about how breastfeeding affects their sex life

'I don't find a conflict between my breasts as part of breastfeeding and as part of my sex life. Or at least, that's not quite true – for the first few weeks of having a new baby, I don't want my husband anywhere near my breasts. But that's during that initial intense period when the baby is feeding all the time, anyway. Once that settles down then it's game-on again.' *PortAndLemon*

'Personally, I have issues with my breasts multi-tasking, if you know what I mean, so made it clear to my partner that even if we have sex while I'm still breastfeeding, breasts are fairly off limits, as it feels entirely unsexy having them manhandled when their day job is feeding the baby! I'll return them to their previous role as part of my body afterwards.' *Hopefully*

'I find my breastfeeding breasts incredibly sexy actually; they look and feel much nicer than when I'm not.' *QueenFee*

Grandparents

Ideally, grandparents will have a real involvement in their grandchildren's lives. Hell, ideally they will be surprisingly youthful, NNEB-qualified child enthusiasts who want to provide all the childcare you need, without ever saying anything even the most uber-sensitive person could construe as criticism. But back to the real world.

Here are some thoughts on grandparents:

- Grandparents may be desperate to help out. And you may need to adjust your newborn baby goggles, so you do not see every effort to help as overbearing interferingness and every bit of ropy, outmoded advice as an affront.

'I couldn't bear to have my parents-in-law near my baby, but I know it was my hormones.' *GoodGollyMissMolly*

- It can be particularly hard to bite your tongue if you don't have an especially good relationship with your in-laws, or indeed your own parents. But they may, none the less, be good and valuable grandparents once you have all knocked each other's corners off. Sometimes they just need you to involve them in the right way:

'I give my mother-in-law little jobs to do, little things to go and find out about. She reads the *Daily Mail* and cuts me out useful articles. I was especially amused as she had been amazed and disbelieving when I told her babies can't have salt. I got the lecture about modern ideas and how modern mums make such a fuss. Six months later, she phoned to say she had posted me an important article about salt; she was quite worried! I nodded and smiled and made reassuring noises.' *TwoFirTreesToday*

- A tactfully given copy of *The Good Granny Guide* might help. OK, there's probably no tactful way to give someone a manual about how not to be an interfering old bat/ male equivalent of a bat, so just send the damned thing anonymously.
- Some things you are entitled to put your foot down about, if they bug you. The mother-in-law who refers to your baby as "my baby". The granny who calls your baby by the name she told you she preferred, rather than the one which is actually on the birth certificate. If you make a stand about things which are really important to you, you are less likely to find yourself bearing grudges.

'When I was going to find out if it was a boy or girl, she said, "Ooh, I find out what I'm having in two days."' *Mumblesmummy*

Or if she's letting baby's poor little head bobble about terrifyingly, advises one mum, 'just gently say next time," "Oh, baby prefers being held like this," and readjust her.'

But do try 'the dance of diplomacy' in relation to the less important things. Sometimes you just need to 'smile, nod and carry on doing it your way'. What they say about toddlers is true of other relationships: pick your battles.

- Some Mumsnetters have found that difficult in-law relationships can improve radically over time:

'Earlier this year I was seriously ill, hospitalised and unable to look after my baby. My mother-in-law was actually the one who went with me to hospital, she was the one who brought down my fever, and then she looked after my son and I when I was recovering. She was a total star. She still comes out with complete howlers, e.g. "Aren't you going to do anything about losing that baby weight, dear?" recently. But I have to remember that what she DOES is kinder than what she SAYS, if you see what I mean.' *thebecster*

'My mother-in-law and I have started to make an effort with each other lately, probably in the last year, and we get along great. To be honest, it was me who had to loosen up a little bit, and my mother-in-law who had to learn to step back when I found it all too overwhelming. She now babysits for me, and I don't fret and worry. I have seen her every day for the past two weeks, and we haven't killed each other yet.' *fireflyfairy2*

- It's easy to feel miffed if the grandparents aren't gagging to have constant contact with the baby. But grandparents are not obliged to offer childcare, to babysit while you go for weekends away or to do anything in particular. They may not, in some cases, be young or competent enough to help out. Or they may just feel their child-rearing days are over and they've had enough nappies, thank you very much. Or they may still be pursuing full-time careers (or full-time bridge on cruise ships). Some may already be committed to helping out with pre-existing grandchildren. And some grandparents just think that grandchildren are there to be served up, clean and delightful on high days and holidays and to appear in photos on the mantelpiece. If yours are like these and you have friends with grandparents who are able and keen to have active relationships with grandchildren, it is easy to get grandparent envy.

'I tend to think the generations should help each other out, if they can; ideally, able-bodied grandparents would help out with the grandchildren, children help with their elderly parents and so on.' *neva*

'Some grandparents may be shy to ask if they can help out, particularly if they are on the paternal side and you and they don't have a fantastic relationship. If they have seen you wincing as baby's head waggles precariously over mother-in-law's arm or baby's ear lobe snags on her large brooch, they may hesitate to offer to babysit. If you would like them to be more involved, try to make this clear tactfully. We were so precious with our firstborn, I think ours just felt a bit out of practice and scared of doing something wrong.' *AussieSim*

- Remember that even where there is willingness to help, overnight babysitting can seem a formidable responsibility to someone who is not the parent, particularly when the child is still a baby.
- And adjust your expectations with grandparents and other relatives who are really elderly:

'The ability to empathise does diminish with age – that is why the very elderly, even if not affected by dementia, can come across as toddler-like in their self-absorption. It's also why they often don't give a !*?@ about being seen with their teeth out/wearing purple/ making outrageous political/racial/religious generalisations. I think the term is social disinhibition ... they don't feel the need to please/be liked any more. How bad this appears is, in my experience, dependent on what their basic personality was like before ageing made its impact. My parents are 78 and 83 and very caring still. But they are less *understanding* of our lives and situations. They don't relate to the grandchildren as well as they used to, despite loving them ... rather *fiercely* shall we say?' *Marina*

- Remember that you 'may not be so nice yourself' as someone's mum used to tell them, especially postnatally:

'I love my mother-in-law, but she doesn't half annoy me, and I am sure I annoy her. She said to me once that as my husband is an only child, she decided years ago that she was going to get on with his wife, regardless ... as it is, we do get on, but I think that was a good mental attitude for her to take. Also, as the mother of three boys, I am very aware of the example I am setting to them about grandparents ... Wait till they all marry horrible women. I am going to keep them at home for ever.' *codswallop*

Childless Friends

Childless friends sometimes do annoying things. Like passing on childcare advice based on something they saw on *Supernanny* that week. And pregnant-for-the-first-time friends often know even more than childless friends; they can be bursting with helpful tips. Consider writing them all down to repeat to them when they have their own kids. Or just let it go ...

Some childless friends may be marvellous, clucky surrogate aunties/uncles and willing babysitters ... who will sit with you and eat pizza in front of the TV, if that's the only kind of evening you can manage. Or take you out for an afternoon at a spa to restore yourself. Or other good stuff that happens in chicklit novels and musical sequences in date films.

Other childless friends may not have a clue about the logistics of your life with a baby. They may ring at bath time/supper time/ when-baby's-screaming-time and be affronted that you can't tarry on the phone for a long yatter. They don't really understand why you can't manage just one night at the pub when baby is six weeks old. Or attend their four-day hen weekend. Or concentrate on their Byzantine sagas of office politics.

It is easy to feel annoyed, to feel that your childless friends are lacking in empathy, to decide that they are self-centred sh*ts. Try to remember that you have gone on a big journey without them. They don't know exactly what it is like to be you. And sometimes they will make mistakes. It can be lonely for you and for them. But be reassured – good friendships can survive cataclysmic change.

'God, when I look back at how I was with friends before I had any kids, I just didn't have a CLUE what they were going through. I don't think I made any allowances for the fact they had babies, purely because I had no idea that their lives were different to mine.' CountessDracula

'Before I had kids, my best friend had two, and she became the most boring person in the world. Didn't mean I didn't still like her, but her favourite topics were kids, sleeping patterns, childcare, etc. I'm sure there are times when I annoyed her – she sure as hell annoyed me! Then I had my three, and I've seen her glazing over as I've started banging on about breastfeeding, sleeping, childcare, etc. She's moved on, but it doesn't matter as long as you have things in common, and you like each other enough to be patient.' OrmIrian

And you may well find that some childless friends will be the ones who work round your constantly cancelled arrangements, and will understand your utter lack of spontaneity:

'Two of our closest friends are childless and yet they put us up in London with amazing care and attention. They buy in all kinds of "kiddy food" and plan nice things for our daughters to do. They are ace.' Enid

Bear in mind that one day you will have a life after small children. In the meantime, some of your childless friends may be harder to deal with and may mess up from time to time. You may see less of each other, but:

'I think it's very important to retain something of yourself, and having childless friends helps that enormously.' mogwai

And while some more peripheral friendships may fall by the wayside, it's worth trying to keep a good old friendship alive. A real friend will probably understand that you are doing your best, even if that means only an occasional text message for a while.

'It's just life. I think you do have to take the initiative and arrange things, otherwise childless friends assume you won't be able to do things, and so don't ask you because they don't want to put you in the position of having to refuse a lot. Think it gets better as children get older.' princesspeahead

While it may feel easier when you have a tiny baby to put relationships with childless friends on hold, and just hang out with other mothers of similar-aged infants instead, remember some 'mummy friendships' will be transitory (like many friendships arising out of shared circumstances). There will be others, of course, which will no doubt turn out to be real friendships which don't depend on a mutual interest in carrots and poo.

Things you can do to not annoy your childless friends

- Talk about things other than your baby, if you can. (But equally they should be able to understand that you need to talk a bit about your baby.) Don't make those, 'You-don't-know-anything-until-you've-had-children' comments. Or smile knowingly. (Actually, no one in any circumstances should ever smile knowingly at anyone. It's a bit of a friendship wrecker.)
- When you can, and as time goes on, try to recapture your pre-baby self sometimes:

  'If we entertain at home, I often get a babysitter in so that we can enjoy being grown-ups with minimal distraction.' moondog

- Also, bear in mind that some childless friends may not be childless by choice and seeing you and your new baby may be hard for them:

  'During the worst times, when I was trying and failing to conceive, I was quite incapable of being at all enthusiastic about friends'

  (continued)

pregnancies. I would dread the Christmas card season, with its clutch of new pregnancy announcements, each of which would have me sobbing and consumed with jealousy and bitterness. I would do my best to smile and congratulate if someone told me face to face, but most of my effort would be taken up with trying not to start crying, so I'm not sure just how enthusiastic I would have come across. I hope those people have forgiven me for failing to demonstrate enough interest in their pregnancies and babies. I didn't enjoy feeling like this, and yes, I was much too absorbed in my own feelings. But now I'm completely absorbed in being a mother and with my wonderful son – and can quite see that what is important to me right now is somewhat tedious to others, especially those without children, and may even be painful for some. I suppose maintaining friendships when life courses diverge is about the overall balance between give and take over the lifetime of a friendship; life would be very boring if we only managed to keep hold of friends who were going through the same life stage as us at the same time.' *elliott*

No Babies Allowed

There are 2001 angsty threads on Mumsnet Talk about weddings to which children are not invited. At last count. Now there are several different views on this one. And some people get very heated.

Some folk take the view that weddings are *family* events, which should – ideally – include some wailing of infants during the vows, some smearing of wedding cake on the bridal party by toddlers, some gangs of small boys headbanging on the dance floor and getting chased by the DJ for trashing the sound system.

'Weddings are anciently tied up with fertility, and if it's a church wedding, there is even a bit in the service about procreating and marriage being a means to have children in a solid union. To then exclude children is wrong I think.' themildmanneredjanitor

'I don't understand how you can invite people to put themselves out so much, and then stipulate their childcare arrangements. Who do couples think they are? God, they want their guests to spend a fortune buying clothes, a present, travelling and staying overnight, and then give them all the grief of palming their children off on someone else.' sobernow

Other people think that it's up to the people getting married to have the kind of wedding they want. And some people approach their nuptials with the firm view that they really don't want to have to pay off the catering staff when the wine fountain gets scuttled. Some parents also confess to having more fun without kids in tow.

A broad middle ground take the view that even a generally child-free wedding should be able to accommodate a new or newish baby who has not been separated for any length of time from his mother, and who will mostly snooze or feed through the festivities.

So before you become irate, check whether 'No children' really does mean 'No tiny babies'. If the happy couple are childless and clueless, explain how often baby needs to feed and how difficult/ impossible it would be for you to attend without her.

'I think before you have kids, you don't have a clue about the difference between a newborn (which is a sleeping, feeding, cuddling, immobile bundle and no trouble to anyone) and an 18-month-old. (I COMPLETELY understand why you would not want one of those at your wedding!)' jasper

'We spoke to the couple and explained about the breastfeeding. They were fine, so we took the baby with us. We were conscientious about taking him out at the slightest squall during the ceremony though.' ProfessorGrammaticus

Try in any event not to get too huffy. Some childless people will not have thought through what a faff it is for you to come without your baby. In fact, they are not really thinking about you at all.

Remember that some people will have said 'No children' because numbers are tight. And those who are marrying late, after many of their friends have already procreated, may not be able to afford to entertain the hordes of children. Some may have booked a venue which is unsuitable for children. But a babe in arms may still be OK in these circumstances.

Even if you think the bride and/or groom is suffering from absurd special-dayitis and self-importance, try to take the long view. Even good friends can be arses at times.

Unmarried Parents

Many people have strong moral, social, religious, political or psychological reasons for their marital choices. Others have a lust for/aversion to being the centrepiece of a wedding ceremony which overcomes any actual rational thoughts they may have on the subject of matrimony.

There are many practical and legal consequences of being married which do not follow from being unmarried and cohabiting, and which may loom large once you have children. Many of these can be addressed through careful planning.

The significant worry is if one parent dies, as a widowed Mumsnetter explains:

'What will happen to you if your partner dies? It is true I don't have a mortgage now; we had life cover to pay that off. So I don't have to pay out nearly £600 a month in mortgage payments. But even so, that leaves me with my wage of £1100 a month to live on.

Because I was married, I am entitled to a weekly widowed-parent's benefit, which adds up to nearly £400 a month. So as we are financially supported through that, my girls and I can stay in our home. Think about it, I am suggesting marriage for financial reasons only. Don't even acknowledge that you're married. You don't have to. And I certainly never thought of myself as a "wife" before being me. But I was very glad I could give permission for the paramedics to attempt to revive my husband that night, and also for the post mortem to be carried out, and to have him repatriated. Please, think about marriage. Marriage for legal reasons is not about becoming a downtrodden wife who loses her identity when she says "I do". It is about protecting what you and your partner have worked for, protecting your children, and giving you financial security if the worst happens. Marriage did *not* change me. But not being able to arrange my own husband's funeral would have *broken* me.' Yorkiegirl

Some people decide it is cheaper and easier to get married than to faff about with the admin of sensible cohabitation.

Others prefer to redress many of the inbuilt disadvantages of unmarried cohabitation through planning ahead.

Here are some practical things to think about (and take legal advice about) if marriage is not for you:

- Parental responsibility: mothers automatically have parental responsibility for children. Unmarried fathers of children born after 1 December 2003 will have parental responsibility if their details were included when the baby was registered. In other cases, there has to be a parental responsibility agreement or order.
- Wills: unmarried parents should make wills because if one partner dies intestate, the other will not automatically inherit anything, including the family home, if that is owned by the deceased

partner. Inheritance is not straightforward for married people either, and really everyone with children should make a will.

- Inheritance tax: this will be paid by the surviving partner where the value of the deceased's estate is worth over the threshold (£312,000 in 2008/2009). Married people and civil partners do not pay inheritance tax on property they leave to each other, and also have more favourable arrangements in relation to property they leave to their children.
- You should seek advice on the arrangements you have as to who owns the family home, and the basis on which you might jointly own it. There are all kinds of inheritance and tax implications.
- Life insurance: think about taking out life insurance to make up for benefits you won't be entitled to as an unmarried person. Make sure you have named the appropriate beneficiaries in any existing policies.
- Pensions: many pension schemes, particularly in the public sector, do not pay benefits to non-married partners. There are also differences to the state pension benefits married people receive. Sit down and have a think about your pension provision and how you might fill any gaps.
- Next of kin: unmarried partners are not automatically treated as each other's next of kin by hospitals. Consider carrying a card naming your partner as your next of kin.
- Splitting up: if one of you is making career sacrifices to stay at home and look after the baby, you need to give some thought as to what financial arrangements would be appropriate if you were to split up. An unmarried partner is not entitled to maintenance, but if you put in place a living-together agreement which provides for the working partner to financially support the partner who is looking after the children, you may be able to provide some security for the non-working partner. Take legal advice as to the enforceability of any cohabitation contract you are seeking to enter into.

(For up-to-date and detailed information on this subject, visit www.marriedornot.org.uk and see Resources, p. 434.)

Single Parenting

Some people choose to go for a baby on their own, and some people just find themselves single – by choice or otherwise – before or soon after the baby is born.

There are lots of issues which may be more acute for single parents, particularly those relating to childcare and finance. If there is another parent on the scene, there are likely to be issues regarding his financial contribution and the contact he has with baby. There are specialist organisations you can contact for advice on benefits and for support (see Resources, p. 434), and Mumsnet and other parenting websites have talkboards where you can exchange advice and chat with other single parents about everything from money to the thrills and spills of internet dating.

A lot of single Mumsnetters advocate a one-day-at-a-time approach to the challenges of being on your own:

'I'm a single mother of a three-year-old boy, no father on the scene. I deal with the boy things as they arise. About six months ago, my son started following people to the toilet (strange, but that's kids for you), and saw that Granddad wees standing up. So now he does his wees standing up too, "like Granddad". So that's one box ticked! I can kick a ball around and drive toy trains with him. The future may raise different issues, but your circumstances could be totally different by then, so I really wouldn't worry about it.' RachelG

Sisters doing it by themselves: how hard is it?

'I was so busy with the baby, I don't know how on earth I would have managed to sustain a relationship at the same time.' *hoolagirl*

'I broke up while pregnant. It was hard at times, but I did (and do) have a supportive family, so that helps. Also my ex is involved, so as my daughter got older I got more breaks. All in all, not too bad. Was so busy with my baby, tired and feeling weird (like whoa, I'm a mother!) that I had enough to deal with!' *LittleSarah*

(continued)

'When I informed my daughter's dad I was pregnant, he informed me he was married, so I left him there and then. It was very, very hard because I had walked away from my family and friends to move to the other side of the country to be near this man, but I got on with it. It's still hard, but I wouldn't change it because I love my daughter and would go through all this again for her. I take one day at a time and I have bad days and good days, and I also have very, very, very bad days, but my daughter makes it all worth it.' *mojosmum*

'I'm lucky that my son's father and I are on good terms and he's very involved (now) in our son's care. I'm happy to be single and have been for years, anyway. Don't like couplehood, and certainly couldn't be arsed having to run around after some man and cater to his ego while raising my son.' *madamez*

'I became a lone parent before my daughter was born – ex walked out when I was four months pregnant. At the time, I was devastated, and desperately hoped that we would get back together – I genuinely didn't believe that I could do it on my own. But as time has gone on, I've come to realise that he did me an enormous favour. Looking back now, I realise that I was never truly happy the whole time we were together. Life isn't exactly easy now, but it is a great deal better, happier, more fulfilling and less stressful than when I was with my ex. I no longer define myself in terms of being someone else's partner; I no longer make all the compromises and all the effort to hold together an unhealthy relationship with someone who, frankly, does not deserve me. I feel liberated. I'm independent, empowered and have learnt just how strong I am. I enjoy a much closer relationship with my wonderful family than I did the whole time my ex and I were together, because he did his best to cause a rift. And, best of all, I have the most amazing and close relationship with my extraordinary daughter. I'll never know for sure, but I suspect that if I were still with the ex, that relationship would be very different.' *BurningBright*

Lesbian, Gay, Bisexual or Transgender Parents

An awful lot of the challenges facing gay parents will be exactly the same as those facing straight parents. One area which may well be different, however, is the whole business of acquiring the baby in the first place – whether that is by adoption, donor insemination, surrogacy or teaming up with a friend or a gay couple to co-parent a child. Those choices can lead to other issues: how do you co-parent with a male friend or another couple? What legal arrangements do you need to make if you are not a biological parent? What should two mums and two dads be called? (There are some useful websites where you can access information and support, including www.pinkparents.org.uk and www.gingerbeer.co.uk, Rainbow Families section.)

Making it Work: a Mumsnetter's story

'My partner and I chose a known donor – an old school friend of my partner's. We wanted someone we knew, who wouldn't necessarily want to help "parent" our children, but who was willing to be named on the birth certificate. This felt really important to us – that our children would know who their father was. We had an offer from a lovely gay friend of mine, but he wanted to remain anonymous, so we said no.

So, our donor is wonderful and also happens to be a lawyer. We drew up a document which indicated how we wanted to parent. It's not legally binding in any way, but if there were any problems later down the line, the document would be evidence of our intentions at the time.

The document stated that our donor would be named on the birth certificate and could have contact with our children. He actually didn't really want any contact at all, but we were happy to have this in as we knew there might be a chance of things turning out differently once children came along.

We spent a year in total discussing it and checking out how we all felt about it. It's worked out brilliantly. Our sons are six and three and adore their dad! He actually sees them and is more involved than he ever thought he would be – and it's lovely. We

(continued)

live very near him now and he sees them every two to three weeks. Takes them out sometimes, but more often than not comes round to tea and then helps with bedtime stories.

It's a lovely developing relationship between them all, and I'm sure as our sons get older (and a bit easier?!) he'll take them out more and have them over. And we're really pleased with that.

I thought I might be jealous at first, but actually, when you see them together, it's just wonderful. And gives us a break every now and then!' *Doddydot*

You may also find that issues arise out of other people's prejudices about how families should look, whether that is strangers you meet at mother-and-baby groups or members of your own family:

'My partner is expecting our first baby in January. I worried for *years* about the attitudes of our families, which led to a situation where we were starting to think we'd left things too late. If there's one thing it's taught me it's that you can't create a perfect world, and you can't take responsibility for other people's reactions. Both my partner and I only have one remaining parent now, and her mother has always been very accepting of me and of our relationship, and is delighted that we are going to be parents. My mother has always had much more difficulty with it, and does too with the idea of our baby. But ultimately, her attitude has ended up hurting her more than anyone else. The only thing that we will not tolerate will be her making any kind of comment to our kid about his or her family not being "proper". But she can say what she likes to me – and frequently does! I won't deny it's been difficult, but we just have to not let ourselves be undermined by it. If you look at some of the threads on the talkboards you will see that problems with in-laws/parents are hardly the exclusive domain of lesbian parents!' drivingmisscrazy

And remember, you can work out your own 'Mummy'/'Daddy' variations to differentiate between two parents of the same gender, or see what develops:

'I know my gay friends are both "Mum" to their daughter, but when talking about being born, etc. she calls the mum that carried her the "tummy mummy".' litterbug

'In our case, our older son settled for "Mummy" if either of us would do, and "Mummy" followed by one of our names if he wanted one of us in particular. The little one has just followed suit. However, both have been known to shout "mums" very loudly when out and about!' bexgirl

And Finally ...

You may also find your relationships with your pets change:

'The first day my husband and I brought the twins home, one of them was crying. My cat was so disgusted at my lack of ability to stop the crying, she came and bit me in the bottom. I then locked myself in the bathroom in tears as even the cat seemed to think I was rubbish as a mother.' MadamDeathStare

Chapter Nine

Childcare and Going Back to Work

In this chapter ...

'Many women (even most, according to some surveys) would like to do a bit of both (work and spending time with children) while the children are small, without it being financially pointless or crippling their later career prospects.' LadyG

'I don't think it's at all selfish to want to work; no one ever suggests it of men do they?' wickedwaterwitch

'I feel as if I am a mediocre parent and a mediocre employee, spreading myself too thinly, never able to do either job as well as it could be done.' Dinosaur

Just as you find yourself, at last, adjusting to the intense and sometimes claustrophobic world of full-time babycare, you may have to confront what Philip Larkin called 'the toad, work'. When are you going back? On what terms are you going back? Are you going back at all? And who is going to look after the baby when and if you do go back?

Many of us may embark on motherhood with a simple plan of action which is a bit vague at the edges. We will stop work for three or six or nine or 12 months, then baby will go into the care of nursery/childminder/nanny/Granny and we will return, full-time, to our old job, full of renewed vigour and enthusiasm, possibly with a novel ready for publication or a fledgling cupcake business to pootle with of an evening. Our renovated bodies will be trim in our work clothes, and baby will be babbling contentedly on our daily return from work, ready for an hour of play before going into his cot to slumber through the night, so as to delight us again over breakfast the next day.

So Much for the Fantasy: Now for the Reality

OK, so maybe not even the most deluded of us seriously entertained these fantasies for more than the odd moment in a hot bubble bath, while reading a women's magazine feature about working mothers with photographs of a model in a pin-striped suit with a baby on her hip, frowning behind her prop-box glasses. Many of us will have seen friends and sisters full of angst over work and childcare choices. Some of us will actually have crappy, unattractive jobs to go back to and no illusions about our childcare choices. Yet, as the end of maternity leave approaches, it can, none the less, be harder to contemplate handing over your real-life baby into someone else's care than you had anticipated. Not to mention expensive.

The choosing of childcare can be somewhat anxiety-inducing (internal monologue: 'How can I tell this nanny is not a psychopath? Perhaps she is just too nice to be plausible? Fret, gibber ...'). And, however much you want – or need – to work, you may be assailed by guilt and concern that what you are doing is not best for your baby. You may just think you are going to miss your baby.

'I am off to cry some more tears into the bucket of guilt that is labelled "Motherhood".' Ghosty

And even with really good childcare, your life is likely to require a level of planning unknown to you in your child-free state. You will have to think about back-up childcare if your baby is sick and cannot go to nursery (or if his childminder/nanny falls ill). And how to cope if you run late at work or transport lets you down. You will also have to figure out how to get you and baby out of the house of a morning in a reasonably hygienic and presentable condition.

But, it's all doable and you will manage. Sometimes it helps to look at the unedifying crowd of adults on a morning tube train and to reflect that each one has been conveyed, alive and apparently relatively unscathed, from the precarious condition of infancy to fully-fledged, grey-complected, newspaper-reading adulthood. By parents who worked or didn't work or worked some of the time and used all manner of childcare.

'You will soon develop highly organised routines, even if you are a chaotic person. You need *very* reliable childcare. Ideally, you would have a relative near by who could step in in emergencies. If you can, it's great to have help in the home. If not, it is perfectly manageable without, as long as your house is not too big and you don't have silly expectations about housework.' pointgravedogger

'Work out plans B (and C and D) if your carefully balanced childcare arrangements fail for any reason (typically, a sick nanny). A mate you can swap favours with? Another nanny (we have an emergency arrangement with my brother's nanny)? A crèche near your office? Being able to work from home? Baby might not be happy all day with someone strange, but it's reassuring to know that if you wanted to, you could leave them somewhere safe for two hours while you did that one thing you really, really had to do that day, the time for which obviously clashes with your partner's similar emergency.' fridayschild

And a word about those childcare studies. Every few months there is more research comparing one form of childcare unfavourably with another. So bear in mind:

- Studies are just that, studies. Some are very small and actually show very insignificant differences in outcome, or arguably, fail to have adequate control groups.
- The results are often hugely exaggerated to make a news story. A news story which, funnily enough, often contains a dig at working mothers. There's not much mileage in a headline which says, 'Study shows marginal and temporary variation in outcomes between children in different forms of childcare'.

Some very basic principles which emerge from Mumsnetters' experiences show:

- that the quality of the care you choose is more important than the form it takes: a good childminder, a good nursery, a good nanny, a competent grandparent will all do a fine job
- that you must do what suits your family: there is no one solution which is best for every family, contrary to all those articles in the press telling women they should all be working/all be staying at home with their children/all sending their children to nurseries/to childminders/to grandparents
- that childcare belongs to both parents and you must divide it in a way which best suits you all
- that some people – male or female – want to work and some need to
- that there probably was no golden age when all children were cared for exclusively by their mothers who were able to stimulate them non-stop while baking scones and building treehouses.

'My granny was a stay-at-home mum, but with six kids and no electricity in the house, she spent all her time boiling clothes in a copper and scrubbing them with a washboard. The older kids raised the younger ones.' hmb

Maternity Leave: It's No Holiday

Basic entitlements

Time

All employed women are entitled to 26 weeks of Ordinary Maternity Leave. You need not have worked for your employer for any particular length of time to earn this right. You will also be entitled to a further six months Additional Maternity Leave. Again, there is no qualification requirement, but there are some technical differences between the two types of maternity leave, although these have become more and more minimal in recent years. The only difference you may notice is that your Statutory Maternity Pay (SMP) will run out after 13 weeks of AML.

Money

Most women will be entitled to SMP, which is 90 per cent of your wage for the first six weeks, followed by (at the time of writing) £117.18 a week for a further 33 weeks (or 90 per cent of your earnings, if that works out at less than the standard rate). You have to have been employed for the relevant minimum period (26 weeks, ending with the week immediately preceding the 14th week before your due date) and satisfy various other technical requirements, including notifying your employer of your pregnancy and due date.

Your employer may run a maternity scheme which offers you more significant benefits, but which may also tie you to working for a certain amount of time after maternity leave. No one can make you pay back SMP, but some contractual schemes will make you pay back any more generous provision the employer has made unless you come back to work for the specified minimum period (often three months).

If you are not eligible for SMP, you may be eligible for Maternity Allowance.

The statutory provisions which regulate all of this remain complex and change from time to time – see Resources, p. 434 for details of where to get the most up-to-date information.

Some women find themselves longing to be back at work. Just to be free of always holding or pushing another human being can give you a remarkable lightness of being. And you can be in control at a desk. No one else is going to disarrange your stationery. Probably.

'I made no secret of the fact that I had come back to work for a rest. A hot cup of tea. A chance to prioritise work, and get it done in the order I want to and with no interruptions.' Flibbertygibbet

Others don't want maternity leave to end. Possibly not ever.

'The real reason the government wishes to get all us mums back to work is so that they can collect taxes from us. In the meantime, we earn (on average) less than our male partners, spend huge amounts on childcare and feel horribly guilty that we are raising dysfunctional members of society. So now I am going to view staying at home as a blow for freedom.' vkone

And many of us, frankly, have mixed feelings and would happily divide ourselves into two selves, one of whom would go to work and enjoy a bit of caffeine and banter, and the other of whom would be charting baby's progress with the zeal of an anthropologist in the field. And, OK, maybe a third self would just be off having a swim and a massage.

If you have a baby who is a very poor sleeper, you may just not be physically and mentally fit for a demanding job until you have sorted out the sleep thing. So if you have gaily promised to be back after three weeks or six weeks or whatever, and you are just not well or strong enough or don't want to leave your baby yet, don't do it:

'Inevitably, if you are a valued employee, people will forget how long you had off quite quickly, and I think it's better to have a longer break and return at a time when you can focus on your job properly and be happy with your decision to leave your baby during the day.' Ringer

The amount of maternity leave you have may also be determined by how much you can afford, either in brute financial terms and/or in terms of how long it will be before your carefully constructed career starts to crumble. On the latter point, it can help to talk to other women with children in your field or at the place you work about their experiences when making decisions about how much maternity leave is right for you.

The no-real-maternity-leave option

For a few people, a very short maternity leave may just suit. One Mumsnetter – who has managed five children and some very short work breaks – makes her case for getting straight back to the coalface post birth:

1. 'The baby does not have a huge wrench when you suddenly return at six months or a year. If you go back to work when she is two weeks old, she can get used to her good childcare from the father, relative, nanny or whatever, so has continuity and no shock to the system of a later return.
2. You don't have time to get out of the swing of work, so it's all less disruptive to your life.
3. You can establish an expressing system early on, without worrying about how to manage breastfeeding when going back at three months.
4. Both parents can be equally as involved with the children. The pattern at home isn't established that the mother does everything to do with the baby.

(continued)

5. You only lose 10 per cent of pay in the few weeks you take off.
6. If I'm allowed say it, being at home with babies can be boring (not for everyone, I know), so you can skip all that and concentrate on the fun cuddles bit. It can aid mental health.
7. You inconvenience an employer or your customers less. No one will like me for saying this, but in the real world, fathers and mothers taking leave is hard to manage.
8. You may find the physical recovery from birth easier in an office than managing small children and domestic work at home. I certainly found sitting still at a desk, time to rest, relax, get drinks at my leisure helped me get back to normal. Dressing in office clothes too helps get you back to being your normal self.' *Xenia*

For others, this would be madness:

'I was still crying every day until about six weeks after the birth. I had a traumatic emergency C-section, breastfeeding didn't work out for us, so I had the emotional trauma of getting over that, my son was waking up every 1.5 hours from midnight to seven a.m., so I wasn't in a fit state to do much during the day. Plus, I certainly wouldn't have fitted any of my work clothes, never mind put my work brain on. And I don't know about other people's jobs, but I certainly don't find that mine gives me time to relax, drink loads of coffee and sit still at my desk all the time. Perhaps I am in the wrong profession. These are just my personal circumstances – there may be a small percentage of the population who feel differently about it and yes, why not let them go back to work? I know that childbirth is not an illness, but a C-section is major surgery.' *rookiemum*

Going Back to Work: How It Feels, Feelingswise

Some women bounce back to work, shouting hooray:

'I went back to work full-time when my son was 4.5 months old and was sooo happy to be back

at work. I love being with my son but the whole mum-and-baby circuit just bored me to tears.' cmotdibbler

'I'm not bored as such, just feel really "out of things" and lonely. I am desperate to get back to work. At home I find the housework tedious and neverending. When I am working, I am more motivated and it gets done (by my husband and me). I have done all the "right" things while I have been off – I am quite involved in the NCT, go to baby music sessions, baby group etc. ... it just isn't working for me.' onepieceoflollipop

Other women cry for weeks in the run-up to going back to work. Sometimes these lachrymose souls are the very same women who are also shouting hooray.

And baby/toddler will no doubt do a fiesta of adorable things as you are preparing to return to work and start rattling through milestones, just to make it all harder for you.

If you do feel heartbroken, remember the following:

- The anticipation is generally worse than the thing itself. There are a lorra, lorra threads on the talkboards started by women who are dreading leaving their babies and returning to work and lots of posters who say, actually, it's all right when you do it.
- It is probably harder for you than for your baby.
- It is normal to feel a bit naked without your baby for the first few days or weeks back at work. Or to feel like you have misplaced something important.
- There is nothing unnatural about going to work:

'I remind myself that for centuries, kids have been raised by lots of people. It is quite unusual for children only to ever have their parents as their caregivers.' beansprout

- It's OK to use childcare:

'I know it is the right thing for me and my family. Some days it is difficult when I leave my son at nursery, but he is happy and thriving and, being blunt, we couldn't manage without my wage. Stop being hard on yourself – does your husband beat himself about this? I bet he doesn't. Tell him how you feel – share your feelings.' *RubySlippers*

- You will probably get some very lovely welcome homes.
- 'Dressing up really helps! Matching underwear and heels for the first time in eight months – it did help a bit!' *Caz10*

Guilt-edged: Mumsnetters talk about guilt

Judging by the talkboards, not many women escape the guilt:

'You will feel guilty, especially if your children are very young. Try not to get dragged down by guilt though. It's not necessary and it's not good for you.' *pointgravedogger*

Here are two radically different views on why mums feel guilty:

'It's been imposed on you by society. You should feel no more guilty than any father going to work whose children are being well cared for in his absence.' *Xenia*

'Maternal guilt at leaving children in childcare is not imposed by society. The maternal instinct to care for one's own child is hormonal/biological.' *Anna8888*

BUT, whatever the reason for women feeling guilty:

'It will get better. It's OK to be sad.' *moondog*

And remember:

'Working to look after your child financially, even when it kills you to do it, is a huge act of love and self-sacrifice.' *anniemac*

'Quality Time'

Plan to make the most of your time at home, however much that is:

- If you can get help with housework, do. Some mothers say it is worth sacrificing other luxuries (such as holidays and eating out) to buy yourself some time to relax and a reasonably hygienic home to relax in. But for some of us, none of those luxuries is a possibility. And being told to sacrifice something you can't afford to enjoy something else you can't afford is annoying (cf those magazine articles about thrift: 'By saving £2000 a month on throw cushions, I was able to purchase a yacht'). In which case, if you can face it, you might try doing bits of housework in the evening, so it doesn't all pile up for the weekend. Which is not to say there is anything wrong with you doing some housework at the weekends and baby hanging out with you while you do it. You just don't want the whole weekend to go on chores.
- 'It might be worth braving www.flylady.net. I mean she is insane, but she can pare down your housekeeping routine. I do very little now and it all seems to work, but she is a bit over the top – just nick the system and run.' *Cappuccino*
- Reduce time spent shopping: 'Menu plan for the week and get shopping delivered,' advises one organised mum. Buy gifts online. In fact, you can buy pretty much anything online. Get non-food items delivered to your office if there will be no one at home during the day.
- Try to declutter your house before you go back to work. Don't toss the book angrily into the bin at this point, muttering 'declutter, hahaha'; you might just get an opportunity to do it.
- Some people batch cook meals and freeze them to free up time in the evening. Doing a giant cookathon every few months and filling the freezer means you can have healthy home-cooked meals without spending the whole evening cooking them. Again, you have to consult your own domestic skills and tendencies here; some of us get by on cheese sandwiches and apples. Others find a slow cooker is a boon for those sufficiently organised to put some ingredients into it in the morning.
- 'When our children were tiny, we spent weekends mostly at home, putting them first and doing stuff with them,' recalls a mum. This doesn't have to be anything fancy and it doesn't have to be soft

play either – swimming, walks, just hanging out at home messing about with toys.

'I definitely enjoy and appreciate every second of time I get with her, perhaps more than I would if I weren't at work. I just love every single weekend these days. I am still the constant in her life, and probably see her as much as her (stay-at-home) dad does. When I am home, I find I wear her in a sling much more than I used to as we both seem to like this more than the pushchair since I went back to work. I am generally relaxed about night wakings (well, usually; I do have some limits!) and never resent having to bring her into my bed, as I enjoy the cuddles. She loves her daddy and has a great relationship with him, which is great for both of them. She still wants to be with me when she is in a room of people and sees me. It is an adjustment, but I don't see how anyone could describe the relationship between me and my daughter as any less loving or close than if I was home with her full-time. Don't let anyone tell you otherwise!' anniemac

'Due to the fact that I work, she spends loads of time with her granddad and her nanna. That's not to say I don't miss her madly when I'm not with her and can't wait to rush home to her – but that's great. I love that I miss her and when I'm with her it feels like real quality time.' Thomcat

Why Work?

This may sound like a stupid question, but it's one that many of us don't analyse in any great detail before we become parents. But if you are a parent who ostensibly has a choice about working, because you have a partner with an adequate salary, a private income or the ability to spin straw into gold, you may find yourself having to think hard about the pros and cons. There are many reasons why parents work.

Money. Of course, many people don't have the luxury of choice. As one Mumsnetter puts it, 'I do what I have to do to get by. Should we not have children because we are poor?' Many families have mortgages to service that rely on two incomes. Some people are very happy with joint bank accounts and a mine-is-yours attitude; others are horrified by the notion of financial dependence:

'I work for two reasons: to maintain my financial independence and to contribute to society (I work in the health service).' scoobysnax

Stimulation and job satisfaction are huge factors for many:

'I went back to work when my daughter was four months because I didn't much like the baby stage. I needed the stimulation, I needed the validation of being good at something again. We didn't particularly need the money, but I wanted to be more than "just" a mother. I also didn't want to give up my career, having worked damned hard to get where I was.' prufrock

Independence and autonomy, not just of a financial sort, are often cited:

'I need my own things, my purpose outside the home and time with grown-ups. I think it helps me to enjoy my family more.' Enchanted

'I like being independent and having my own mental space without toddlers all around me the whole time.' Fennel

'I work. My reasons for doing so are very personal – my grandmother was widowed at 30 with four small children to raise (one just six months old) and my mother's memories of childhood poverty and my gran's lack of employment options are big drivers. Also, my dad was made redundant when I was at university and I had to work four jobs to pay my living expenses, so I could stay on and get my degree.' sprogger

Some women work in part because they realise they are not cut out for full-time childcare and that their children benefit from being with other people:

'I work because I was going crazy at home. I did not cope with it at all. I didn't have PND, but I did have depression and it was caused by being at home with the baby. It just did not suit me. I love the challenge and variety in my day. I love the rush and the adrenaline. So I know that it is a highly personal choice.' fisil

Some jobs do not easily accommodate career breaks:

'I love what I do – effectively, I have a vocation. Also, it's not something you can give up for five years and just skip back in, at least at my level.' tamum

Dealing with People Resenting You as a Parent in the Workplace

Your own sternest critic in this respect may be you. Especially if you were the person who always worked late, who was always in before everyone else, who took work home at night, who was never ill. And now your working life is affected by things you do not always have control over – childcare failures, child illness, the fact that every hour you work may be an hour which you have to fork out money for. But you can still do a good job – the truth is that oftentimes, work expands to fill the time available to do it in. If you have to be more efficient because there is a nanny knocking off at 7 p.m. or a nursery fining you for lateness, the chances are you will be.

But you may also be in an environment where not working long hours is perceived as slacking. Mumsnetters' experiences suggest that in a decent workplace, if you show you are not taking the piss, you should be able to win round difficult colleagues:

'There are some skivers who are parents and some skivers who aren't. Likewise, there are some grafters who are parents and grafters who aren't.' jbr

But this is by no means universally true. And it's not always just the childless who are the problem:

'The other thing that is really doing my head in is older female colleagues with kids not showing solidarity. They seem to have forgotten ...' Lotsoftoys

If the culture is really unfriendly to families, you may have to accept you are in the wrong place:

'Last week my child was ill and I wasn't able to take him to his childminder. I managed to pick up some work to do at home, and pop into the office for the odd hour or two while grandparents took over. On the whole, I found my colleagues were very supportive. The only comment I had about "working hard" came from a 25-year-old bloke who received a very short comment back. Annoyingly, I had to use up holiday, but because I managed to fit in some work, I actually only took two days out of the four I was off as holiday. It depends on where you work – we have a lot of women in my workplace, two thirds of whom I'd say have kids, so they've been there, done that and got the (vomit-covered) T-shirt.' Emmam

Changing Work Patterns

See, the good side to all the miserable, challenging, how-do-I-manage-this-work-and-childcare-thing angst is that it can sometimes be an opportunity – to change the way you work or the work you do in one of a number of ways. None of this is easy and everyone's solutions will depend on a huge range of factors. But here are some things to think about.

Part-time work – the best or worst of both worlds

The truth is, there is full-time work and there is full-time work with bells on. You might be happy with a genuine 35-hour week with some commuting, but find that in *your* job, full-time really means 50 hours or more. Life with a child can be very tough if both parents do full-time plus because there may be no one to pick up the pieces if childcare falls through or simply no time to do the family administration which you cannot delegate to paid help. For some really very energetic and organisationally gifted couples this all works fine, particularly if they are in a position to pay for stacks of help.

For other families, however, having one parent working part-time while the other works full-time is a good solution because there is someone to do all the life admin that otherwise falls by the wayside. And to spend more time with the baby, while still making a contribution to the family finances and having some time to maintain a career or develop a new one.

The downside is that in many careers, this means one of you ending up on the 'mummy track', i.e. not being in line for big promotions or pay rises or whatever the glittering prizes are in your particular field. But if one parent was looking for a change of direction anyway, this might be a boon. Although finding really interesting and stimulating part-time work can be a struggle.

Another potential downside is that, in some types of work, part-time workers find their part-time work constantly requires attention on days when they are 'not working' or that they wind up feeling they are doing two things badly (but then a lot of full-time working parents feel this, anyway). These are the poor souls at soft play whose whole frame vibrates as another message fizzes through on their BlackBerry. Talking to other parents in your field/place of work who are working part-time is a good way to get a feel for whether it is likely to be a viable option for you. Working out what level of part-time work is really feasible in your job may be key:

'Going from three days to four has made a big difference with me. My job makes no concessions to part-time hours; we have to do the job in whatever time is available, so when I was working three days, I felt that I wasn't doing well at work and I wasn't doing well at home either, trying to do work at home. I had to think it over quite a lot; obviously it's tipping the balance from "mostly at home" to "mostly at work", but I am lucky in that my daughter loves nursery and is very happy there, which made the decision easier.' Angelene

Many families find that the patterns continue to change if and when more children are born, children get older and the family circumstances change. Some parents take a break, work part-time for a period, study for a new career:

'I left a job that I knew wouldn't be the same part-time and changed my career after I went back, after some time off with my first daughter. I'm not using many of the same skills, but I'm using *me* which is, after all, what I have worked for all the time – my ability to change and grow. I think it's good to change; it's good to live a few lives. One would be *really* boring.' Cappuccino

Part-timers' ups and downs

'I am part-time and think it is the worst of both worlds. I feel like I am either trying to mentally prepare for my days off (what we are going to do/where we'll go, etc.) or trying to prepare for my days at work (checking email at home on days off, juggling two wardrobes, being ORGANISED). If I were full-time, I'd have more paid help (I have two hours' cleaning, which is great, but doesn't achieve much) and if I were a SAHM, I'd take life day by day, I think.' *MarlaSinger*

'I went back three days per week days after my daughter turned one, and although I dearly wish I could jack it in at times, we're better off with me staying here. So many people would kill to have a flexible well-paid part-time job. Remember your childcare costs will go down as your children age, and you keep your foot in the door with the option of increasing your hours in the future when the children are older and you want to concentrate a bit more on your career again. You are also getting pension benefits and are eligible for pre-tax childcare vouchers if your company does them.' *Kiwinyc*

'I am about to go back to work part-time for no financial gain and what will prove to be a logistical nightmare, but it will be worth it just to be something other than Mummy.' *Ihg32*

'In my experience, part-time is very hard. It means that you aren't always there when meetings are held, when decisions are made; you might be walking out of the door when vital stuff is happening. You are not able to stay on when needed. You cannot be flexible. I did it for five years, and I didn't realise how bad I felt about it till I stopped. Back full-time now and I am loving my job and my home life is better too. Luckily I have a husband who has been able to step into the breach.' *OrmIrian*

Career Change

Apart from the fact that your old career may not allow you as much time as you'd like with your baby, there are other reasons you might think of changing job post-baby. Some parents find that their priorities have changed and they want an opportunity to use different skills and experience. Some women who have deferred childbearing until their 30s or later may find they have worn out their existing career or it has worn them out. Or that long-hours high-stress jobs no longer work for them once their home life is also challenging:

'I realised that I would have to do two difficult and demanding and stressful full-time jobs. And there weren't enough hours in the day to do both of them properly. And that somebody else could do my "work" job at least as well, probably better, than I could, but NO ONE could do my parent job anywhere near as well as I could.' seeker

Some parents just wake up and realise they were hating their old jobs. Searching for greater flexibility about work hours and patterns, many find themselves looking at the public and voluntary sectors, possibly at jobs in education and childcare. Some take up working freelance, running their own businesses or doing work which can be done flexibly at home.

Here, just to give you some food for thought, are some Mumsnetters' career changes:

- From sales analyst to working in the voluntary sector with women suffering domestic violence.
- From advertising to manager in a charity, via working in PR for charity.
- From marketing/business consulting to technical writing.
- From police officer to teacher.
- From HR manager to teacher.
- From teacher to adult education lecturer.

Applying for flexible working: the technical stuff in a nutshell

If you have a child under 17, you have the right to request to work flexibly and your employer has an obligation to give your request consideration. Flexible working might involve part-time working, changes to shift patterns, a job-share, home-working, working in term time only or working annualised or compressed hours. Your application must be in the appropriate form (in writing, signed and dated). Although your employer is not obliged to allow your request, he is obliged to follow a proper procedure, including meeting with you, before refusing your request. And he must provide one of a limited number of permissible explanations for refusal. He also has to stick to a timetable and he has to give you a right to appeal if he does refuse your request. Have a look at www.acas.org.uk for more detail on the procedure to follow.

If you are proposing to go part-time, think about what you might suggest to your employer about how to cover the remainder of your tasks. It may erode goodwill with your colleagues if you simply suggest that they have the spare capacity to do, say, two days' worth of your work.

It's pretty easy for your employer to find a reason to turn your request down. Try to get your boss genuinely on side by demonstrating practically how your proposal will work.

'Do consider offering a trial period. It provides a bit of a "safe" environment to test your proposal. Your employer is protected as they can withdraw the arrangement if it's not working, and it gives you the opportunity to make damned sure it works brilliantly, so they can't possibly turn it down.' *flowerybeanbag*

Remember that it is not appropriate for your employer to grill you about your childcare arrangements during the course of discussions about flexible working.

Working from Home

Working from home can be a good way of arranging hours so that you get some more time with baby in the morning or evening, while cutting out the time and fatigue of travelling. Obviously, it depends on your job – it will be hard to work from home if you are, for example, an actor or a factory worker or a cleaner. And working from home has the disadvantage that you are stuck with your own four walls, your own sandwiches and your own company. But there are advantages too:

'Being based at home is ideal, as I get to hang out with my daughter until 9 a.m. and then see her at lunchtime, and am here for her when she gets home in the evenings.' CountessDracula

And many people find that working from home one day a week or a couple of days a month is a good balance and allows them to cope with things like GP appointments and being in to receive all that internet shopping.

Mumsnetters' three golden rules of home working

1. You need childcare. Although there are a few impressive/ demented Mumsnetters who manage freelance activities such as writing while a baby naps and in the evenings, for most types of work, e.g. those requiring uninterrupted telephonic communication, you will be doing yourself and your employers/ clients no good at all if you are working from your laptop at the soft-play centre.
2. You need to be disciplined. You really have to make the most of the childcare you have and shut your eyes to the dust on your skirting boards. If you wear glasses, consider removing them any time you leave your work area, e.g. to make a cup of tea or use the loo, so that you will not see any of this alleged dirt.
3. (OK, maybe this is a variation on Rule 2, but it's an important one.) You need to ignore your dishwasher. Do not stack and unstack it during working hours. Ditto washing machine.

If you work from home and baby and childcarer are on the premises, you need to observe boundaries:

'I've done it and it was fine. You have to let go, let the nanny be in charge, let your children know you're not really "at home" – you're *working*. However, I didn't do it with a baby, and that might bring with it a whole other set of issues, a bit different from ones you get with a six- and eight-year-old. I'd recommend some dummy-runs – disappear into the workroom for a few hours at the weekend. Don't crack and come out when the child cries. Then (obviously) there's the whole feeding thing. Are you still breastfeeding? If so, you need to work out what you'll do when working – plenty of options, but be prepared (e.g. if you want to express and have nanny give it in a bottle, you'll have to get your baby used to bottles).' hatwoman

When Work Isn't Working: Becoming a Stay-at-home Parent

The moral of the many angry, angsty, sometimes funny, sometimes murderous threads on Mumsnet Talk on the merits of being a stay-at-home mother (SAHM), versus the merits of being a working-out-of-the-home mother (WOHM) (and the occasional thread about SAHDs) is simply this: there is no one right answer for every parent and every family.

'I think in my case, personally, some of the choices I made earlier in life indicated to me that I was more the "have children, stay at home with them, do lots of crafty things and make lovely messes and enjoy all their milestones and cook a lot" person than a "get a high-powered job in the City, work all the hours God sends, have high-powered friends and live a very adult-centred life" person. I appreciate that not everybody is the same, things are not clear-cut and other people's choices are every bit as valid as mine – but I had a few "crossroad moments" when I was younger, making choices about jobs/locations/ etc., that taught me stuff I needed to know about what would make me happy in the long run. And although I do sometimes get that "grass is greener" feeling, I do think I've done the right thing for me and my particular children. I'm just not the sort of person who would lie on their deathbed saying, "I wish I'd spent more time at the office".' Greensleeves

For some parents, having both partners working is just too stressful, or they may have no money left over from one salary once they have paid the cost of childcare and of the work itself. Some people just want to stay at home and look after their babies themselves:

'When I had my son, I initially returned to work with him in a nursery in the City. I thought this would be a good idea, until I kept finding myself detouring past there on the way to meetings. One day I found myself standing at the window looking at him and realised I would have to rethink.' pagwatch

As many SAHMs point out, there will be plenty of time to work when your kids get older, as long as you recognise that you are coming off the career track – at least in your existing career. In some jobs, you may even be able to take a sabbatical or a career break.

You can always decide to work again. OK, so you may not make Chief Exec, but you can go back. Emmagee

We're not brainwashed cupcake-baking numpties: lots of reasons why some Mumsnetters stay home, at least for a while

'We're now entering my third year of a career break. Every now and again I think, should I go back to work? And resoundingly, I think no. It hasn't all been plain sailing. My car gets older and rustier in the driveway. And I don't remember the last time I bought something for myself clotheswise that wasn't from a supermarket!' *squilly*

'My job is now looking after my son, and I have to confess I have probably turned him into a little project of my own. I just love filling his day up with exciting new things to do or see – even if it's just poking woodlice in the garden. It's great to see his responses to even the most mundane things. Love it, love it, love it and would live in a shed if it meant I could get these first few years to spend with him.' *muddaofsuburbia*

'Most days, I am counting the hours until bedtime, just like when I was working I was counting the hours till quitting time. And I loved my job.' *KateandtheGirls*

'I know it can drive you nuts to be at home all the time, but I guess I've kind of got used to it and – almost like an addict – I need to see what she's up to and be there when she needs me or hits a milestone or whatever. We're not going to have any more, and that's partly why I feel like this. I know soon enough she'll be at school and the week will be mine and I'll pine like a nostalgic old fruit about the long (sometimes magic, sometimes tedious) days at home with her.' *Evita*

'I did earn a pretty comfortable salary. I gave it up and I don't regret it for a second.

I loved my career, I was very committed to it and I was good at it. But this life is seriously f**ing priceless, honestly. I get to spend all day every day with two beautiful, wonderful people and get

(continued)

to share in their lives in a way that I simply would not have had the time or the energy to do had I continued in my career. If you want stimulation, then there are many ways to find that. Your self-esteem does not have to come from work, and it is a myth put about by capitalists that it does. You can find a place for yourself and a happy life for yourself in your family and in the community. Every woman I know in her 50s talks about how important her children are in her life, beyond anything else.' *harpsichordcarrier*

'I like being a SAHM because it means I don't have to be arsed doing things that other people tell me to do. Staying at home being silly, talking gibberish, painting and watching cartoons, or being out of the house first thing in either a uniform or a bloody suit, being bossed about and bored? No contest in my opinion! But SAHM is not for everyone, so each to their own. That's my 2p worth, anyway.' *nbg*

Tips for stay-at-home parents

Wine tends to feature rather heavily on threads about how to survive being a SAHP. Some Mumsnetters heartily disapprove of this tendency and wonder why beer and cocktails don't get more of a look-in.

But here are some tips less likely to end in 12-step programmes:

- 'Plan things to do. 'The key is to do something every day,' reckons one mum.

'You have to be quite businesslike about how you organise your day. It's not like a dreamy drift from Play-Doh (shudder) to play group.' *codswallop*

'Split the week into sessions – mornings, afternoons, evenings, whatever works for you, and know what you are going to be doing for those sessions. Just roughly – like park, CBeebies, café, painting. It keeps you sane, and then the long day doesn't seem neverending and overwhelming. And everyone is so right about the evening drink.' *suzywong*

- See adults. Find local friends who are not at work:

  'If you find another reasonably sane human mother, don't lose her!' *maisystar*

- Try fitting in some studying/evening classes, other things which are not infant-centric:

  'You have to rely on your own resources more to enjoy being a SAHM – I do enjoy it.' *belgo*

- See it as a career change:

  'When I do return to work, it will hopefully be to a job I can feel good about. Motherhood certainly changes your view of life.' *magnum*

- 'Try to read a newspaper and AVOID DAYTIME TELLY AT ALL COSTS (it's the slippery slope).' *tatcity*
- Do not be in your own home too much. If you go out, you don't see the mess at home and get tempted to do anything about it. And the mess cannot worsen on its own.
- Cultivate an alternative philosophy of life:

  'Leave behind the corporate mentality of efficiency and task completion. You will drive yourself mad if you think, "But such-and-such *has* to get done now, but Junior won't let me!" In a way, you'll be happier if a kind of "surrender" takes place – if you don't think too much about the tasks you really *ought* to be doing (or would rather be doing). For me, that's the key: there's so much I'd *rather* be doing than Play-Doh, but I've learnt to dismiss those thoughts and enjoy the moment to whatever extent possible.' *expatkat*

- Establish an early(ish) bedtime for your child or children. Ahem.

Getting gender specific for a moment: stay-at-home dads

There are lots of circumstances in which it may make sense for the father to be the primary carer: he may be less happy in his job or the mother's career may be particularly important to her or more lucrative than his. He may simply be better suited to full-time childcare. Or it may be that each parent can take consecutive time out of their careers, or perhaps both can work flexibly for a period. Like mothers who stay at home, fathers may find they can do things to keep their CVs looking reasonably sprightly during a period of looking after children – some consultancy work, some studying, some creative dressing up of the period out of remunerative employment.

'The challenge of caring for your children, earning an income and finding some level of personal fulfilment is not an exclusively female one. Or it shouldn't be.' Issy

'It is wonderful to go back to work knowing you are leaving your child in the care of the one person in the world who loves them as much as you do.' smallwhitecat

One of the significant downsides for the out-at-work partner of a stay-at-home parent is what they call 'provider pressure' – being the person financially responsible for your whole leaky boat/family. You need to be honest with each other about what you feel about that pressure and how you can share the burden. Many parents who have been on the 'provider' side suggest that having joint responsibility for the financial admin – budgeting and paying bills – helps to share the burden.

A more gender-specific issue is that dads can find it harder to feel accepted in mum-dominated environments. But, hey, someone has to turn those mother-and-toddler groups around.

Before either partner makes a decision to give up working for a period, you should consider this:

'Be very, very clear from the outset between you as to the time horizon you are looking at. Is it going to be three years? Until your children reach school age? Secondary school age? What if you lose your job? Be very, very clear also as to what each one's role in the home is. How are household chores going to be split? Make sure the balance is struck and everyone is happy with what they are expected to do. As a working-out-of-the-house mother, it is very easy to overcompensate and end up doing childcare and housework before going out to work. Then you do a full day's work and come home and do some more childcare and housework ...' citronella

(Of course, the person who goes out to work, male or female, should not generally expect to come home to slippers and a pitcher of martinis, however.)

A father who is at home with his children makes these (again not gender-specific) suggestions:

'Make sure that you and your partner get some quality time together. Recognise that it will be like starting a new job for your partner and help him through the mistakes he makes. Watch out in case he begins to feel isolated and encourage him to have regular time for himself, when he can get out and do what he enjoys. (I have a wargaming evening with friends once a fortnight.) Let your partner know if he's doing well. I try to really look after my wife; I know she has huge demands from her job and I am very appreciative that we have structured our lives so I can take care of the children. Try and show your partner how much you appreciate his taking care of the family.' permanentvacation

Consider what would happen if you split up. A SAHD may well be entitled to maintenance payments and may be more likely to end up with the children residing with him. You need to have a ponder about how you feel about that, and also about whether you will feel jealous about him being the primary carer. If you will, can you overcome that feeling if having him stay at home seems the best option for your family?

With the right characters involved, Dad caring for the children can work really well:

'I think that as a woman, I'm more likely to understand that having children at home all day is full-time work and have sympathy and understanding for him; and ditto, that as a man, I think he'll understand the pressure I face at work.' Blinglovin

But as another working mother and partner to a SAHD says, ruefully:

'The best thing really (and I wish I had had this advice myself at the time) is for both parents to work, but part-time or flexible hours.' SixSpotBonfire

Money Too Tight to Mention? Getting by on One Salary

Obviously, this is not a problem if the working person is a premier-league footballer or a retired banker on a plush pension (plus state-subsidised security arrangements). Otherwise, you are likely to have to adjust your spending habits. Many people's salaries are eaten by childcare costs and the costs of working (clothes, travel, lunches) so, if you do the sums realistically, you may find you are not much worse off if one of you stays home. And you may come to realise how much you were spending on crap you can do without, like lattes and taxis. If you were in a stressful job, you may have spent a lot of your spare cash treating yourself to takeaway food and new tights and buying guilt presents for your kids. It's always worth looking to see whether you are entitled to Working Families Tax Credits (see Resources, p. 434).

You may, however, have to redefine necessities:

'Simple things become great luxuries, and you learn when to shop to get the bargains.' tarantula

'We budget on a monthly basis and give up holidays, don't buy new clothes for ourselves or go out much. It's only for a few short years.' Twiglett

Find a cheaper supermarket. Buy clothes second-hand or on eBay. Buy reduced-price food and freeze it. You can do 'smarter' shopping if you have more time. And smarter cooking. Sell stuff on eBay or old books on Amazon, if you are good at wrapping things up and don't mind spending time at the post office.

'Someone mentioned growing your own veg – we save a lot of money by having an allotment. I also now have time to do a major shop at Aldi for the basics (rice, tins, etc.) and then go elsewhere for other stuff – butcher, etc. This saves me a fortune, plus I've time to plan meals and cook properly. If you're at home, you don't buy sandwiches and have other work expenses.' tearinghairout

Some Mumsnetters find downsizing is the only way:

'We moved – the only way we could have stayed in London was if I went back to my full-time, full-on job. And even then, money would have been tight. So we downshifted to a small town in the southwest. We have a house that would have cost a fortune in London, whereas here we hardly have a mortgage. So we can survive on my husband's salary; haven't needed to eat into my savings too much yet. By downshifting, we've also saved tons. And I'll probably make £4k or so via eBay this year, but that's a bonus, and keeps me entertained.' vonsudenfed

Childcare

Here, before we start wrestling with specifics, are three general points about childcare:

1. Remember, as you take a deep breath and set out on this course, that there will be many things that your child gains from the childcare experience:

'I was at my son's nursery for a parents' meeting. While I was there, he was doing some sand and water play and, later on, tootling around on a ride-on toy in the fresh air with the other children. He was quite clearly having a ball. Quite apart from the developmental and social opportunities his nursery offers him, he would also not have a roof over his head if I didn't work.' Marina

2. Start your childcare research early, if you can. You will feel much better if you don't have to panic buy.
3. Look at a variety of forms of childcare, unless there is a very strong reason for you to go for a particular option. You may have the world's best childminder on your doorstep or a fantastic nursery down the road.

'With my first baby, I visited lots of childminders on the council's list and, frankly, I wouldn't have left a gerbil with half of them – TV on at mega-volume, too few toys, main outings seemed to be trips to Sainsbury's, that kind of thing.' *frogs*

Equally, however, lots of mothers say they wouldn't leave a puppy/cockroach at the nurseries available to them. So keep an open mind while doing your research.

I can't liiiive, if living is without you: separation anxiety

Separation anxiety is that bit when you hand your baby over to the nanny/childminder/nursery key worker and he attempts to graft himself on to your suit jacket with his little, soft, papery fingernails and his surprisingly strong leg muscles. And then he screams inconsolably as you attempt to leave. And when you return, his little face is all puffy and pink from weeping and he holds his little arms out to you *bonelessly* ...

Pull yourself together, woman:

'Separation anxiety is a perfectly normal stage of development when a child starts to realise s/he is a different person from Mum (or whoever has been the main carer) and gets freaked out when you leave the room, etc.' *bundle*

'Separation anxiety usually starts at around nine months of age and then starts to diminish from about 18 months (this does vary a bit from child to child, like most other areas of development). It's believed that they become distressed when their carer is out of their sight because they cannot understand that the situation is temporary and believe they've been abandoned. Therefore, they are distressed for an understandable reason from their point of view.' *northshield*

A lot of parents report peak time for onset of separation anxiety at about eight or nine months. For some, the answer is to ensure

(continued)

your baby is well settled with alternative care before the onset period. Or to wait until significantly after, if this is a realistic possibility. Other parents find that even when the child is settled with an alternative carer at under six months, there can still be a period of separation anxiety. Although it may be less distressing if the baby is already used to new carer/environment.

Some children never seem to show any particular signs of separation anxiety. Apart from making you feel like maternal chopped liver, this is a good thing and not a reflection of how much your baby loves you. Really it's not.

'I do sometimes feel a bit paranoid that while other babies are flinging themselves into the pits of despair, mine is happily waving and kissing, or just running off to play!' *fisil*

Different children develop separation anxiety to different degrees and at different stages. Try not to be too melodramatic yourself. Or at least save the sobbing for your bath. Your anxiety will only increase his.

'You can help your baby to feel secure by gently giving them more space from you, and letting them find out they are OK with other people and with you at more of a distance. It is more that you are "weaning" the baby from their fear that they can't be without you, than "weaning" them from you.' *spink*

Peek-a-boo games can, apparently, work to show that you don't actually disappear permanently when not in view.

'I found that not taking a child from the person they are crying at makes them realise that there is nothing to fear. I would just say, "You're fine, it's OK," and smile. Try to do it with people who are confident handling babies though, not someone who can't deal with it and gets stressed.' *mytetherisending*

Try not to go from all Mummy to all childcare in one mighty blow. See some of the advice below for adjusting to nursery. If your baby is going to a childminder, see if the childminder will agree to visit you at home – this can help to make her familiar to your child in an unthreatening milieu. Similarly, if your nanny can come for some shorter trial periods, this may ease the transition.

Choices, Choices

For many people, the nature of their childcare requirements may effectively make their choices for them. Others will have more freedom to window shop. What follows is Mumsnetters' collective wisdom as to the differences between the various sorts of childcare, and what is good, bad and ugly about each of them.

Spot the difference: nanny and childminder

The nanny:

- is your employee, you can tell her what to do and how to do it
- cares only for your children (unless you have arranged to share a nanny with another family)
- comes to your home, for the hours you require her
- has to be taxed like any other employee; you need to operate PAYE for a nanny, deducting her tax and National Insurance from her salary, plus paying employer's National Insurance (you can get a payroll company to do this for you and there are several which specialise in nannies – they usually have 'nanny' in their title, so are easy to spot if you do an online trawl)
- is generally paid in arrears, which may be in line with how you are paid
- needs a spending kitty – for outings, activities, etc.
- is entitled to paid holiday – as the employer, you have some say as to when she takes this; some families operate a system whereby the nanny chooses say two weeks a year and the rest are selected by them
- can (in England) be part-paid via Childcare Vouchers/Tax Credits if she is Ofsted registered
- tends to do some household tasks, usually related to the children (such as their washing, looking after their toys and bedrooms and cleaning up after meals she has prepared for them)
- will charge per hour, rather than per child, so:

'The more children you have, the better value they are – although this isn't in itself a sufficient reason to have a bus load.' *bigbertha*

The childminder:

- is self-employed
- can care for many children (within regulatory limits), often of varying ages; in England, a childminder must, by law, be Ofsted registered
- works from her own home
- may have fixed opening times – and may not be able to accommodate certain pick-up times; you have to take your child there and collect her
- will dictate the terms of contract; you will pay her as per that contract, usually a month in advance
- will bill you for outings/activities (although some may include certain outings, such as a toddler group in their fees)
- will tell you when she is on holiday and you have to work around it; she may or may not charge you for these periods – it depends on the terms of the contract
- obviously won't do any household tasks apart from those relating to her own household
- charges per child and sets her own prices.

The nursery

Option Three is a nursery. This is an establishment which provides all-day care for babies and pre-school-aged children. There will be a number of adults providing childcare in ratios which depend on the age of the children being looked after, and your child will almost certainly have a 'key worker' especially assigned to him. The facilities usually include some outdoor space and lots of toys and stimulating activities, and nurseries are rigorously controlled by Ofsted.

Nannies, Childminders and Nurseries – For and Against

Each of the three types of paid childcare has its own advantages and disavantages. There really is no universal best solution for every parent and every baby, but here are some things to think about.

Nannies – pros and cons

Well, a nanny can be the most de luxe form of childcare, but the quality of individual nannies is as variable as it is with any other form of childcare.

Pros

- There is significant flexibility about the hours of work, provided you are clear about what you require when you recruit.
- She provides one-to-one care in your own home. You don't have to struggle to get your baby out of the house in the morning.
- She will look after your child when he is poorly.
- You are the boss in relation to food, routines and activities.
- Most will do the bits and bobs around the house you would do – preparing food, cleaning your baby's clothes, looking after his toys.

Cons

- Cost is the big downside. This is likely to be your most expensive option unless you have two or more children or do a nanny share.
- The fact that she is in sole charge means she is not being supervised in the way a nursery worker would be. A mediocre nanny may spend all her time drinking coffee with other nannies and sending text messages, rather than doing the things you have asked her to do.
- She is your employee, with all the responsibility and admin that that entails: tax, NI, possibility of maternity leave, redundancy pay, etc.
- You may have to deal with your own jealousy that someone else is getting to spend significant amounts of time with your baby (although this can be true with a childminder also or, indeed, a key worker at a nursery).
- The level of regulation is lower than that for nurseries or childminders, although some nannies are Ofsteded and you can (should) ask for a CRB check, as well as up-to-date references.

Childminders – pros and cons

Note: a lot of the horror stories about childminders will pre-date the regulation of childminders (banish your mental image of child sharing a Big Mac with the Rottweiler in front of *Jeremy Kyle*, while childminder puffs her way through 40 Silk Cut, before setting her copy of *Take a Break* on fire with some spilled nail varnish and a smouldering dogend). Childminders are now very strictly regulated by Ofsted and have yearly checks for health and safety and hygiene (smoking, for example, is not allowed in the Ofsted rules).

Pros

- They provide your child with the security of ongoing care from one person.
- It is usually possible for children to follow their own routine.
- Some childminders will still take your child when she is ill. (But this may not be a pro if yours is the other non-ill child at the childminder's, about to be infected!)
- A childminder can care for up to three children under five years (one under one), and these children may turn into playmates and surrogate siblings.
- Childminders may have more flexible hours than a nursery. Depending on their arrangements with other children they may be able to provide ad hoc childcare other than that which you have contracted for.
- A childminder will be cheaper than a nanny and may well be cheaper than a nursery too.

'The benefit of a childminder is that children have the same constant care from one person and lunch is prepared for them when they need it, be it 12 p.m. or 2 p.m. It is a home-from-home environment.' Alibubbles

- Some parents say that sensitive children do better with childminders.

Cons

- 'You have no control over pets, visitors, outings, etc.,' says one mother. BUT:

'Many childminders do not allow any visitors at all when minding. I certainly don't and I'm not unusual in this.' *malovitt*

- Childminders often have their own and other children to look after, and there is generally a mixture of ages (although, again, many parents find this a good thing):

'When I take my daughter out in the buggy myself, she finds it boring. With the childminder she is with another mindee in a double buggy and the dog. She loves it.' *onepieceofbrusselssprout*

- Your child's days may be punctuated by school pick-ups (but not for all childminders and, again, you may think this is a good thing – exercise, an outing, sometimes a chance for your baby to visit the school she will eventually attend):

'A school run is really not a bad thing for younger children to experience. The excitement among toddlers, or even younger children, when I say, "Let's go and pick the big children up," is wonderful. All the children are happy to see each other in the school playground, and the interaction continues at my house. The mix of older and younger children can also provide many positive life experiences.' *ThePrisoner*

- If your childminder is ill, you will have to make alternative arrangements. And you will have to work around her holidays.
- Childminders have their own routines and ideas about parenting. You cannot dictate to her.
- A childminder is perhaps more likely to give notice than a nursery, e.g. if her family circumstances change.
- There is no collective responsibility. No other adult is necessarily watching how the childminder looks after the children in her care on a particular day (cue the paranoid *Jeremy Kyle* Rottweiler house fire fantasy above ...).

Nurseries – pros and cons

Pros

Here, according to Mumsnetters, are the good things about nurseries:

- A nursery provides a consistent care environment. It is likely to provide stability and continuity (unless there is a high staff turnover), and you should be able to keep your child in a nursery you are happy with throughout their pre-school period.

- They don't shut because of staff illness (well, major epidemics aside).
- Nurseries have more varied facilities than your own home or that of a childminder: child-sized loos and basins, a wide range of toys and equipment, sometimes good outdoor spaces.
- Nurseries are more highly and publicly regulated than other forms of childcare.
- You are not leaving your child with one single other person, but with a group of people with 'collective accountability'. For some parents this kind of arrangement feels safer.
- There is lots of social interaction with other children. Some parents report that their children who have been at nursery since babyhood have almost sibling-like relationships with other children.
- There are lots of activities.
- Some nurseries can accommodate your baby's own routines:

'The nursery where my daughter goes is fairly flexible about meal and sleep times.' *Bugs*

- Children who have been to nursery often seem to find the transition to school relatively easy.

Cons

Not all parents are fans of nurseries. The debate mainly centres on how suitable nurseries are for children under two – whether they get enough individually tailored attention, and whether nurseries make them antisocial (as some studies have suggested) or the opposite (other studies ...):

- 'Nursery workers I know felt it was not right for the under-twos. They say no matter how hard you try, you can never give the babies the attention they need. Babies cannot sleep when they want, feed when they want. There is such a strict structure and with so many children it has to be kept to. Key workers, in theory, are supposed to alleviate the situation, but some babies are in daycare 12 hours a day, staff work shifts, have meal breaks and rest breaks, holidays and sickness, so no child is going to be able to attach firmly to another carer.' *Alibubbles*

- 'I used to run a baby room in a day nursery. It was a warm and happy place. I have always said that nursery is great for the over-twos, but I would never put my baby into one, for the simple reason that I always felt that although we did our best, we could never give them all the attention they needed. It's very difficult to deal with things if three are crying at one time and one might be trying to sleep and you're in the middle of a messy activity with the other two.' *Aero*

Others, however, suggest that some nurseries do cater well for younger babies:

- 'I worked in a private day nursery. In my baby room, babies were cuddled, sung to, entertained, loved. They do get one-to-one when others go to bed, and if you are a stay-at-home-mother, you don't give your child ten hours of one-to-one, anyway. You know your child better than anyone. If they're happy, then the childcare they receive – whether childminder, nanny or nursery, is good.' *cuppy*
- 'Well, it's hard to counter research with anecdotes, but my children went to nurseries in the mornings from babyhood. They were with me or my parents in the afternoons. I thought that was a good balance. They are now six and nine and are very happy, well-adjusted and well-behaved children. They are both very empathetic and moved easily. I believe the quality of the interaction and the general atmosphere of the nursery is the key feature.' *tamum*

Many parents believe simply that some babies do not thrive in a nursery setting and others do:

- 'My daughter is much happier with a childminder because she is a shy child and needs continuity of care, which she wasn't getting at her nursery.' *Acinonyx*
- 'My son is a very loud, lively two-year-old who thrives with other children. He was originally with a childminder who could not offer him as many activities as the nursery.' *jrsmum*

As well as the ongoing suitability for the under-twos debate, there are some other, less controversial, downsides to nurseries:

- Expense: private nurseries can be extremely expensive, especially in London.

- Lack of flexibility: the nursery may be unable to accommodate a parent arriving late for pick-up and may charge a significant overtime fee.
- There may well be waiting lists for good and popular nurseries.
- Bugs travel through nursery populations like, well, bugs. Be prepared for lots of them in the first year, particularly if baby is at nursery, but remember that the upside is that he is building his immunity. Try filling your (weaned) baby with superfoods, fruit and vegetables.

Eenie Meenie Miney Mo: Making the Choice

Whichever form of childcare you choose, you are likely to be asking yourself the same basic question: do I think my baby will be safe and happy with this person/in this place? There is a lot to be said for listening to your instincts, provided you have some (and they aren't completely addled by new-mother anxiety). But there are also specific ways of investigating the different kinds of childcare.

Selecting a nanny

What you want, ideally, is someone who can be a partner in caring for your child. How much of a 'friend' she becomes depends on you, her and what you feel comfortable with, given that she is also your employee and there may come times when you have to deal with tricky issues, like performance.

Note: we refer throughout this section to the nanny as 'she' – there are, of course, male nannies (or mannies), but the same rules apply.

It is worth starting your search with an idea of what your irreducible minimum requirements – in terms of experience, qualifications and other qualities – are. How important are childcare qualifications? There are different views on this one:

'Experience and good references are worth more than a bit of paper, but a qualification in my opinion shows a certain amount of commitment, and means that the nanny does actually know a bit about children at all their different developmental stages, whereas someone with three years' experience and no qualification may have worked with only one specific age group and be clueless about any other.' frannikin

It is also increasingly easy to check that your nanny candidate is not an actual convicted murderer and baby trafficker. Ofsted-registered nannies will have enhanced CRB checks. More and more nannies are becoming registered.

'There are criteria that need to be met – training requirements – which some people may not want to do, but there will be others who already have the necessary training and thus becoming registered is quite easy.' nannynick

There are lots of ways to trawl for nannies: agencies, adverts in the *Lady* magazine, websites such as gumtree, nannynet, nannyjobs and mumsnet, of course.

Agencies charge large fees (often a month's salary), but they do sift out some of the real duffers for you, if you can't face the work involved in conducting your own recruitment exercise from scratch. Some agencies are more stringent than others about references and so forth, so if you are going to pay them a hefty fee, make sure they are actually doing something for the money. But then check the references yourself, anyway.

You can get hundreds of phone calls/emails after advertising, 90 per cent of which will be from candidates who have entirely misunderstood the job and what you are looking for. It can be easier to operate through an email address, rather than a phone number, although you may find yourself subsequently getting some odd 'friend' requests from social networking sites.

You should start looking, ideally, at least six weeks before your planned start date, although there is no harm in starting earlier. Some very covetable nannies will know that their jobs are coming to an end months in advance because, for example, their existing charges are off to school.

Always press the references hard. Cross-check dates and details. Would they employ her again? What was the best thing about her? What was the worst thing? If you are lucky, you will get a reference for the nanny you like which just glows, in a genuine way. A really good nanny inspires such pitiful excesses of love and gratitude in the parental heart, it will spill down the phone line at you. So beware the hesitant or lukewarm or technically-OK reference:

'Having had quite a few nannies (some significantly better than others), I now feel I know what to look for in references. What you don't want is just a list of what she did and a few platitudes. What you're looking for are things like, "We will miss her for ever", "She was always cheerful and did all her jobs with a smile on her face", "Whoever gets X next will be in for a treat". If you don't get this, but still think she might be the one for you, follow up the references on the phone – you can usually tell by the tone of their voice what they really thought of her.' Hollee

The interview: sorting the Mary Poppinses from that scary one in The Hand that Rocks the Cradle

So here's a starting point. (You will no doubt have your own particular quirks and queries.) Do you agree on the basics – food, discipline, routine? Do you think you can get on with her and communicate well? Ask her what was her favourite job and why? And what was her favourite aspect of her most recent job? (The nanny who frankly says it was the swimming pool or the plasma screen TV may not be what you are looking for.) Ask what activities she likes to do with a baby, how she would plan her day and whether she'd be happy to fill in a daily diary? Does she show interest in the baby?

Make clear what housework you would expect. Generally clearing up after children and their meals, looking after their bedrooms and laundry are par for the course for a full-time nanny. As one mum says, 'If you're working full-time, it can be demoralising to come home and have to do all the stuff that you've presumably paid someone else to do.'

Discuss overtime and what the deal would be if you got stuck at work, how frequently that might occur and what payment she could expect. Don't set an unrealistic finish time which you are regularly going to exceed: 'Don't think that being late won't be a problem because she is being paid for it,' warns a wise Mumsnetter. But if you can let her go early sometimes, you will build up goodwill for times when you are late. And try to warn her whenever you are going to be late. Allow for some handover time in your schedule.

You should also talk at the interview about any babysitting you might ask for and whether that would be acceptable to her. Discuss petty cash with her: what is she responsible for buying? What would you expect her to spend on outings, snacks etc.?

Talk to her about the contract you propose. You can get lots of off-the-peg contracts (and your payroll service may be able to help you, if you are using one). But however you do it, be very clear about the following:

- Notice periods (either side)
- Sickness absence and pay
- Holiday entitlement
- What happens if there are conduct or performance issues
- What she should do if she has concerns/grievances

Consider asking your top one, two or even three nanny candidates to do a paid trial day.

Note: a nanny who brings a photo album of pictures of her charges and the birthday cakes she made them is likely to be a good bet (or very cunning).

Choosing a childminder

Here's how to go about it:

Source childminders. If you can get a recommendation from someone you trust, that is ideal. Otherwise, your local council should be able to provide you with a list of registered childminders with vacancies. Also, have a look at Child Care Link – a government service which provides information and advice on childcare (see Resources, p. 434, for contact details):

Once you have candidates, you should look at their Ofsted reports. Then, consider Alibubbles' questions (not all of these points may be important to you), as well as her Top Ten Quality Pointers in the box, opposite:

Alibubbles' list of questions to ask childminders and things to check out

- How long have you been working with children?
- What training have you had? Any qualifications? Are you part of a network? Have you achieved a quality-assurance qualification (look at her registration certificate and insurance details)?
- Do you have up-to-date first-aid training?
- Have you got a food hygiene certificate?
- Do you enjoy being with children and why?
- Can I look around, see the rooms and outside playspace? (If there is no outside playspace: how will you make sure my child gets the chance to play outside?)
- Where will my child rest?
- What kind of food and drink will you give? Can I see a menu?
- What will my child do all day?
- How do you encourage good behaviour?
- Will my child be with a regular group of children? How old are they? How will their timetable fit in with my child?
- How will you make sure I know how my child is getting on?
- What hours are you open?
- How much do you charge? What about when my child is sick/on holiday?
- What do you do in an emergency?
- When was your last Ofsted? Can I see the report?
- Can I see your contracts and record forms?

Alibubbles's Top Quality Pointers

'When you visit possible childcare options, look for these Quality Pointers:

- Are the children calm, safe, happy and busy?
- Do children play and talk together?
- Is the childminder listening to the children and answering them carefully?
- Is the childminder friendly and proud of her work?
- Is she joining in with what the children are doing?
- Are there lots of fun activities planned to help children learn and play? Can children plan some of these activities themselves?
- Are there plenty of clean toys and equipment for children to use?
- Are the premises clean, well kept and safe for children?
- Do parents have plenty of chances to say what they want for their children?
- Listen to your child and find out more if he/she is unhappy.
- Always trust your own feelings about your childcare – you know your child best.' *Alibubbles*

Choosing a nursery

Local authorities keep lists of nurseries but, again, if you can get a recommendation, it's a good start. As ever, you need to ask the right questions and make the right observations. Many of these may be covered in the nursery's prospectus:

- Check the Ofsted report.
- Are there opening hours which suit? What happens about holidays?
- What is included in the fees? What is the deal with nappies and food?
- Look at the care ratios: some are better than those required by law; the minimum is one carer for three children under the age of two.
- Is there a good outdoor space to play? How much time is spent outdoors?
- Look at the loos.

- Ask about the food. Look at a menu. Does it seem healthy? Or is it all turkey twizzlers and novelty-shaped meat by-products with chips (probably less likely in these post-Jamie Oliver times than it might once have been)?
- What happens if a child gets sick at nursery?
- What happens if a child needs to sleep? Will his naptimes be catered for?
- Ask what staff turnover is like. High staff turnover is a bad sign. How many staff members are qualified?
- What activities are the children engaged in?
- Is there a key-worker system, i.e. where each child is assigned a carer who builds a special relationship with him and monitors his development. What happens in the absence of your child's usual carer: at lunchtime, when there is staff holiday or sickness?
- How does the nursery deal with worms and nits?
- What is the average age of employees?
- Bring your child to visit the nursery and see how he and it respond to each other. Watch what goes on. Get a feel for the place and the staff. 'I saw nursery nurses caring for their charges – holding them, cuddling them and playing with them,' recalls one mum. On the other hand, you may see staff spooning food into babies while nattering about their nights out.

'Ask how many staff have left in the last year. (DON'T let them squirm out of this one.) How many kids in one room at any time? (Because although the ratios are set by law – 1:3 for babies – the reality of a huge room with lots of crying babies is pitiful. I've seen it. It's utterly grim. When visiting, do they allocate a member of staff to babysit your baby while you look around? Good Nursery – will look after your baby and bring him to you the minute he asks for you. Bad Nursery – you leave your baby in the room but no one really makes an effort to include him in play or reassure him (my son was actually ignored on a visit and he came screaming after me).' Highlander

Instincts you didn't think you had may kick in: 'I did truly just know which one was right on walking through the door,' asserts one mum.

'Our son went full-time at eight months to a local university nursery which has a low turnover among its largely mature and 100 per cent qualified staff and is only small. I think size does matter.' Marina

Settling in to Nursery

Some nurseries will have a very gentle settling-in process. This is great, but obviously, you need to plan your return to work accordingly.

'1st visit – me and my daughter stayed in the room for an hour; I sat and played with her and chatted to the staff. 2nd visit – me and my daughter stayed in the room for an hour, but I left her to it as much as possible. 3rd visit – me and my daughter arrived together, I stayed for 15 minutes, then went upstairs to the staff room for a coffee and to fill out forms; was gone about 20 to 30 minutes, then came back for her. 4th visit – dropped her off for 30 minutes. 5th visit – dropped her off for an hour, including a snack time.' amidaiwish

'Ask the nursery what their experience is and their induction processes. My son was a bit clingy when he first started, but very, very quickly settled in and is extremely happy at the nursery. IF they are a good nursery, they will be happy for you to phone any time for an update, and will be honest about how long it takes him to settle. At my nursery, induction for my son took place over a four-week period, building up from me staying, to me leaving for an hour or so, to an eventual dry run, where they asked me to get him in for 8 a.m. on the Friday before I went back to work, so that we had a rehearsal of getting out on time. That day he stayed till lunchtime.' Waswondering

It helps if you can leave your baby with the same person on each visit, and changing the person who drops baby off may ease the transition, if this is possible:

'Our son was 8.5 months old when he started nursery, three months ago. Our initial settling-in visits went quite badly, with both him and me ending up in tears. Our nursery then recommended my husband did the drop-off instead of me as he was more used to Dad leaving. It took a couple of weeks for him to settle, but he now seems to love it and is much much better at being left with friends and relatives at home too.' Liff

Check out things like sleep times and meal times, if the nursery is not able to accommodate a baby's existing patterns. If you can mirror the nursery routine at home in the run-up to going to nursery, that will be one less adjustment to make.

'You can also check about taking in a sleeping bag/cuddle blanket to help your baby feel at home.' riab

Even the most hand-reared chicks can settle nicely:

'My daughter was 11 months when she started nursery. She was still breastfed, rejected bottles, hardly ate solids, had separation anxiety, would only fall asleep with nursing or in moving buggy, co-slept in my bed. We settled her in very gently. Grandma did the drop-off. Take about five minutes chatting with carers, then say goodbyes casually, like nothing is wrong, hand to carer to cuddle, then LEAVE. The howling, if any, should stop after a few minutes. The carers will call you, anyway, if it goes on for too long. When I pick up, I always peep through the door (out of my daughter's sight) to make sure she is not crying. If you are worried about cuddling to sleep, make sure the carers are prepared to do that for your baby.' blueshoes

Do not sneak out. It doesn't work and can lead to hysteria:

'I've found it easier to hand over my son after a brief chat with the nursery staff about how he is that day, with a big smile and kiss for my son (even when I feel like crying), say "Bye bye, see you later," then walk out ... quickly ... without looking back. It's horrible, but I think it's better for both of us if I don't hang around, otherwise I think I would get distressed trying to calm down my son, he would sense my anxiety as well and it would just make him worse.' preggersplayspop

Be upbeat and hide your own anxiety; give the nursery all the help you can to settle your baby:

'Don't be afraid to tell the nursery exactly what your baby likes and dislikes, how you settle her, everything you can about her, no matter how trivial – it will give them a much better idea of her personality and this may help them to calm her quicker.' pinkandsparkly

Adjusting your baby to something other than your home-cooked messes and ergonomically correct finger foods may take a little while:

'With regards to not eating nursery food, that is something that will come in time. Ask nursery staff to introduce a little of the nursery food alongside their stuff brought from home. I had one baby who was fed baby food jars at home, so I used to mix it with some cooked fresh veg at nursery to get them used to the taste.' glitterandsparkle

You may find there are three stages to adjustment (yours and baby's):

1. Horror and alcohol:

'Pass me the gin. Had to leave my son crying this morning. It's broken my heart. I went back in after an hour to see how he was getting on – he was fast asleep in a cot; they said he cried for a while, then fell asleep. I have this horrible image of him crying himself to sleep because his mum wasn't there.' PuppyDogTails

2. Stiffening of upper lips:

'I had the oh-no-training-like-a-dog moment. And then I thought, it is all very *well* doing attachment/instinctive/caveman parenting when they are tiny, but you cannot do it and go back to work. You just can't. So training may be contrary to the spirit of what you've done so far, but unless you're up for eternal SAHM-dom, you're going to do it. My daughter did two weeks of wailing (including food/milk refusal, them having to come and fetch me from the car park, etc.), a week of three-minutes-of-tears, a week of mild-whimper, and, ultimately greeting the staff with smiles, holding her arms out for a cuddle. So long as you like and trust the staff, you'll get through it and, more importantly, so will your child.' MrsBadger

'She falls on the toys without a backward glance and I skulk off unnoticed ...' MrsBadger

Granny

Granny here is a code word for any family member who may have agreed to provide some childcare. There are lots of advantages to this – it is often free and your baby will be with someone she already knows and whom you trust.

Obviously you cannot look at Granny's Ofsted report or demand a CRB check, and you may have to accept that she is not going to do everything exactly as you would. Drawing up an extensive manual for her to follow is likely to be a trifle insulting. ('Seven typed pages of instructions is an awful lot! Your mother-in-law brought up your partner – it's not as if she's never seen a baby before,' as one mum correctly points out.)

But you can discreetly and tactfully explore whether the arrangement is likely to work. Is she happy to parent – at least broadly – as you do (food, discipline, etc.); or are you happy to live with the differences? If the whole thing is going to drive you both mad, open a fault line in the bosom of your family and other histrionic mixed metaphors, this may not be the mode of childcare for you.

'The downsides potentially come when grandparents are doing full-time (or close to it) care. It's difficult to make requests assertively when someone is "doing you a favour", rather than being paid by you/your employee. For a day a week, it's not a big issue. Five days a week – well, they are seeing more of your child than you are and you want to be "the boss" of what happens, how and when. A day a week, though, is a lovely arrangement, and one that I think would hugely benefit any child (having that special bonding time with Granny), Granny (gets that bonding time with her grandchild) and parents (saves you a bit of dough!). My mum has my son two to three afternoons a week, and while we don't pay her (she wouldn't accept money), we try to make sure all "expenses" are paid for (i.e. if she takes my son out anywhere or buys him little treats) and we try to treat my mum now and then, with a nice meal or theatre tickets, etc. – just to let her know we are very grateful for all that she does for our family.' MrsMattie

If money is going to change hands, remember you are allowed to pay a family member to look after your child in your own or the relative's home, without them being registered as a childminder. However, if you are considering having a friend look after your baby (in her own home), she would have to be registered as a childminder in order for it to be legal for you to pay her. If she's looking after your baby in your home and you are paying her, you would just treat her like a nanny, i.e. she wouldn't have to be registered, but you would be liable for her tax, NI, etc. If she is looking after your baby either in your home or hers and you're *not* paying her (lucky you), then you can do what you want.

Mumsnetters' Tips for Getting Everyone Out of the House in the Morning

There is no greater organisational feat than preparing an adult for its working day and a child for its childcare in a way that ensures each is appropriately arrayed and equipped for its tasks, and arrives at its place of business/play on time. This is where other mothers' hard-learnt multitasking tips and survival skills can make the crucial difference between arriving at work with everything you need and finding nothing in your handbag but Tombliboos.

The baby side of this doesn't apply, if your childcare comes to you. But even if you just have to thrust your baby at your nanny, you will still require a certain organisational genius.

Bags and stuff

Advance preparation is absolutely vital in this area. All bags (including your handbag) should be pre-packed. Your clothes and your baby's clothes should be laid out. Do check the weather to make sure the clothes you select are weather-appropriate. And do all of this before you rest at night. Any packed lunches or other foodstuffs should also be prepared the night before.

Have a stash of stuff your baby needs at your nursery/childminder – e.g. ready-made formula if appropriate, cups, spare clothes and nappies.

Your toilette

Get yourself ready before your baby is awake if possible.

'BUT put dressing gown on over work clothes until baby has eaten.' lou99

Or a large shirt.

'I am aware that this will be perceived as really grotty, but could you shower and blow-dry hair the night before? I reckon this saves me 20 minutes in the morning, and I don't smell too badly.' PerkinWarbeck

And you can always use a baby wipe to freshen up.

'When you've washed hair night before, get some dry shampoo. Good spray, good brush. If you need to restyle somewhat, quick spray of dry shampoo can help. I also keep in my office for when I'm running REALLY late:

- spare make-up bag
- face wipes (also do for underarms and, er, fanjo if really scummy)
- deodorant and cologne spray
- gas-powered styling brush/tongs combo
- mirror.' WilfSell

Practice

Do some trial runs before you actually start work to see where the potential problem areas are.

Breakfast

If you have to accommodate a long and leisurely morning breastfeed, you will have to get up that bit earlier:

'If you need to get up at 5.30 a.m. for the next year, then just do it. You WILL cope, but just make sure you adjust your and baby's bedtime so that you still get enough sleep.' findtheriver

A bigger baby/toddler may be able to breakfast in the car/bus. Or can your baby breakfast at his nursery/childminder. Can you breakfast at work or on the way to work?

Some mothers recommend a plastic booster high chair which you can stick on a wipeable mat, so that your baby/toddler can be self-feeding while you run around like a headless chicken dressing and grooming yourself.

Share the load

Divide the tasks between the available adults:

'When I worked, I would get up at six and have my shower and get ready (hair/make-up, etc.) and my husband would get up for our son. If the baby woke later than six then that would be a bit of a lie-in for my husband. He would give our son his breakfast and/or bottle. Then, when I was ready, I would come down and take over getting our son dressed, etc. while my husband got showered and dressed.' Ghosty

'Bath baby the night before. Pack baby's bag the night before and make sure your clothes and underwear are set out the night before as well.' Ledodgy

Baby's toilette

If you are really desperate, dress your baby the night before. Put a T-shirt and bib over the baby while breakfasting, then remove at nursery/childminder: ta-dah, clean baby.

'Another Mumsnetter told me this and it's been unbelievably helpful. Buy your child a selection of long-sleeved bodies which are quite T-shirty, rather than vest in style (GAP do really nice ones) and tracksuit bottoms. Put them in the body the night before, then the next morning all you need to do is change their nappy and yank up some trackies. Takes seconds. You can chuck a zip-up fleece over the top when it's chilly or swap for short sleeves in high summer. Genius.' spicemonster

Sleep Management

Well, there is no bigger issue than sleep, and no sleep and work is a horrible combination. To make sure you get 'enough' sleep to stay sane:

'One night a week, go to bed at the same time as your child. Sounds utterly ridiculous, I know. But my God, it works, in terms of avoiding burnout. Take a book/newspaper, if it's too early for you to sleep. I read this on Mumsnet, thought it was rubbish, but actually it is a great piece of advice.' wobbegong

Multitasking – Mumsnetters who can't quite separate home from work

'When a patient – an adult, grown-up patient – new to contact lenses managed to put his contact lens in first go, I exclaimed, "Good boy!" Please tell me I'm not the only one to have done things like that!' *chipmonkey*

'I am famous in my office for taking a carload of engineers down the M11 and pointing animatedly at the roadworks: "Look – diggers!" I think they were interested, actually – just too embarrassed to admit it.' *gizmo*

'I took the hand of my head of department to help him across the road. He is in his 50s. He knows how to cross roads.' *Libra*

'I am an anaesthetist. On one of my first days back to work after maternity leave with my daughter, I put someone out saying, "Sleepy time now, sweet pea ...". I suppose I could have added, "Here's blankie".' *rempy*

Resources

Breastfeeding

Mumsnet.com (www.mumsnet.com/Talk/ breast_and_bottle_feeding)
For advice and support from thousands of other breastfeeding mothers.

Association of Breastfeeding Mothers (www.abm.me.uk)
A charity run by mothers for mothers, committed to giving friendly support and supplying the right information to all women wishing to breastfeed.

La Leche League (www.laleche.org.uk)
Breastfeeding support from pregnancy through to weaning.

Breastfeeding Network (www.breastfeedingnetwork.org.uk)

The Twins and Multiple Birth Association (TAMBA – www.tamba.org.uk)
Information on breastfeeding twins and multiples, plus links to local support groups.

How Breastfeeding Works (www.howbreastfeedingworks.com)
Support, articles and blogs.

Kellymom (www.kellymom.com)

NCT (www.nctpregnancyandbabycare.com/home)
For breastfeeding information and support.

NHS (www.breastfeeding.nhs.uk)

Childcare

Mumsnet.com (www.mumsnet.com/Talk)
Has a childcare section covering nannies, nurseries and childminders.

Child Care Link (childcarefinder.direct.gov.uk/childcarefinder)
Government online search facility to help you find childcare and nurseries in England by postcode or town.

Daycare Trust (www.daycaretrust.org.uk)
Information and services to help you make the right decision
about childcare for your child.

**Early Years Foundation Stage (www.direct.gov.uk/en/Parents/
Preschooldevelopmentandlearning)**
The structure of learning, development and care that all early-
years providers have to follow for children from birth to five years.

**The Department for Education and Skills
(www.dfes.gov.uk/nanny)**
The DFES publishes a guide to choosing a nanny called 'Need a
Nanny?'.

Ofsted (www.ofsted.gov.uk)
The official body for inspecting childcare providers, such as
nurseries and childminders. Provides links to reports and official
publications, as well as FAQs and contact details.

**Professional Association of Nursery Nurses (PANN –
www.pat.org.uk)**
Note: you can also visit www.doula.org.uk for doulas and
reputable childcare agencies for maternity nurses.

Childcare benefits (www.direct.gov.uk/en/Parents/Childcare)
Government information on financial and practical help you
can get with childcare, from tax credits to flexible working
arrangements.

Health – Babies' Health

Mumsnet.com (www.mumsnet.com/Talk/childrens_health)
Share your concerns with other parents.

Bliss (www.bliss.org.uk)
Information and support for parents of premature babies.

Eczema (www.eczema.org)
The National Eczema Society provides information about all types
of eczema, articles and fact sheets that you can download, plus a
really useful helpline for info on treatments and support groups.

Great Ormond Street (www.childrenfirst.nhs.uk)
Comprehensive guide to children's health.

Group B Strep support (www.gbss.org.uk)
Information on testing and symptoms, plus support and advice.

The Meningitis Research Foundation (www.meningitis.org)
Has lots of information. See also the Meningitis Trust
(www.meningitis-trust.org), which has a downloadable symptoms
card you can carry around with you.

Royal Horticultural Society (www.rhs.org.uk)
For information about poisonous plants. Or if you are concerned
about poisons, ring the poisons unit at your local hospital.

NHS (www.nhs.uk/Pages/HomePage.aspx)

Health – Maternal Health

**Mumsnet.com (www.mumsnet.com/Talk/general_health,
www.mumsnet.com/Talk/feeling_depressed)**
General health discussions here, plus help and support with
mental-health issues.

Association for Postnatal Illness (apni.org)
Telephone helpline and information leaflets, plus volunteers
network, to help women with postnatal illness.

Birth Trauma Association (www.birthtraumaassociation.org.uk)
Supports all women who've had a traumatic birth experience.

Healthtalkonline (www.healthtalkonline.org/Pregnancy_children)
Carefully researched patient experiences of pregnancy, post-
pregnancy, immunisation and health screening.

**Royal College of Psychiatrists (www.rcpsych.ac.uk/
mentalhealthinformation/mentalhealthproblems/
postnatalmentalhealth)**
Expert advice about postnatal depression.

Sands (www.uk-sands.org)
Support for anyone affected by the death of a baby.

Health – Special Needs

Mumsnet.com (www.mumsnet.com/Talk/specialneeds)
For help, support and empathy from parents of children with
special needs.

Birth Defects Foundation (www.birthdefects.co.uk)

Birthmarks (www.birthmarksupportgroup.org.uk)
For information and support.

Cerebral palsy (www.scope.org.uk)

CLAPA (www.clapa.com)
Support for babies and their families affected by cleft lip and/or
palate.

Contact a Family (www.cafamily.org.uk)
Support, advice and information for families, no matter what their
condition or disability.

Cystic Fibrosis Trust (www.cftrust.org.uk)
Information, support and, where appropriate, financial help for
families affected by CF.

Down's Syndrome Association (www.downs-syndrome.org.uk)

**Association for Spina Bifida and Hydrocephalus
(www.asbah.demon.co.uk)**

Parenting and Families' Support

Mumsnet.com – local (www.mumsnet.com/Local)
Meet other mums with babies in your area, find out what's on
and pick up tips on everything from local playgroups to reliable
plumbers.

Advice Now (www.advicenow.org.uk/living-together)
For information on your rights as co-habitants vs your rights as a
married couple.

The Citizens Advice Bureau (www.citizensadvice.org.uk)
Can advise on questions about maternity leave, pay, etc.

Department for Children, Schools and Families: Early Support (www.dcsf.gov.uk/everychildmatters/healthandwellbeing)
Also, visit www.direct.gov.uk for good up-to-date guidance on your entitlements.

Disabled Parents Network (www.disabledparentsnetwork.org.uk)
Information, advice and peer support for parents with disabilities.

Gingerbread (www.gingerbread.org.uk)
The UK's largest organisation for lone-parent families.
Also, talk to other lone parents at Mumsnet.com:
www.mumsnet.com/Talk/lone_parents

Working Families Tax Credits (www.direct.gov.uk/WorkingTaxCredit)

Relationships

Mumsnet.com (www.mumsnet.com/Talk/relationships)
Rant, rave and be reassured on Mumsnet's (very busy) relationships boards.

Relate (www.relate.org.uk)
Relationship counselling, sex therapy, mediation and support face-to-face, by phone and via the website.

Sleep

Mumsnet.com (www.mumsnet.com/babies/sleep)
To share the pain and talk to other mums in the middle of the night, plus advice and support, visit Mumsnet.com/Talk/sleep; and for more in-depth info:

NHS (www.nhs.uk/Livewell/childhealth0-1/Pages/Babysleeptips)

Cot death (fsid.org.uk)
For the latest information and advice.

Cry-sis (www.cry-sis.org.uk)
Support for families with excessively crying, sleepless and demanding babies.

Twins and Multiple Births

Mumsnet.com (www.mumsnet.com/Talk/multiple_births)
Talk to other parents of multiples.

Multiple Births Foundation (www.multiplebirths.org.uk)
Support for families with twins and triplets.

Tamba (www.tamba.org)
Provides information and mutual support networks for families of twins, triplets and more.

Weaning

Mumsnet.com (www.mumsnet.com/Talk/weaning, www.mumsnet.com/Recipes, www.mumsnet.com/babies/weaning)
For advice on weaning and Mumsnetters' favourite recipes

Baby-led Weaning (www.babyledweaning.com)

Food Standards Agency (www.eatwell.gov.uk/agesandstages/baby/weaning)
For the latest Government advice on weaning.

INDEX

boredom, difficult babies 297
bottle brushes 85
bottle-feeding 57–8, 84–91
    bottles 9–10, 85
    and colic 253
    and constipation 256
    demand-feeding 87
    equipment 85
    formula milk 86–7
    introducing bottles to breast-fed
        baby 95–6
    mixed feeding 89–91
    night feeds 170
    overfeeding 88
    preparing feeds 87–8
    windy babies 89
bottle warmers 14
bottoms
    nappy rash 269–70
    thrush 270
botulism 211
bouncy chairs 13, 43, 168, 171, 225, 313
bowel disease, and MMR vaccination
    280, 283
bowel movements
    after birth 134–5, 136
    constipation 255–6
    diarrhoea 259–61
    and weaning 219
bowls 225–6
bras
    expressing milk at work 104
    nursing 12, 99
BRAT diet, for diarrhoea 261
bread, salt content 227
breakfast, getting out of the house
    in the morning 431
breast milk
    cure for conjunctivitis 255
    see also breastfeeding
breast pads 12, 97
breast pumps 13, 92, 93

breast shells 92
breastfeeding 53–84
    after-pains during 115
    alcohol and 67
    antibodies 91
    attitudes to 55–6
    biting nipples 101–2
    caffeine and 67
    clothes for 79–80
    cluster feeding 62
    and co-sleeping 176
    colostrum 61
    demand-feeding 56, 67, 73–6
    dummies and 328
    expressing milk 83–4, 92–4, 98
    expressing milk at work 103–4
    foremilk and hindmilk 64–5
    introducing bottles 95–6
    latching on 77, 97, 328
    let-down reflex 62, 64
    milk coming in 61
    mixed feeding 89–91
    night feeds 170
    nursing bras 12, 99
    positioning 63, 82–3, 100–1
    in public 35, 76–81
    and reflux 274–5
    return of periods 145–6
    routines 56–7, 67–76
    second-time mothers 75–6
    and sex 352, 355
    and sleep problems 195
    sore nipples 96–9
    stopping 105–7
    support for 58–61
    twins 81–4
    'wanting-a-feed-now' signs 75
    and weaning 209
    and weight gain 141, 142
    and weight loss 141
    what to eat while 66
    and working from home 397

breasts
blocked ducts and mastitis
99–101, 106
see also nipples
breathing problems
bronchiolotis 249–50
choking 222
colds 251–2
croup 258–9
stridor 259
broccoli 220
bronchiolitis 249–50
broodiness 50, 156–7
bruising 120–1, 247
brushes, bottle 85
bubble bath 263
building blocks 315
Bumbos 16, 271
bump, disappearing 111–14
bumshuffling 300
burns 247

C
cabbage leaves, for sore
nipples 98
Caesarean section
after-effects 382
lochia after 116
recovery from 130–3
café-au-lait spots 248, 249
caffeine
and reflux 274
and sleep deprivation 199
while breastfeeding 67
cakes 230–5
calamine lotion 251
calendula cream 247, 270
candles 170
car seats 9, 11
cardigans 9
career breaks 388–9, 397–401
careers *see* work

carrots, for diarrhoea 261
carrycots 171
cars
daytime naps in 184
driving after Caesarean section
131
casein, in hungry-baby formula
88–9
catarrh 247
cats 371
cauliflower 220
Cetraben 263
chairs
bouncy chairs 13, 43, 168, 171, 225,
313
high chairs 225
chamomile tea 247
Chamomilla 247, 278
changing mats 12–13
changing tables 14
chewing
and teething 277
and weaning 221
chicken pox 250–1
Child Care Link 420
childcare 41, 373–8, 406–29
adjusting to 408
choices 409–10
conflict over 341
experts 291–3
by family members 357–8, 428–9
feeling guilty about 384
by friends 429
getting out of the house in the
morning 429–32
nannies 409, 416–19
nurseries 410
separation anxiety 407–8
studies of 377–8
and time for yourself 347–9
working from home 396
Childcare Vouchers 409

crying 43
    baby blues 32–3
    colic 252–4
    controlled crying 185, 186,
        188–93, 196
    difficult babies 297
    hunger cry 75
    pre-sleep grizzling 166
cuddling, newborn baby 168
cues
    cue-feeding 73–4, 88
    sleep 165, 194
cups, introducing to breast-fed baby
    96
cushions, valley 121, 124
cutlery 220–1
cuts and grazes 247

D
dairy intolerance 262
dancing, with colicky babies 253
daytime naps see naps
death, cot
    and co-sleeping 176
    dummies and 328
    mattresses and 10
    preventing 171, 172
defecation see poo
deformational plagiocephaly (flat
    head) 270–2
dehydration
    bottle-feeding and 88
    and diarrhoea 260
    mother 199
    signs of 240
demand-feeding
    breastfeeding 56, 67, 73–6
    bottle-feeding 88
dental health 234
Dentinox 257
depression
    baby blues 33

postnatal 33, 111, 146–52
    in pregnancy 295
    and returning to work 388
    and sleep problems 194
dermatitis, seborrhoeic 48, 257,
    270
Dettol 121, 247
development milestones 298–305
diaries 6, 331, 332
diarrhoea 259–61
    homeopathic remedy 247
    rehydration sachets 247
    and teething 277
diet see feeding; food
dieting, getting figure back 143–4
difficult babies 296–8
digestive problems
    constipation 134–5, 136, 240,
        255–6
    diarrhoea 259–61
    and early weaning 206–7
    vomiting 222–3, 278
diphtheria immunisation 279
discharges, lochia 114, 116–19
diseases, vaccinations 279–83
dishwashers 5, 396
disinfectant 247
doctors
    six-week checks 136–7
    when to go to 245–6
donor insemination 369–70
door bouncers 16, 315
doulas, postnatal 30–1
dream-feeding 72
dribbling, and teething 277
drinks 239–40
driving, after Caesarean
    section 131
drugs
    administering medicine 267–8
    and co-sleeping 176, 177
    cold and cough medications 252

forks 227
formula milk
    cartons of ready made-up
        formula 87, 88
    choices 86–7
    preparing feeds 87–8
    temperature 87–8, 89
    see also bottle-feeding
freelance work 395–7
freezing
    breast milk 94
    meals 385
    purées 214, 225
friends
    childcare by 429
    childless 359–62
    'mummy friendships' 361
fruit 144
    finger foods 221
    foods to avoid 211
    juices 239–40
    preventing constipation 134,
        255–6
    purées 212–19
    sweetness 235
    and weight loss 144
fungal diseases, thrush 98–9,
    101, 270
fussy eaters 236–7

G
gagging 222–3
gastroesophageal reflux disease
    (GERD) 272–5
gastrointestinal infections
    260
gay parents 369–71
gel pads, pain relief 124
general anaesthetic, Caesarean
    section 130
genitals, after birth 119–22
Germolene 122

gloves, rubber 247
glue ear 262
gluten 211
glycerine tablets 135
Gordon, Dr Jay 186
GPs
    six-week checks 136–7
    when to go to 245–6
'gradual withdrawal' sleep-
    training 192
grandparents 355–8
    childcare by 428–9
    sugar battle 230–3
    visitors after birth 33–7
grazing, labial 121–2
grommits, for glue ear 262
growth spurts, and weaning 209
guilt, returning to work 384
gum massagers, for teething 278
gurus
    breastfeeding 67–73
    childcare 291–3
    sleep-training 185–97
gynaecologists 129

H
Haemophilus influenzae type b (Hib)
    immunisation 279
haemorrhoids 135–6
hair
    hair loss 138–41
    newborn baby 47
    washing mother's 430–1
hallucinations 154–5, 198
hands
    fingernails 267
    hand-eye co-ordination 300
    milestones 299–300, 301, 302
Hardyment, Christina 293
harming baby, fear of 151
hazards, eating the wrong things
    275–6

head
    cradle cap 48, 256–7
    lifting 299
    plagiocephaly (flat head) 171,
        270–2
health 243–83
Health and Safety Executive
    (HSE) 103
health visitors 111
heartburn 112, 273
hemangionas, strawberry 248
herbal remedies
    for eczema 263
    for labial grazing 122
heuristic play 316–17
high chairs 225
high-need babies 296–8
hindmilk 64–5
hobbies 349
Hogg, Tracy 71–3
holidays
    childminders 413
    nannies 409
home ownership, unmarried
    parents 366
home working 395–7
homeopathy 247
    teething powders 278
homosexual parents 369–71
honey 211, 247
hormones
    after birth 137–8
    and hair loss 139
    stopping breastfeeding 107
    stress 194
hospitals
    coming home from 29
    taking bottle-feeding equipment
        to 84
hot weather, eczema and 264
household cleaners, safety 275–6
housework

after Caesarean section 131
before birth 6
conflict over 341–7
entertaining babies with 315
help with 39, 385
nannies and 409, 419
relaxing about 39
and returning to work 385
stay-at-home parents 403
humidifiers 251, 258
husbands see fathers
hygiene
    diarrhoea 260
    preparing formula milk 87

I
ibuprofen
    for after-pains 115–16
    for babies 246
    and breastfeeding 66
    for chicken pox 251
    for colds 251
    for fever 265
    for mastitis 101
ice packs 247
    for piles 136
    reducing swelling 120
illness
    and childminders 412, 413
    immunisation 279–83
    nurseries 416
immunisation 279–83
incontinence, after tears 126–7
incubation periods, chicken pox 250
independence, reasons for working
    387–8
Infacol 253
infections
    ear 261–2
    gastrointestinal 260
    and stitches 123, 125
    uterus 117

probiotics, in formula milk 86
projectile vomiting 273
prolactin 352
prolapse, uterus 127–8
protein
    and early weaning 207
    in hungry-baby formula 88–9
    purées 212
    vegetarian diet 237
prune juice 256
psychosis, postnatal 154–5
Pulsatilla 247
pulses, vegetarian diet 237
pumps, expressing milk 13, 92, 93
purées 209, 210, 212–19
    Annabel Karmel and 217–19
    freezing 225
    introducing 213–14
    making 215
    ready-made vs homemade 215–17
    and strange poo 219
Purelan cream 97
pushchairs
    choosing 11–12
    daytime naps in 184
    snowsuits and 17
    sleeping in 168

Q
quality time 307
    and returning to work 385–6
    stay-at-home parents 403
quilts 171
Quorn 237

R
rashes
    chicken pox 250–1
    meningitis 268, 269
    nappy rash 269–70
raspberries 211
references, nannies 417, 418
reflux 67, 272–5

registering birth 365
rehydration solutions 247, 260
relationships 335–71
    sex 352–5
    unmarried parents 364–6
    with childless friends 359–62
    with father 337–55
    with grandparents 355–8
    with pets 371
relatives
    childcare by 428–9
    see also grandparents; mothers-
        in-law
relaxation, and postnatal
        depression 149
Rescue Remedy 247
respiratory problems
    bronchiolitis 249–50
    colds 251–2
    croup 258–9
    stridor 259
respite care, special needs babies
        311–12
responsibility, parental 365
Rhus tox 251
rice 214
ring slings 78–9
rocking 73
rolling over 299, 300, 304
routines
    bedtime 169–70, 182
    breastfeeding 56–7, 67–76
    daytime naps 183
    newborn baby 168
rubella immunisation 279, 280–3

S
safety
    bottle-feeding 89
    co-sleeping 176
    eating the wrong things 275–6
    preparing formula milk 87

St John's wort 148
salt
    in baby food 220, 227–8
    salt baths 120, 121, 123
sanitary towels 118–19, 132
Savlon 247
savoury food, weaning 228–9
scalp, cradle cap 48, 256–7
scar, Caesarean section 132–3
school runs 413
scissors 247
scrapbooks 331–3
scratch mitts 14–15
Sears, Dr William 172, 174–5, 186–8,
    245–6, 296, 298
seborrhoeic dermatitis 48, 257, 270
seborrhoeic eczema 257
second-time mothers
    breastfeeding 75–6
    coping with toddlers 44–5
security, separation anxiety 407–8
separation
    stay-at-home parents 404
    unmarried parents 366
separation anxiety 407–8
septicaemia 268, 269
sesame 211
'settle-and-leave' sleep-training 192
settling baby 164–6, 339–40
sex 352–5
    after birth 130
    and co-sleeping 180–1
shampoos
    for cradle cap 257
    'thickening' 140
sheets 171
shellfish 211
'shhh/pat' sleep-training 192
shock 247
shoes, buying 326–7
shopping 8–18
    carrying 12
    managing on one salary 405

and returning to work 385
    what not to buy 14–15
    what to buy 8–14
Silverette nipple devices 98
single parents 366–8
sit-ups 142–3
sitting up
    milestones 300, 301, 302–3, 304
    and weaning 208
six-month-olds
    abilities 300
    entertaining 315
six-week checks 136–7
six-week-olds
    abilities 299
    entertaining 313–14
skin
    birthmarks 248–9
    chicken pox 250–1
    eczema 46, 206, 211, 262–4, 319–20
    nappy rash 269–70
    newborn baby 47–8
    stork marks 48–9
    stretch marks 145
    thrush 270
skull
    asymmetry 272
    cranial osteopathy 253
    plagiocephaly (flat head) 171, 270–2
sleep 159–201
    bedtime routines 169–70
    changing sleep patterns 181–3
    co-sleeping 172–81
    cues 165, 194
    daytime naps 162, 183–5
    and difficult babies 297
    first night 28, 29
    lie-ins 348
    and plagiocephaly (flat head) 271
    and returning to work 433
    settling newborn baby 164–6
    sleep associations 170
    sleep counselling 197

vomiting 222–3, 278
and diarrhoea 260
homeopathic remedy 247
meningitis 268
posseting 278
projectile vomiting 273
rehydration sachets 247

W
Wakefield, Andrew 280, 283
walking
baby 301, 303, 305
getting figure back 141–2
overcoming depression 149
settling baby 41
shoes 326–7
washing baby 14
washing clothes 344–5
washing machines 396
washing up 5
water, drinking 124, 134, 144, 199, 239, 255
weaning 203–41
baby-led weaning 209–10, 220–2
baby using spoon 226–7, 302
bought baby foods 215, 216–17
encouraging baby to eat 228–9
equipment 225–6
foods to avoid 210–11
from bottle-feeding 105–7
gagging, choking and vomiting 222–3
how to wean 209–11
purées 212–19
and strange poo 219
when to wean 205–9
weddings, no babies allowed 362–4
weeing
after birth 112
with stitches 123–4
weight loss, after birth 141–5
wheat 211

white noise, settling newborn baby 164–5
whooping cough immunisation 279
widowed parents 364–5
wills, unmarried parents 365–6
wind, postnatal 132
windy babies
bottle-feeding 89
and colic 252, 253
wipes 9, 15, 247
witch hazel 121, 122
womb see uterus
wooden objects, in treasure baskets 316
work
career changes 393–5
changing work patterns 390–3
expressing milk at 103–5
feelings about returning to 382–4
flexible working 394–5
getting out of the house in the morning 429–32
giving up 397–404
managing on one salary 404–6
maternity benefits 379
maternity leave 379–82
multitasking 433
and quality time 385–6
reasons for working 387–9
resentment of working mothers 389–90
returning to 373–8
sleep management 433
working from home 395–7
wounds
Caesarean section 132–3
stitches 122–5

Y
year-old babies, abilities 301–2
yoga 6, 141

Z
zinc oxide 270

www.mumsnet.com

" **Feeling desperate, baby waking every two hours at night** Any recommendations for ballet-themed novels for an 8 year old? **Single and pregnant – tips needed** Calling Coronation Street watchers **Would you send your kids to private school if money were no option?** Any IVFers out there? **Where can I buy large quantities of plaster of Paris?** Ever wonder how life got like this? **Separating – how do you explain it to a three year old?** Are school secretaries all jobsworths? **Alexander McCall Smith: Is he pure genius?** My four month old doesn't like Grandma **Need a saucy read...** I am rubbish at expressing – tips please? **What does a contraction actually feel like (kinda urgent)?!** Can I cook a shepherd's pie from frozen? **Things to do in South Wales** Feeling broody – should I try for baby number three? **Best treatment for nits?** Personal trainers – do they work? **Does your child know the f word?** Pooing in the bath... "

...another day on **www.mumsnet.com**

by parents, for parents